SEPTEMBER 1918

SEPTEMBER 1918

WAR, PLAGUE, AND THE WORLD SERIES

SKIP DESJARDIN

REGNERY
HISTORY

Regnery History™ is a trademark of Salem Communications Holding Corporation; Regnery® is a registered trademark of Salem Communications Holding Corporation

Excerpt from "September 1918" from THE COMPLETE POETICAL WORKS OF AMY LOWELL. Copyright (c) 1955 by Houghton Mifflin Harcourt Publishing Company, renewed 1983 by Houghton Mifflin Harcourt Publishing Company, Brinton P. Roberts, and G. D'Andelot Belin, Esquire. Reprinted by permission of Houghton Mifflin Harcourt Publishing Company. All rights reserved.

Cataloging-in-Publication data on file with the Library of Congress

ISBN 978-1-62157-620-4
e-book ISBN 978-1-62157-621-1

Published in the United States by
Regnery History
An Imprint of Regnery Publishing
A Division of Salem Media Group
300 New Jersey Ave NW
Washington, DC 20001
www.RegneryHistory.com

Manufactured in the United States of America

10 9 8 7 6 5 4 3 2 1

Books are available in quantity for promotional or premium use. For information on discounts and terms, please visit our website: www.Regnery.com.

For Karen,

who always knew

CONTENTS

PROLOGUE   xi

1 WORK OR FIGHT   1

2 OVER THERE   15

3 OUTBREAK   27

4 LODGE   35

5 THE BABE   45

6 SPANISH FLU   65

7 FENWAY PARK   73

8 THE BATTLE OF ST. MIHIEL   95

9 EPIDEMIC   115

10 THE HOMEFRONT   139

11 DON'T NAG   161

12 STATE OF DENIAL   171

13 COOLIDGE   189

14 THE HORROR AT DEVENS   199

15 THE YANKEE DIVISION   207

16 THE PATH OF PROGRESS   223

17 TURNING THE CORNER   237

EPILOGUE   253
ACKNOWLEDGMENTS   257
NOTES   261
INDEX   281

Some day there will be no war,
Then I shall take out this afternoon
And turn it in my fingers,
And remark the sweet taste of it upon my palate,
And note the crisp variety of its flights of leaves.
To-day I can only gather it
And put it into my lunch-box,
For I have time for nothing
But the endeavour to balance myself
Upon a broken world.

—"September 1918," by Amy Lowell

PROLOGUE

Just a month after President Woodrow Wilson was inaugurated for a second term—won in the fall of 1916 under the slogan "He kept us out of war"—he felt he had to ignore the will of American voters and commit the United States to history's first global conflict. In April 1917, despite his mandate for peace, Wilson asked Congress to declare war on Germany.

Over a year later, as the summer of 1918 waned, Wilson and his administration had succeeded in what he believed to be his biggest challenge: not just changing the minds of most voters about the need for war, but somehow building a groundswell of public support, which he knew would be critical for success in waging that war. "It is not an army we must shape and train for war," he acknowledged, "it is a nation."[1]

It was not an easy process, nor a period of American political history about which, in retrospect, we should be particularly proud. Wilson pursued this imperative with the single-mindedness of a missionary zealously determined to save his new converts. "To fight you must be brutal and ruthless," the president said, "and the spirit of ruthless brutality will enter into every fiber of our national life, infecting Congress, the courts, the policeman on the beat, the man on the street."[2]

President Wilson understood from the start that the great power potential of the United States could only be wound up and let loose if there was near unanimity of purpose among the public. The very nature of the American populace made this difficult. America was then, as now, a collection of diverse religious and ethnic groups. The country was founded, in large part, on the principle of dissent: the reluctance of early settlers to adhere unanimously to any single philosophy or policy dictated by a government. In September 1918, nearly 15 percent of Americans were foreign-born. What's more, a very sizable number of Americans were recent immigrants from Germany, still speaking the language, with family remaining abroad. Where were their loyalties? Could they be trusted?

Somehow, Wilson had to get all of these disparate factions onto the same page. How to convince the American people of this? How to mobilize them to action? His options were limited. Many Democrats felt betrayed by his policy reversal, and Republicans were not about to embrace a political opponent despite their muscular calls for war throughout his first term. Complicating matters, as historian David Kennedy has noted, was the fact that Wilson was an academic, not a traditional politician. He had been president of Princeton University before being elected governor of New Jersey in 1910 and then president of the United States just two years later. As such, he had no base of knowledge of how to "manipulate the traditional levers of influence, nor how to move comfortably within existing structures of power. Without well-established bases in either party or Congress, he still had one constituency to which to turn: the public at large."[3]

As a byproduct of its democratic system, the United States was "a country governed by public opinion," as Wilson's attorney general Thomas Gregory noted.[4] By means of the emerging art and science of "public relations," the president and members of his administration believed that Americans could be swayed to accept, even embrace, the shared sacrifice that would be necessary to fuel a massive war effort.

Almost immediately after the declaration of war, Wilson turned to a former journalist and champion of progressive causes, George Creel, to build public support for his concept of "total war," which would require the coordinated participation of virtually every American citizen, institution, and organization. By Executive Order, the president established the Committee on Public Information (CPI) and put Creel in charge. "Woe be to the man or group of men that seeks to stand in our way," Wilson said.[5]

Creel decided to wage a war of his own—on American hearts and minds. He was certain that his own role was critical to the country's chances for victory and willing to employ every tactic imaginable in the service of his cause. As one historian described it, the mission of CPI was to "organize patriotic enthusiasm where it existed and create it where it did not."[6]

"What we had to have was no mere surface unity, but a passionate belief in the justice of America's cause that should weld the people of the United States into one white-hot mass instinct of fraternity, devotion, courage and deathless determination," Creel explained. "The 'war-will,' the will to win, of a democracy depends upon the degree to which each one of all the people of that democracy can concentrate and consecrate the body and soul and spirit in the supreme effort of service and sacrifice. What had to be driven home was that all business was the nation's business, and every task a common task for a single purpose."[7]

By late summer of 1918, Creel had been at work for over sixteen months, building public support, if not obsession, for the cause of the war. Typical of the all-out effort was the work of what became known as the Four Minute Men. Some 75,000 volunteers were organized and instructed to give short speeches nearly everywhere a crowd gathered: civic meetings, theaters, churches, union halls, and rural granges. Speakers were advised to be simple and concise, to organize their thoughts or memorize their speech in advance, and to focus on a single theme—often a patriotic or motivational slogan supplied to them by the CPI. By Creel's count, the Four Minute Men spoke to over 134 million people in 755,000 presentations, "every one having the carry of shrapnel."[8]

Creel's success had had a profound effect on the American homeland in the period since war had been declared. "It was the fight for the minds of men, for the 'conquest of their convictions,' and the battle line ran through every home in every county," he recalled.[9]

No aspect of American life was untouched: not home or church, not work or school, not a Sunday drive or an afternoon at the ballpark. No opportunity to drive home the message was missed. The Massachusetts state government, for instance, asked Boston Symphony founder Henry Higginson to establish singing groups across the commonwealth. These "Liberty Choruses" would perform a selection of patriotic songs at nearly every kind of public gathering, often in tandem with a speech from a Four Minute Man. Even the normally staid *New York Times* was caught up in the fervor. "Our people are aroused to the stern necessity of organizing victory and overwhelming Germany, because civilization and human liberty and all that thinking beings and freemen hold dear can be saved only in that way," the newspaper editorialized. "The whole country is aflame with rage."[10]

In Boston particularly, life would be plunged into chaos as the month of September began. Nowhere would the tentacles of the all-consuming war effort be as far-reaching, or squeeze as tightly. There, the battle for hearts and minds would whip up unwavering support for a division of home town soldiers off to fight the Kaiser and keep the world safe for democracy. Also there, ironically, the government effort to maintain morale at all costs would contribute to death on a massive scale—right in the communities those soldiers were fighting to protect.

In a single month, a tremendous cross-pollination of American policy, politics, and culture would occur in and around this one city. Famous athletes, artists, and politicians intersected with ordinary people in Boston, simultaneously caught up in both heroics and tragedy. Some of these unfolding stories were classic instances of individuals simply in the wrong place at the wrong time. Fascinatingly, in some cases the right people were in the perfect place at precisely the right time—yet helpless to bend history to their will.

Events that would shape America and the world in the twentieth century were playing out on a single stage in and around Boston that month: the restlessness of workers and the emerging labor movement, the growing roles of women in all aspects of society, the dawn of a "golden age" of sports, swift advances in science, and the defining of two political parties. All of these were on display in Massachusetts over a single, thirty-day period. Even in the preeminent world event, the Great War, Boston men were playing a central role.

Under the constant influence of war and in the midst of the greatest health crisis the nation had ever known, Boston truly lived up to its reputation as "the hub of the universe."

CHAPTER 1

WORK OR FIGHT

SEPTEMBER 1–3

The Boston Red Sox were tired. September 1 was a Sunday, and therefore in many American League cities, like New York, it was an off day for baseball. Sunday games were still banned in New York City by local ordinance, and the team needed the rest after playing double-headers on both Friday and Saturday.

With the Great War underway, baseball team rosters had been decimated by the war effort and the draft. The Red Sox bench was so thin that manager Ed Barrow had been forced to send starting pitcher John Watson to the mound for both games of Saturday's double-header; Watson had somehow managed to hurl a one-hit shutout in the second game for a 1–0 victory.

It was Labor Day weekend, and another double-header was scheduled for Monday against the New York Yankees at their home field, the Polo Grounds. But it was a Labor Day weekend unlike any the Red Sox—or any big league team—had ever experienced. For this Labor Day was also to be the last day of the 1918 season, perhaps the last regular season day ever for professional baseball. Certainly there would be no more baseball for the duration of the war; that much was clear. Whether big league baseball would ever return as America knew it on that late summer day was very much in question.

The Red Sox, winners of four of the fifteen World Series played to date, were the most dominant team of the era, but they were still a franchise in a near constant state of upheaval. The club had changed owners six times over that stretch despite—or perhaps because of—its success on the field, as a string of wealthy men with healthy egos saw opportunity for profit. The team also was backed by the most loyal fans in the game, including a raucous band of followers who billed themselves as the Royal Rooters, led by the owner of a popular bar in the city's Fenway neighborhood, Michael "'Nuf Ced" McGreevey. Recent years, when the Red Sox won World Series titles in 1912, 1915, and 1916, were particularly heady times to be a Boston fan. The Rooters and their ballpark marching band celebrated win after win to the strains of "Tessie," a popular show tune of the time adopted as the team's theme song.

In 1918, a theatrical agent named Harry Frazee owned the team. Frazee had left home at sixteen and took a job as a janitor at a theater in Peoria. By nineteen he had produced his own show, on which he profited $14,000, and an impresario was born. A string of hits followed. By age twenty-seven he built his own theater in Chicago; five years later he built one on Broadway and another in Boston. All this in spite of the problem, as one songwriter noted, that "Frazee never drew a sober breath in his life."[1] In 1916, Harry Frazee bought the Red Sox at the height of the club's success. American League president Ban Johnson, the league founder who liked to think he ruled it with an iron fist, was not consulted regarding the transaction, contrary to custom. Johnson was so angry that he told the press he might disallow the sale. But Frazee prevailed, and the Red Sox became a source of amusement for the diminutive thirty-eight-year-old theater producer, a means of gaining publicity for himself and his latest production.

In the middle of the 1917 season the previous summer, Johnson offered to shut down the American League for the duration of the war.

But President Woodrow Wilson intervened, and the game continued. Frazee echoed Wilson's feelings on the diversionary benefits of the game. "People must be amused," he said. "They must have their recreation, despite the grim horrors of war."[2]

Yet Johnson, sensing a growing distraction among fans by far more pressing matters, wondered how the game could survive when most able-bodied men, both fans and players, were facing a patriotic duty to serve their country. After the 1917 World Series he proposed that eighteen players per team be exempted from the military draft to ensure that enough players remained to field teams. The idea went nowhere. By 1918, across the major leagues, nearly a third of all players from the prior season were serving in the military. A total of eleven Red Sox players from the previous year's squad joined up during the offseason. Unlike Johnson, Frazee was convinced that the war was quickly winding down, even before America became fully engaged. Over the winter of 1917, he went so far as to very publicly wager that hostilities would be over by Opening Day, laying 6-to-1 odds.

Frazee was certain he would get his former stars back just as soon as the war ended. So, with an eye toward peace and prosperity, he boosted his roster for 1918 with player acquisitions, making a big trade with the cash-strapped Philadelphia Athletics (the A's). Frazee sent $60,000 and three marginal players to the A's owner, Connie Mack, in the largest cash transaction in baseball history. In return, he got young, twenty-one-year-old pitcher Joe Bush along with Wally Schang, who was the best catcher in the game, and up-and-coming outfielder Amos Strunk.

The press was outraged that this brash, young owner, as well as Charles Weeghman of the Chicago Cubs, would engage in such unsportsmanlike behavior and simply purchase the best players in the game. As the *New York Times* huffed, the two had "stirred up no end of commotion in the two major leagues by starting out to monopolize the two pennants next season. Baseball owners of the past never knew the methods in accord with which these two owners have started to buy players who can land them a pennant at any cost."[3]

Ever the producer, Frazee knew how to draw an audience. "You can't fill a theater with a poor attraction," he said, "and you can't interest the fans with a losing ball club. Boston has been educated to expect winners in the American League, and when I discovered that the war had deprived the Red Sox of their best players, I was compelled to act or play to empty benches."[4]

Frazee's time and attention for baseball were limited, however. He wanted to focus on his theater business and needed someone to run the baseball team full-time. He offered part ownership of the team to Ed Barrow, the outgoing president of the minor-league International League, but Barrow couldn't come up with the cash. So, instead, Frazee hired Barrow to oversee the team.

It had been thirteen years since Barrow last managed a big league baseball team. He had never been a professional player, so he wouldn't wear a uniform in the dugout. Frazee gave Barrow final decision on player transactions, effectively also making him the equivalent of today's general managers. So Barrow had full control over the team in both the front office and on the field. The Red Sox went to the well a second time and grabbed another player from Mack's A's, bringing in Jack "Stuffy" McInnis, a slick-fielding first baseman from nearby Gloucester, Massachusetts. Barrow filled in the rest of the holes in his lineup with journeymen and minor league call-ups and headed off to spring training in Hot Springs, Arkansas.

Barrow's ornery style did not win over many people. Between the opening of spring training and the start of the season, two of his coaches quit. Players groused about the heavy workload. The new manager stood for none of it. He was going to run the team the way he saw fit, the way a team *should* be run.

As the season moved into its second month, Frazee's vision of a quick victory for the Allies and the rapid return of his former stars evaporated. He lost his "peace by Opening Day" wager, and it was evident that the war would drag on, requiring an even greater commitment from the American people.

On May 24, Secretary of War Newton Baker issued an order that became known as "work or fight." It dictated that every able-bodied man between the ages of twenty-one and thirty must either be employed in industries essential to the war effort or be subject to induction into the military. Provost Marshall General Enoch Crowder, the man tasked with building the American military through the draft, was in charge of enforcing the "work or fight" order, which was to take effect on July 1. The Red Sox found themselves in crisis. While the government was not shutting the game down, most of the players remained eligible for, and vulnerable to, the military draft. The need for able-bodied men for the war effort was dire, and professional baseball players were nothing if not able-bodied.

"The spectacle is not a satisfying one of a contingent of drafted men from Class 1 being marched down the street to camp while other men of their own age, watching them from windows, remain behind," Crowder said of the logic behind the order. "If these men of the same age are to stay behind, let them at least get into work more effective to help the war. They are of military age and therefore have the primary duty to do war work."[5]

The order exempted the entertainment industry, specifically theater employees, but the status of baseball players and coaches remained unclear. Was the game, like the theater, morale-boosting recreation and therefore contributing in its own way to the war effort? Or were the young, healthy players prime examples of the type of men who needed either to get to work supplying the military or to get down to the enlistment office?

One of the best players for the Red Sox, pitcher Dutch Leonard, decided not to wait around until the July 1 deadline to find out. Trying to stay ahead of his local draft board, Leonard, who had thrown a no-hitter for Boston on June 3, left the club in late June for a job at the Fore River Shipyard outside the city. One of his duties there, apparently, was pitching for the company's baseball team. At the time, the Red Sox were in a three-way tie for first place with no idea how long the season was going to last. Barrow needed pitching once Leonard departed, which made a young lefthander on the roster even more critical to the staff.

As a skinny twenty-three-year-old from Baltimore, George Herman "Babe" Ruth was the undisputed new star of the Red Sox. Already in his fifth year with Boston, Ruth was among the top pitchers in the game. He had won twenty-four games the previous season, compiling a 2.01 earned-run average per nine innings and leading the league with thirty-five complete games. Amazingly, however, Ruth was becoming the most fearsome hitter in baseball as well.

Ruth was hitting home runs at a pace never matched by any pitcher and few pure hitters. He badgered his manager to play more often than every fourth day, when his turn to pitch came around, but Barrow was certain that he would be "the laughingstock of the league" if he turned one of the game's best pitchers into an everyday fielder. Outfielder Harry Hooper, a veteran player and unofficial coach, tried incessantly to get the manager to change his mind. Ruth could clearly hit, he argued, and it was evident the kid didn't have the patience to spend three out of every four days sitting on the bench.

"I like to pitch, but my main objection is that pitching keeps you out of so many games," Ruth complained. "I like to be in there every day. If I had my choice, I'd play first base. I don't think a man can pitch his regular turn and play some other position and keep the pace year after year. I can do it this season all right. I'm young and strong and don't mind the work, but I wouldn't guarantee to do it for many seasons."[6]

The war of wills between manager and player went on with Ruth agitating to play every day and his manager resisting. Finally, on May 6, when the Red Sox played the New York Yankees at the Polo Grounds, Barrow gave in. Babe Ruth started his first big league game as a hitter, playing first base. Of course, he hit a home run. The Yankees' owner, Colonel Jacob Rupert, was sitting with Frazee at the game and jokingly offered $150,000 on the spot to buy Ruth's contract.[7] It was a concept just a bit ahead of its time.

A successful first day was one thing, Barrow thought, but wait until Ruth fell into a slump at the plate. "He'll be down on his knees begging me to pitch," the manager predicted to Hooper.[8] Three days later Ruth went five-for-five with a triple, three doubles, and a single at the start of a ten-game hitting streak. By early June, Ruth was a full-time hitter, though still much against Barrow's better judgment. The American League record for home runs over an entire season was sixteen. By June 30, Ruth had eleven. No one considered the manager a laughingstock now.

As the "work or fight" deadline arrived, the tension between the unruly Ruth and the hard-nosed Barrow reached a breaking point. Happy to be playing daily instead of going stir-crazy on the bench, Ruth begged off from pitching, insisting that his left wrist was sore—though not too sore to hit. He hadn't been to the mound in over a month. But with Leonard gone, Barrow was thin on options and increasingly annoyed with Ruth's unwillingness to help the team. The pot boiled over in Washington on July 2.

During the game, Barrow ordered Ruth to take a few pitches when he went up to bat, but the overeager kid swung at the first pitch he saw. The manager exploded with frustration, calling it "a bum play." Ruth gave it right back to him, threatening to punch him in the nose. Barrow fined his player $500 on the spot. Ruth decided he had had enough of this disciplinarian; he took off his uniform and watched the rest of the game from the stands. After it was over, he packed his bag and went home to nearby Baltimore.

By this time Barrow was used to Ruth's hotheadedness and figured he would return by the next afternoon's game in Philadelphia. In fact, when local reporters tracked Ruth down at his father's bar in Baltimore later that night, he was already cooling down. "I was mad as a March hare and told Barrow then and there that I was through with him and his team," Ruth said. "I know I was too mad to control myself, but suiting the action to the word, I did leave the team and came home. I am all right and willing and ready to get back to playing. But I do not want to be fighting and fought with all the time."[9]

As Barrow and Frazee met with the press in the dugout the following day, however, sportswriters stunned the pair by telling them Ruth had announced he had taken a job at the Chester Shipyards Company in Baltimore and would be playing baseball for the factory team instead of the Red Sox.[10]

Frazee unloaded with threats of legal action. Barrow just spoke of how important Ruth was to the team. In the end, Ruth was gone only two days. Barrow sent coach Heinie Wagner, whom Ruth trusted, down to Baltimore to retrieve the slugger. In true Ruth style, he returned with an enthusiastic greeting for his teammates as if nothing had happened. Barrow, concerned that he was wearing out his three remaining starters with overwork, slipped Ruth back into the rotation gradually. Ruth's point about the grind of trying to pitch and play the field apparently had some validity, though. He did not hit another home run the rest of the season. The tension between Ruth the pitcher, Ruth the hitter, and Barrow the manager would linger and, almost inevitably, would become an issue again on the game's biggest stage—the World Series.

By July 11, the ten-day grace period that American men had been given after the effective date of the "work or fight" order to get their personal affairs in order had expired. The government wasted no time in taking action. Between games of a double-header at Weeghman Park in Chicago, home of the Cubs, the gates of the ballpark were locked, and no one was allowed to leave without clarifying their work or draft status with authorities. Over 500 men were detained in the first of what became known as "slacker sweeps," aimed at finding men who were defying the government's order to take a job or take up arms.

Unsure of how or whether play should continue, baseball owners sought answers from the federal government. Were players exempt from "work or fight" like actors? Should the season be shut down? The National Commission, baseball's governing authority, petitioned the War Department for an exemption through October 15 so that the season could be completed and the World Series played, after which the professional game would be shut down for the duration of the war.

American League President Johnson, who had advocated shutting baseball down during the 1917 offseason, was ready to pull the plug again. In late July, he took it upon himself to announce that the rest of the season would be canceled. "The Boston American League club does not propose to abide by that arbitrary ruling," Barrow immediately replied on behalf of the Red Sox.[11] The rest of the American League owners concurred and simply ignored Johnson's decision and kept playing games. The National League, under president John Tener, also decided to keep playing. Johnson fumed.

Upset that they could not get clarity on a definitive status for the game from the government and frustrated by the ineffectiveness of the two league presidents in getting some kind of resolution, owners decided to go to Washington in search of answers. A twelve-man contingent appealed to Secretary of War Baker and Provost Marshall Crowder to be allowed to finish the baseball season on schedule in October. On July 26, Baker compromised and gave them until September 1 instead.

At the beginning of August, the National League owners met and decided to play through Labor Day. American League owners met the next day, with Johnson once again vigorously arguing for an early end to the regular season, followed by a World Series that would wrap up by the end of August. "I will not be a party to a baseball game played after September 1," Johnson bloviated ahead of the meeting. "I think the owners of the American League will unanimously agree with my views after the situation is thoroughly discussed."[12]

Instead, his league's owners ignored him again, voting to play through Labor Day and petition Baker for a further extension for just the two, pennant-winning teams to play the World Series. Johnson had no choice but to back down, but he seethed at the uprising, which he saw as having been orchestrated by Red Sox owner Frazee. "If the clubs wish to take a chance on acting contrary to the ruling of the War Department, that is their business," he growled.[13]

Baker granted the World Series exemption through September 15. Every ballplayer on every other team would be subject to the "work or fight" rule at the end of the regular season. Once the World Series was finished, players from the two league champions would also face the same prospects as millions of other American men, including big league star players like Cubs pitcher Grover Cleveland Alexander, who had been drafted into military duty in late April after pitching just twenty-six innings for Chicago and was currently at the front in France as a member of an artillery unit.

While baseball pushed the limits of the "work or fight" order, prevailing American sentiment was not with ball players. Too many families had members serving in some capacity to garner support for giving professional athletes special privileges. Households struggling to make financial ends meet had little sympathy for those being paid well to play a child's game. As Labor Day approached, workers in Massachusetts had enough trouble of their own. Streetcar operators at the Boston and Middlesex railroad company were on strike, virtually shutting down the trolley system in the city. Boston's firemen voted to strike as well if the mayor didn't agree to their demand for a $300 per year raise from their current annual salary of $900. In the suburbs, 800 lasters in the Brockton shoe factories went on strike to support their fellow cutters union. When they were ordered back to work by the National War Labor Board, they found that management had locked them out and were training replacements. They had lost their jobs and their draft exemptions.

Even with American productivity at peak performance and industry operating nonstop to supply the troops overseas, few workers felt any real job security. "Today, the mind of the public is burdened by great responsibilities, and cares about the World Series at best can be but a momentary diversion," is how the *Boston Sunday Advertiser* put it on the first day of September.[14]

On the last day of the regular season, while most professional baseball players worried about how to provide for their families if they weren't conscripted and sent to the European front, the Red Sox at least knew their immediate fate. As they took the field for their double-header against the Yankees, they had already clinched the American League championship. Regardless of the outcome of the day's two games, they were headed for Chicago to play in the World Series against the Cubs.

Across baseball the regular season was ending like a weak grounder to second base. The Cleveland Indians didn't bother to travel to St. Louis for their double-header. A pitcher for the Browns threw five pitches to an empty batter's box and the umpire declared a forfeit. A half hour later, they repeated the formality for a second-game forfeit. As other games ended, players on every team except the Red Sox and the Cubs were informed that they had been waived by the club and their contracts for the rest of 1918 and any future seasons had been terminated. Baseball was truly shutting down for the duration of the war. When and if it returned, however, the released players would not be free to sign with any team they chose, even though they had been freed from their contracts and though the owners did not have to pay for what would have been the last month of the season. No, the owners had a gentleman's agreement not to poach each other's players. If baseball started back up again, players would be bound to their old team—just not their old salaries.

Boston split its meaningless double-header, with manager Barrow pulling all of his regular players off the field part way through the second game. No sense risking an injury to any of the stars he would need to rely on in the World Series.

After the games, the team boarded the 5:04 p.m. train from New York's 125th Street station for the twenty-three-hour trip to Chicago. While players would undoubtedly be looking ahead to the games with the Cubs, baseball was not the only topic of conversation on the train. A number of Red Sox veterans, led by Harry Hooper, regularly used evening dinners and long train rides to catch up on the latest war news. *Boston Post* columnist Arthur Duffey called it the Board of Strategy, describing how the group was "following the movement of the allies by means of maps clipped from various newspapers."[15] Hooper, a college-trained engineer before his big league career, was the chief thinker on the Red Sox, whether it was helping Barrow with in-game decisions or leading an ongoing study group on the war. As a result, he would soon be thrust into a leadership role on behalf of the players from both teams, though no one knew it at the time.

For now, Ed Martin, a sportswriter for the *Boston Globe*, was previewing the World Series for his readers, and he thought he knew exactly who would be the center of attention. "Ruth is the magnet that will draw thousands of fans to the Series," he wrote, "and they will want to see him as a principal in every performance and not as a 'prop' on the coaching lines. It is believed that they will have their wish."[16] The *Boston Herald*'s Burt Whitman saw Ruth's role the same way. "Regardless of whether or not the Babe pitches, you may be sure he will be in every game," he wrote. "His stick is too valuable an asset to be idle."[17]

Things would not work out that way.

The Chicago Cubs practiced at Comiskey Park on the morning of September 3, an off-day scheduled to allow the Red Sox to make their way across half the country by rail. The Cubs needed the practice because Comiskey Park was the home of their cross-town rivals, the White Sox, and the players were unfamiliar with the field. In fact, the Red Sox were far more accustomed to playing there, since it was a regular stop on their American League schedule.

The Cubs' management had chosen to play the team's World Series home games on the south side of Chicago because Comiskey Park held more people than their still new home stadium, Weeghman Park, on the north side of the city. In later years, when ownership of the team changed hands, the field was renamed after the new team owner and his popular chewing gum and became Wrigley Field. The team had high hopes that the added capacity of their temporary home would mean additional ticket sales. They had every belief that attendance and revenue would surpass the 1917 World Series, won by the White Sox.

The Red Sox arrived in Chicago and checked into the Hotel Metropole at East Twenty-Third and Michigan Avenue, luxury accommodations two miles from the ballpark, which would later become famous as gangster Al Capone's headquarters. In the evening, they worked out at Comiskey Park to stretch their train-cramped muscles and in anticipation of the next day's opening game. Barrow practiced the already age-old tradition of saying nothing of consequence in his conversations with reporters. "The best thing I can say is that the Red Sox are ready for a fight, and I, of course, feel certain that we shall bag the championship," the manager told the *New York Times*. "I realize we are playing a wonderful team. The games, I think, will be close and will arouse more interest than expected."[18]

Newspapers in both teams' cities were filled with stories looking forward to the start of the series as well, and much of the anticipation revolved around young Babe Ruth.

"Babe stands supreme as a super hitter," wrote Eddie Hurley in the *Boston Record*. "In fact, Babe is the mightiest driver of them all. More than anything else, victory or defeat of the Red Sox is up to the big Baltimore kid. If Babe falls down, it is feared he will drag his mates with him; if he goes through as expected, it is thought the Sox will have smooth sailing."[19]

Fred Mitchell, the Cubs' manager, also saw Ruth as the key to the World Series. "The Red Sox are a one-man team, and his name is Ruth," he maintained. "But we have studied his ways and his mental processes so much this season that we will spike his guns."[20]

On the eve of the scheduled World Series opener, all of the pressure seemed to be squarely on the young, immature, but immensely talented kid from Baltimore.

"The mighty shadow of Babe Ruth falls athwart Chicago tonight like a menace," wrote Whitman in the *Herald*. "Never did one man count so heavily in the before-the-game pressure of the World Series. Take him out of the way and the Cubs would be superior and would have enough confidence to do harsh things to the men from Massachusetts. But there he is, a huge, horrifying prospect for Mitchell and his men. He is the difference between defeat and victory."[21]

Even those partial to the Cubs acknowledged Ruth's importance. "The one big interrogation mark is Ruth," noted the fabled Hugh Fullerton, a Chicago-based, syndicated columnist and the newspaperman who would break the 1919 Black Sox story. "In my opinion Ruth, the superman, who won the pennant almost alone for the Red Sox, is the only thing that can stop Chicago."[22]

Times may have been good for Red Sox fans in the late summer of 1918, but the larger world in Boston and beyond was under a darkening cloud. Inflation was rampant, the latest in a cycle of boom and bust that had plagued the economy since the latter part of the previous century, and the little money most families had was buying less and less. Nevertheless, gambling was rampant, in organized sports and beyond. A faction of society, particularly in Puritan Boston, was driving the country toward a prohibition on the sale of alcohol. Terrorism, in the form of anarchist bombings or labor violence, was common.

But mostly, there was the Great War.

CHAPTER 2

OVER THERE

SEPTEMBER 1–5

While the baseball teams prepared for the World Series, people in the Bay State were paying close attention to more than the sports pages. Anxious families scoured newspapers for the latest on the war and tried to read between the lines to guess what it meant for their loved ones fighting in Europe. One newspaper spun casualty announcements from Washington as positive news for Massachusetts troops. "The fact that the 26th Division has been withdrawn from active fighting in the first line trenches is borne out by the constantly decreasing number of casualties from New England," surmised the *Boston Post*.[1] In fact, as the month began, the Twenty-Sixth Division of General John "Black Jack" Pershing's newly formed American First Army was tramping through the darkness and heavy rain through France on their way to the front once again.

Marching was nothing new to these soldiers. The Twenty-Sixth— numbering over 30,000 primarily state guard soldiers from New England and, therefore, known as the Yankee Division—had been the very first

American division organized for the Great War. After the men of the Twenty-Sixth completed their training at Camp Devens in central Massachusetts, they were the first Americans shipped overseas to fight in Europe and the first to enter battle as a unit, albeit as part of larger French and British commands. From their initial action in February, the Yankee Division had been in the thick of it practically every day for seven months. Still, as they moved under the cover of darkness to avoid detection by German forces, something was definitely different. The men knew that this time, for the first time, they would enter the fight as an American division, under American command, alongside fellow American soldiers.

Pershing had assembled a force of more than a half million American soldiers by consolidating U.S. divisions, like the Twenty-Sixth, that had been fighting under the command of various French or British generals. He had not liked what he had seen of a number of French and British commanders, nor did he trust them to always work in a coordinated fashion for Allied good rather than for their own nationalistic goals. He had insisted on, and been reluctantly granted, command over all American forces following the Battle of Chateau-Thierry.

For the sake of efficiency and effectiveness, the Allies needed to shorten the front. Salients, or bulges, extended the length of the lines that both sides needed to attack or defend. By late summer, it was decided that the salient that extended into French territory east of the town of St. Mihiel needed to be smoothed out. The area in question formed a rough triangle with a twenty-five-mile base and an apex extending some sixteen miles into Allied territory. The American plan was a massive attack from two sides that would act as a pincer, thereby cutting off German troops, material, and supplies.

At the end of August, however, the top Allied commander, Marshal Ferdinand Foch, nearly reversed Pershing's plan and re-dispersed American troops. The French general was having second thoughts and argued forcefully with Pershing that his men should be integrated with other Allied units and that the St. Mihiel plan should be scrapped in advance of a major offensive at the Meuse-Argonne. Pershing disagreed just as forcefully. "Marshal Foch, you may insist all you please," he told the Allies' commander-in-chief. "I decline absolutely to agree with your plan. While our army will fight wherever you may decide, it will not fight except as an independent American army."[2]

Foch, aware that the French had been unsuccessful in several attempts to reduce the St. Mihiel salient over the previous four years, conceded, perhaps figuring that a stinging setback in their first engagement would bring the Americans back in line.

Unaware of the simmering dispute between Pershing and Foch, the Yankee Division found itself moving stealthily, or as stealthily as an entire army can, through the French countryside on its way toward St. Mihiel. As it turned out, they were not unexpected. It seemed that everyone living on their side of the front lines was aware of the Americans' plans.

"Late in August, as far away as Biarritz, they heard that the Americans were going to have a little offensive of their own, and would attack on the Saint-Mihiel salient on September 1," recalled Frank Sibley, a reporter with the *Boston Globe* who was embedded with the Massachusetts men of the Yankee Division. "Even the 26th Division was named as one of the units in that attack, and the whole French public was perfectly aware of the plan. The only people in France who did not know were the men in the Division itself."[3]

Private Connell Albertine of Company A in the 104th Infantry and the rest of the men of the Yankee Division were slogging through rain and mud at night and hunkering down beneath the cover of French forests every day on their way to the first coordinated American engagement of the war.

"The orders were no lighting of matches, no cigarettes, no smoking, and no talking," Albertine remembered.

> We hiked all night with an occasional rest until daybreak, when we pulled into dense woods. Cold corned beef and hardtack were served, and then we pitched pup tents and tried to get some sleep. Even though it was daylight, the density of the woods made it almost pitch dark. Some fell asleep, while

others just sat in their tents singing or having a bull session. At dusk we were again served a cold meal and then took our tents down, rolled our packs, and soon we were on what was supposed to be a road but turned out to be a cow path. It was very dark, we couldn't see a hand in front of us, and to make it worse it started to rain.[4]

In this case, rain was good. It made for darker nights, and the inclement weather meant that there would be no German reconnaissance planes or observation balloons aloft to track the American soldiers' movements by day. Even the Division's artillery could be transported unseen on these rainy nights.

"The night turned out dark and stormy," Fritz Potter of the 101st Field Artillery wrote home. "In fact, it was so dark I could not see the horse's head I was riding. Strange as it may seem, you do not feel the hunger at night that you would in the day time. You do get rather sleepy and more than once I have fallen asleep in the saddle."[5]

Of course, rain also meant mud. "The cow path, having just dirt for a foundation, became very muddy," Albertine recorded. "Our trench hobnail shoes, having been impregnated so many times with dubbin, were as waterproof as any shoes could be. No other kind of shoes would have lasted so long under such adverse conditions. But the mud stuck like glue, and the farther we marched the deeper it got, and it just kept on raining."[6]

In all the history of human warfare, moving armies had always foraged for food. For these men, covering ground that had been traded back and forth between the Allied and German armies over the course of the war, there was little to scavenge as the landscape had been all but stripped bare of food and supplies. Some signs of life, however, peeked through the destruction. Some soldiers managed to find berries amongst the devastation, though the results were mixed.

Dr. Harvey Cushing had been the chief of surgery at Peter Brent Brigham Hospital in Boston and a professor at Harvard Medical School. Now he was lieutenant colonel in the Army Medical Corps and moving with American troops toward St. Mihiel, and he noticed something about the sick troops appearing in his medical unit during that first week of September. "Eight out of the first ten patients admitted to this hospital had widely dilated pupils with hallucinations—a few being actively excited," he noted in his journal. "One of them this morning was clearheaded enough to recall that, in addition to some blackberries, he had eaten about five large ripe berries which grew on a bush four or five feet high, and they left his mouth puckery. The big black berries were poison—belladonna, as every Frenchman knew."[7]

Others had a better experience. "Most every place we stopped on our trip we found plenty of blackberries (nice big ones) and I picked my share of them," Private Robert Shepherdson of the 103rd Infantry said in a letter home. "My! But they tasted good."[8] But not every soldier was as enthusiastic. Some took up another age-old tradition of men at war: griping about the food. "I never want to see another cherry again," complained George Kirkpatrick. "But that's the way of the army; eat all you can while you can because you may never see any more cherries."[9]

Ever vigilant to keep up stateside morale, however, a Boston newspaper ran an article on September 4 that made it seem as if the soldiers were enjoying the culinary comforts of home. "New England's famous doughnuts are coming into their own on the Western front," it cheerily reported. "Salvation Army and Red Cross caterers find the American soldiers greedy for this delectable creation of the mothers they left behind. There is only one delicacy that outranks the doughnut with our boys, and that is the flavorsome, flaky-crusted apple pie."[10] The article was undoubtedly planted—the work of George Creel's massive PR campaign—and the kind of detailed effort designed to ensure that nervous families kept up their stateside morale and support of the war cause.

Alas, there were no doughnuts for these doughboys. The New England men who made up the bulk of the Yankee Division just kept pushing on, through the slop, night after night, ever closer to the heavily entrenched German front lines.

"The rain finally stopped, but not until we had reached our bivouac area, which was another small forest," Albertine wrote in his war memoir.

> The Boche planes were up every day to see what they could observe. They seemed to sense something was up, either through their intelligence or by clever spies. They would fly very low. Of course during the daylight hours we were well concealed in the woods, and sentries were posted all around the edge of these woods to stop any Yank from venturing outside. This forced march went on for several days. We figured we were hiking from twenty to thirty kilometers a night. No hot meals were served, because smoke would make the Boches suspicious. As far as we could ascertain, no one fell out. It only goes to show you we were all tough soldiers and in good health. Toward the end of this march the roads were jammed with all kinds of troops, artillery, machine gun carts, ambulances, trucks, and it seemed as though everything was being massed for the big drive.[11]

In fact, German commanders strongly suspected that Allied forces were planning an offensive of some kind, somewhere. Throughout August and into September they persistently tried to gain intelligence. Almost daily, scouts were sent out to probe the area beyond the salient front lines in the hopes of capturing and interrogating prisoners. Despite all the efforts by the Americans to conceal their movement and plans, the Germans sensed that a battle was imminent at St. Mihiel and contingency plans were being readied, including one for a rapid retreat. This was the last of the wars fought in the old ways, where battlefield commanders were still often blind to their opponent's positions, numbers, or plans until armies met—sometimes accidently—on the field of battle. Keeping the Germans in the dark was the key objective of the pre-battle air campaign, designed to prevent German planes from sussing out the precise location of Allied armies and preparing for those attacks.

Airplanes had become a dominant factor in warfare, in fact. Near Toul, France, the First Pursuit Wing of the U.S. Army Air Service was redefining war. For centuries, men had fought exclusively on land and sea in a two-dimensional give and take to determine a winner, but now, in the skies above Europe, everything had changed. From above, one could see the field of battle from a new perspective. Terrain could be studied, the opponent's forces could be seen, an accurate assessment of his strengths and weaknesses could be made, and armies strategically moved to counter. Most importantly, the other side could be attacked, with bombs and bullets that would rain down in a storm of death.

For over a week, the First Pursuit Wing had been clearing an area on the front lines between the Meuse and Moselle Rivers, in preparation for an Allied offensive. From daybreak to dark, day after day, patrols of aircraft in shifts that overlapped by fifteen minutes kept a constant control of the skies. Now the airmen, mostly French and American, had pushed German aerial activity back about five kilometers from the front lines and held an observational and strategic advantage over their enemy.

The 139th Aero Squadron was temporarily under the command of First Lieutenant David E. Putnam of Newton, Massachusetts. A descendant of Revolutionary War hero Israel Putnam, who was second in command of colonial forces in the Battle of Bunker Hill, David Putnam was unquestionably a hero in his own right and the closest thing America had to a war celebrity at the time.

Fighter pilots were the glamor boys of the Great War, setting the precedent for wars to come. For soldiers and sailors in other branches of the military, the seamless execution of specific orders by masses of troops and seamen, each a part of a larger, more critical whole, spelled success or failure in battle. Pilots, on the other hand, largely operated alone and without pre-planned maneuvers. A soldier who deviated from strict discipline in battle might get himself or others killed. But fighter pilots were freelancers and artists who lived and died on spontaneity, imagination, and daring.

The introduction of aircraft into war led to a new kind of battle, the three-dimensional dogfight—a looping, swerving dance of kill-or-be-killed that a pilot fought alone. The ultimate prize was to bring down the enemy's plane at the end of one of these dizzying fights. Any pilot who managed to down five enemy aircraft was bestowed the new, unofficial, but enticing title of "ace."

Lieutenant Putnam was America's "Ace of Aces." With thirteen confirmed enemy kills, and at least another twenty victories in which the other plane went down so far behind enemy lines that it was impossible to verify, he was an undisputed celebrity with more dogfight victories than any U.S. pilot alive. It was an important distinction because Putnam had taken over the top ace position when fellow Massachusetts native Frank Bayliss of New Bedford, with thirteen kills, had himself been shot down in June. To stay at the top of the pyramid, a pilot had to stay alive.

"Mingled with this natural desire to become the leading fighting Ace of America was a haunting superstition that did not leave my mind until the very end of the war," wrote Eddie Rickenbacker, who eventually became the most successful and famous American aviator of World War I, with more than two dozen confirmed kills. "It was that the very possession of this title—Ace of Aces—brought with it the unavoidable doom that had overtaken all of its previous holders. I wanted it and yet I feared to learn that it was mine!"[12] Rickenbacker would survive the war to achieve even more fame as a race-car driver and, later, as president of Eastern Airlines.

Born in Jamaica Plain, Massachusetts, Putnam had attended nearby Newton High School before entering college at Harvard at age sixteen. He was an athlete, starring on the football, baseball, swimming, and hockey teams, and he was also a leader—class president and class orator. While at Harvard, with war raging in Europe, he passed the exam to enter the Aviation Service but was rejected for being too young. After completing his mid-year exams in early 1917, he visited with his mother, Janet, who was ill and in the hospital. He bid her goodbye.

"Why, where are you going?" she asked her son.

"To France," he told her. "I'm going on a cattle boat, and it leaves in one hour."[13]

Once overseas, Putnam joined an ambulance corps and then the famed Lafayette Escadrille, made up of American volunteer pilots attached to the French Army. It was Norman Price of Pride's Crossing, Massachusetts, who had the original idea for an American squad of pilots in the initial months of the Great War in 1914. With the United States committed to neutrality at the time, many Americans were seeking ways to join the battle against Germany. Rebuffed at first, Price eventually convinced the French government to allow for a squadron of American pilots. The French saw the unit as a potential means of swaying American public opinion toward the Allies and, in August 1915, formed the *Escadrille Americaine*, otherwise known as the Lafayette Flying Corps.[14]

Putnam enlisted at the end of May 1917 and spent six months in flight school, training in biplanes near Nord, France. By Christmas he was shipped to the front. It did not take him long to stand out.

From the start, Putnam was an aggressive fighter. Other pilots called him fearless. "Putnam was famed for the reckless bitterness of his attack," fellow Lafayette Corps pilot James Hall remembered. "Always on the offensive, he cruised far within enemy lines, attacking with a ruthlessness and a disregard of odds which ran up his victories like magic."[15]

He had a penchant for flying deep behind enemy lines to seek out and engage German planes. Once he found them, he was a deadly foe. In April alone, he shot down six enemy planes. On the first day of the month, he emerged victorious from a thirty-five-minute dogfight with a confirmed kill. The very next day he went up against an eight-plane German "circus" and brought down two of them. Later in the month he earned his "ace" title by ringing up three wins in a single day.

"If we wanted to fight we had to go to a long way hunting behind the lines," a fellow Lafayette Escadrille pilot said of those early days. "This was especially forbidden by our Commandant; you know how cautious the French are in giving young pilots permission to do any *chasse libre*. When we were fortunate enough to get this permission you could rely on Putnam to stretch the privilege to the limit. I speak from experience, remembering that it was he who led me into my first scrap, when we were 25 kilometers in German territory."[16]

Putnam earned headlines in America on June 5 when he engaged ten German planes at once over Rheims and, in the course of the battle, shot down five of them. "One afternoon when I was with Putnam we attacked ten Albatross," remembered fellow pilot David Guy. "I had motor trouble and was forced to quit. It was certainly a revelation to watch Putnam attack. He showed absolutely no fear, and waited until within a few yards of the enemy plane before opening fire."[17]

Putnam's own recounting of the dogfight reflected all the youthful exuberance with which his colleagues said he fought.

I was with three other fellows when I saw two Boche biplanes. They saw us at about the same time and started to drive for home. Putting on all the speed I could I gave chase. As my machine happened to be slightly faster than the others of my patrol, I arrived first. With both guns shooting murder, I slowly closed with one of the Boches. Nearer and nearer I drew. One gun stuck, but the other rattled on. When I was about ten yards from the German, up came his nose. A perfect target, and just at that moment my remaining gun stopped. The German gunner (I could see him clearly) took one look at me and commenced to fire. A quick turn and I was out of range. I looked back and there was the unlucky Boche falling. Suddenly, his left wing broke off and he dashed into the ground. I looked for the rest of my patrol, and there they were, some five hundred yards above me watching the fight. We got together again and started to patrol some more. I kept on, for I was able to fix my guns, which weren't very badly jammed. Suddenly, I saw five more Germans and gave chase immediately. As the biplanes had done before them, they, too, turned toward home, and in following them I passed through a cloud and lost the rest of my patrol. The Germans, however, went so far that I turned back. I had flown perhaps three minutes

towards our lines when a German balloon loomed up directly
ahead of me. "Well," I said, "I've got no incendiary bullets,
but there's no harm in shooting at it." No sooner said than
done. I pulled both triggers. Pfoof!!! The balloon burst into
flames, and it did look queer. I supposed that there would be
just one burst of flame and that would be the end. No; the
thing remained in the air, a flaming mass, for perhaps twenty
seconds, and then dropped slowly to the ground where it
continued to burn. But how the anti-aircraft guns did shoot
at me. Bang! Bang! Bang! Just a continuous roar. "Flaming
onions" were also coming up from the ground. Into a cloud
I went. The shooting was even more terrible there, so out I
dove. Twisting, turning, circling. I finally reached our lines
and made tracks for home. The others arrived about the same
time, having witnessed the entire performance. That makes
nine official planes and thirteen unofficial for a total of
twenty-two in six months.[18]

When America officially declared war, the Lafayette Escadrille was
incorporated into the U.S. Army Air Service. Putnam accepted a commission as a First Lieutenant on June 10 and was shortly thereafter
assigned to the 139th Aero Squadron. Stateside, he was a bona fide war
hero, with his exploits chronicled in newspapers from coast to coast.

   "Combat after combat comes my way," he said, "and without boasting, I'll say that I generally meet them head on."[19]

CHAPTER 3

OUTBREAK

SEPTEMBER 2–3

The war in Europe was always on the minds of Americans, but it was not the only cause for concern. As September 1918 began, American workers, in Boston particularly, were facing their own set of problems closer to home.

"Labor Day 1918 is not like any Labor Day that we have known," President Wilson told his "fellow citizens," calling for Americans involved in war-related industries to take to the streets in a national show of support. "Labor Day was always deeply significant with us. Now it is supremely significant. We know that every tool in every essential industry is a weapon, and a weapon wielded for the same purpose that an army rifle is wielded—a weapon which if we were to lay down, no rifle would be of any use."[1]

The annual Labor Day parade in Boston was unlike any the city had seen before—more a military display than a celebration of civilian workers. One local newspaper described it as "largely a Navy Yard demonstration" and "patriotism with a genuine punch to it."[2] Most of the 4,000 marchers were government employees who worked in area shipyards, such as the Fore River plant in Quincy. There was a float depicting the Kaiser getting boiled head first in a huge cauldron, and a giant replica battleship with guns that fired confetti into the crowd. Parades around the country held to a common theme. "'Win the War for Freedom' is inscribed upon the banners of America's workers today in every city and hamlet," said Samuel Gompers, founder and president of the American Federation of Labor, who was in London. "It is the message that will be spoken from every platform. It is the song of every heart. It is a war for freedom because only through victory can there be freedom."[3]

Back home, however, unions were not as united as Gompers's statement made it seem. While Gompers was out of the country, John Alpine of South Boston, former business agent for the Boston Gasfitters' Local 175, was the acting head of the national AFL. In his home town, infighting among local labor unions resulted in the city's largest union group, the Boston Central Labor Union (BCLU), which Alpine formerly ran, calling for a boycott of the parade. A dispute over hiring by the federal government at the naval docks, resulting in three union members not being used to fill open jobs, had the trade group up in arms. After a heated meeting, the BCLU membership voted unanimously to decline Mayor Andrew Peters's invitation to march and have union officials join him on the reviewing stand at City Hall. Other local unions were totally on board with the parade, especially the Metal Trades Council of Charlestown, home of the Navy Yard. As a result of the dispute, the number of participants in the Labor Day parade was less than half of what was typical.

Even so, there was a large crowd, and when the parade stepped off at Arlington and Beacon Streets on that sunny Monday morning, there were thousands of marchers, including 1,000 sailors from Commonwealth Pier. These patriotic men and women were unaware that a deadly invisible enemy had silently invaded their ranks. The sailors and factory workers packed the streets, walking side by side, jostling one another, unavoidably breathing and coughing on the people around them. They had no idea that nearby, in military facilities at the Chelsea Naval Hospital and the Army's

Camp Devens, a biological fuse had ignited that would explode in Boston and the rest of Massachusetts, moving outward like a devastating shock wave that would reverberate around the world.

The man in charge of Camp Devens, Major General Henry P. McCain, was a stickler for details. McCain had been adjutant general of the Army, the top administrative officer in the service and the key assistant to Judge Advocate General Enoch Crowder. Together, the two had been responsible for filling the ranks of the Army through the draft and organizing it into a battle-ready command structure. But as General Pershing was organizing the disparate American Expeditionary Forces into a single American army in Europe, McCain volunteered to leave his Washington desk job to organize and take command of the Army's newly-formed Twelfth Division, made up primarily of New England recruits, and he came to Camp Devens in Massachusetts in mid-August to assume his post. Like dozens of similar facilities around the country, the cantonment in the hills outside of Boston had been thrown up quickly when America declared war on Germany the year before. Built for 36,000 troops, it now held over 45,000 soldiers amassed and ready to burst forth as if from a fire hose pointed at an enflamed European theater.[4]

In the meantime, McCain would make damned sure that the brand new Twelfth Division, to be known as the Plymouth Division, was prepared. The fifty-seven-year-old West Point graduate and veteran of the Spanish-American War insisted that the men of Camp Devens train and drill and drill and train some more. He worked them to the point of monotony, knowing full well that rote became instinct and that discipline could be the difference between victory and defeat once his men were in battle. All the while, McCain attended to the detail work that falls to commanders. During his first two weeks at his new post, he inspected every building in the camp with meticulous care. He checked and rechecked every aspect of camp operations, from food supplies to the motor pool, even the latrines. Camp Devens had 199 company barracks, another seventy-four barracks for officers, ten regimental headquarters buildings, ten quartermaster storehouses, and a variety of support buildings—including a refrigerating plant, a post office, a bakery, fire stations, garages, stables, and recreational buildings.[5]

Among the only quiet places in what amounted to one of the largest cities in Massachusetts were the nearly twenty medical buildings. All told, Camp Devens had 1,800 hospital beds, but as September began there were only a couple dozen patients, almost all with the routine kinds of problems that arise in a large community with an inordinately high percentage of young men. So it was of little note when four soldiers were admitted with flu-like symptoms and were diagnosed with pneumonia.

About thirty miles away, on the Boston waterfront, a few dozen seamen from nearby Commonwealth Pier were also suffering with similar symptoms and were being cared for at Chelsea Naval Hospital under the supervision of Lieutenant Commander Milton Rosenau.

Rosenau was no stranger to public health. Earlier in his career, he had served for twenty years in what had been called the U.S. Marine Hospital Service but became known as the Public Health Service during his tenure there. He built the service's Hygienic Laboratory from a one-doctor outpost to a thriving research center specializing in bacteriology, chemistry, biology, pharmacology, and pathology, one day to be renamed the National Institute of Health. It was his responsibility, in many ways, to solve America's most vexing public health problems. Along the way, he wrote "Preventive Medicine and Hygiene," a hugely influential text-book. At age forty-nine, he was among the country's foremost authorities on infectious disease.

"It was very clear early in my career that I took a dislike to the actual practice of medicine and developed a distinct liking for investigation and for public health work," Rosenau said. "The old days of fads and fancies have passed and we realize today that doctors and public health officers are two different, distinct branches; the doctor thinks of his sick patient, while the health officer thinks in terms of the health of whole communities."[6]

Like many other American doctors, Rosenau had left his day job—in his case, as an esteemed professor of epidemiology at Harvard—to join the military. He was commissioned a lieutenant commander in the

Navy and was posted at the Chelsea Naval Hospital across the harbor from downtown Boston. As one of the country's top experts on infectious disease, he was in the perfect position to recognize the emerging contagion, identify it, and take the necessary steps to prevent it from turning into a full-fledged epidemic.

It wouldn't matter.

In those first days of September, Rosenau and his assistant, Dr. John Keegan, noticed an uptick in the number of respiratory cases at Chelsea—namely pneumonia and influenza. Going into the war, pneumonia had been the chief medical concern of military doctors. Experts feared that pneumonia, often as a byproduct of some other disease such as measles, could become an epidemic that would ravage a fighting force in time of war. Influenza, they believed, was far more controllable and not even remotely likely to cause death among otherwise healthy soldiers and sailors.

As far back as 1913, William Gorgas, currently the Army's surgeon general, claimed that influenza could actually be eradicated, and somewhat easily. "You might ask why, if we are so boastful of our efficiency in getting rid of diseases, do we not abolish grippe altogether," he said in a *New York Times* profile, referring to influenza by its more common name. "Doubtless we could abolish it if we chose. It could be abolished everywhere if people became convinced that it was worthwhile to take the requisite trouble."[7]

Simple steps, like refraining from spitting in public, using a handkerchief, spending time in the open air—in essence, avoiding the spread of germs—was all that was needed to manage widespread influenza infection. Or so the popular thinking went.

Three years later, in 1916, Rosenau spoke about how advances in the study of communicable diseases had deepened medicine's understanding of the how the flu moved from one person to another and how that could be prevented. "It makes comparatively little difference to us from the standpoint of preventive medicine, from the standpoint of the health officer, whether this disease is due to the bacillus influenza," he said. "If we know how they are spread, we may be able to control them."[8]

What was unknown at the time was how resilient influenza is, how it has an ability to adapt and evolve in ways that make it difficult to fight and impossible to fully defeat. Even now, a century later, influenza and resultant pneumonia remain among the top five or six causes of natural death in the United States, despite tremendous medical advances.

Still, at the time there may not have been a doctor in America better equipped to identify and quash an infectious disease before it could erupt into an epidemic, so Rosenau knew immediately that the Commonwealth Pier cases that were appearing in his hospital were influenza. He and Keegan did everything right, applying all the knowledge the scientific community currently had about the disease. First, they checked blood counts and took throat and blood cultures. They isolated sick men and traced the people with whom they had come in contact then tried to isolate those people as well. The idea was to contain the virus in a finite set of subjects, allow it to run its course, and essentially starve it by denying it new people to infect.

Ever the researcher, however, Rosenau also realized that the sick sailors presented him with a chance to learn. Here was an outbreak of infectious disease in its earliest stage, with victims who were also on active duty in the military and therefore easily manipulated and tracked. To Rosenau, it was a living laboratory environment, and he was not about to waste the opportunity. He and Keegan set about testing the symptomatic sailors.

"This is the first time the disease has prevailed since we had the modern scientific methods to study it," he noted. "This is the first chance that has come to doctors to study the disease since doctors have had proper methods to fight it."[9]

On September 3, the first civilian case of influenza was reported at Boston City Hospital as well, though that was only notable in retrospect. At the time, a single flu patient was unremarkable, one of a stream of patients with a wide variety of ailments admitted to a big-city hospital on any given day.

At Camp Devens, the number of patients in the cantonment hospital was starting to climb. While four soldiers had been admitted on September

1, there were thirty-one new cases the next day.[10] Presenting symptoms gave doctors no reason to think they were anything but the normal aches and pains associated with a heavy cold—perfectly normal in a community of nearly 50,000 people. A few inevitably developed pneumonia. Still, there was no cause for real concern. The day after Labor Day, 1,400 fresh recruits from Massachusetts arrived at the camp to begin training, hailing from every corner of the state but heavy on natives of Boston.[11]

"We're going to write 'South Boston' across the signposts in *Unter den Linden*," one enthusiastic new recruit reportedly said between his arrival at the camp and his quick dispatch to a lesson in proper rifle handling.[12]

How many of these brand new inductees had attended the "Win the War for Freedom" parade the day before? How many lived or worked by the waterfront naval yards, where Rosenau and Keegan were trying to isolate anyone exposed to their influenza cases? The soldiers were as ignorant as their superiors to the fact that many of them were undoubtedly bringing death to camp in their bags, on their clothes, and in their lungs. Doctors at Devens had not yet correctly diagnosed a single patient, but influenza was already silently spreading through the camp.

And the virus was just getting started.

CHAPTER 4

LODGE

SEPTEMBER 1–17

W hile the fate of Massachusetts's military men came under the deadly threat of influenza, one powerful Boston man was busy attending to the political fate of the nation. Henry Cabot Lodge was a man of considerable accomplishment even before he went to Washington. He was a three-time graduate of Harvard, with a bachelor's degree, a law degree, and the first doctorate in history the school ever conferred. In the thirty-two years since he was first elected to Congress, however, Lodge had risen to a pinnacle of power unmatched anywhere but 1600 Pennsylvania Avenue. Though the office had not yet been officially established, he functioned as what today would be the majority leader of the U.S. Senate.

Lodge was the quintessential Boston Brahmin. He grew up on the city's exclusive Beacon Hill, as the great-grandson of one of Massachusetts's first U.S. senators after the ratification of the Constitution, and as the scion of a wealthy merchant family that dated back well before the American Revolution. At sixty-eight years old, with a neatly trimmed, gray beard giving way to a luxuriously full mustache, he was small in physical stature but a political giant, the self-styled leader of the entire Republican Party. As such, he saw his opposition to President Wilson and his Democratic allies as a moral imperative—particularly now, with the country at war. Unlike many of his colleagues, who would argue passionately on the House or Senate floor all day only to retire to a nearby bar to socialize at night, Lodge was highly partisan and allowed little room for cross-aisle compromise. But in any event, it is unlikely that many members of Congress were interested in socializing with him; he had a reputation for being condescending, humorless, and prickly.

Wilson had been elected in 1912 when Lodge's one close friend, Theodore Roosevelt, split from the GOP, formed the Progressive Party, and set up a three-way presidential election that opened the door for a Democrat to win the White House for the first time in two decades. When he was an academic, Wilson had held quite conservative views, but as governor of New Jersey and in his 1912 campaign for president, he changed his position on a host of issues to far more liberal positions. What Lodge saw as a lack of consistency on Wilson's part offended him.

"He is a man of ability, but he has no intellectual integrity at all," Lodge wrote just before Wilson was first elected. "I think he would sacrifice any opinion at any moment for his own benefit and go back to it the next moment if he thought returning to it would be profitable."[1]

In the years since, the relationship between the two men had become increasingly acrimonious. When it came to foreign policy, the first priority of both was an Allied victory in the war, and each initially felt it important that the United States remain neutral. Lodge, however, was more vehement in his opposition to Germany and suspected that Wilson was too soft. He worried that Wilson's commitment to neutrality might outweigh his willingness to see the Germans defeated at all costs. During Wilson's first term, Lodge and Roosevelt had been the chief proponents of what they referred to as "preparedness"—shorthand for a massive American military buildup—while remaining nominally in favor of neutrality.

The doctrine of "peace through strength" was not a new position for Lodge. As far back as 1897, in the run-up to the Spanish-American

War, Lodge had argued that "armies and navies organized to maintain peace serve the ends of peace because there is no such incentive to war as a rich, undefended and helpless country, which by its condition invites aggression."[2]

Throughout Wilson's first term, Lodge kept the partisan heat on. "It is not our business, as the opposition party out of power, to construct bills and frame policies," he told a fellow Republican. "Our one business is to drive from power the present Administration, and that must be done by attack. We cannot make our attacks and criticism too pointed or too strong."[3]

So Lodge, Roosevelt, and their allies banged out a constant drumbeat for America to step up to the precipice of war, if not to actually take the fateful last leap. Massachusetts Congressman Frederick Gillett, Lodge's Republican colleague and a twenty-five-year veteran of the House, put it in unmistakably partisan terms when he noted that, "after the European war began, it was the leaders of the Republican party who agitated for an immediate arming and forecasted the future so accurately that, if their advice had been followed, this war would long before have been ended by our victory; while it was the leader of the Democratic party who discredited their fears and sneered at them as unnecessarily nervous and excited."[4]

As his re-election campaign drew nearer in 1916, Wilson made no bones about his feelings for Lodge and the Republicans. "I think you cannot know to what lengths men like [Elihu] Root and Lodge are going, who I once thought had consciences but now know have none," the president wrote a friend. "We must hit them straight in the face, and not mind if the blood comes."[5]

Lodge's Massachusetts colleague in the Senate was John W. Weeks, and the two were opposites in almost every way. While Lodge was a short and wiry political junkie with a patrician air of self-importance, Weeks was a barrel of a man with a shiny bald head and drooping mustache who had no real appetite for the "public" aspects of public service. While Lodge was a Machiavellian schemer, Weeks was what we now refer to as a "wonk"—which is not to say he wasn't a partisan. Weeks simply preferred to remain in Washington working on policy; he did not ravenously devour news from back home about whose political fortunes were up or down, in the way so much of Lodge's time was consumed. Both were impressed with their own intellect and skills, however, and both harbored quiet ambitions for themselves.

A graduate of the Naval Academy at Annapolis and a veteran of the Spanish-American War, Weeks was appointed to the Senate in 1913 after four terms as a congressman. Despite the undercurrent of rivalry between the two, he and Lodge got along fairly well. In 1916, when the Republicans were choosing a nominee to oppose President Wilson's re-election campaign, Lodge placed Weeks's name in nomination.

"The first duty of the Republican Party in the coming campaign is to drive from power the Administration and the party which have so gravely injured us at home and so deeply discredited us abroad," Lodge told the delegates at the GOP convention in Chicago, touting Weeks's "preparedness" credentials. "Our candidate must be a man who believes in the protection of American rights by land and sea and who will maintain an honest and real neutrality: who loves peace, the peace of justice and right, and who at the same time thoroughly believes in a preparation both in the army and navy which will absolutely defend and secure, not only our peace, but our rights and honor."[6]

Even as he publicly supported his colleague, however, Lodge briefly entertained the possibility of his own candidacy. He believed Wilson could only be defeated by a united opposition and that the ongoing split between the Republicans and the Progressives would doom the country to a re-election. Behind the scenes, as the author of the GOP platform, Lodge was working with his Progressive counterpart to see that the two campaign documents were as closely aligned as possible, so as not to hinder a possible unified ticket. His friend Teddy Roosevelt, who had created the Progressive Party for his own run at the White House in 1912 and opened the door for Wilson to win a three-way race, harbored hopes that he could be the person to heal the rifts he had created.

When it became apparent that Republican resentment would block his own path, Roosevelt suggested Lodge as a possible unity candidate.

A committee from both parties visited Lodge in his convention hotel room and floated the idea. "Oh! that this honor should come to me at my time of life!" he reportedly replied, still clad in his pajamas.[7] For a moment, he could see the possibilities.

It didn't last.

Reaction at the Progressive convention was swift and loud, and the Lodge trial balloon was definitively shot down. Days later, in a letter to Roosevelt, Lodge claimed never to have been interested at all, except in the cause of defeating Wilson. "Of course, I readily assented," he said of the offer, "for I thought it would at least tend to bring us all more together, which was the main object, and I cared not what happened to me. Personally, I am of course glad that I could not be nominated. I am not fit to run a campaign, and I not only have no desire for the Presidency, but I should dread the mere thought of it."[8]

As events unfolded, neither Lodge nor Weeks could unite the factions of the Republican Party. Weeks finished second among eighteen candidates in the first round of convention balloting then faded on the second ballot before withdrawing his candidacy. The GOP instead nominated Supreme Court Justice Charles Evans Hughes, and Wilson won his second term. Lodge's frustration mounted. The president's reluctance to commit to what Lodge now believed was a dangerous threat to America and to democracy around the world convinced the senator that Wilson was not only weak, but a coward.

"His one desire is to avoid war at any cost, simply because he is afraid," Lodge wrote to Roosevelt. "He can bully Congressmen, but he flinches in the presence of danger, physical and moral."[9]

When Wilson finally declared war on Germany in April 1917, Lodge faced a dilemma: how to fulfill his patriotic duty to support a wartime president while also leading the political opposition? The Republicans' elder statesman settled on what Weeks described as "a program which will of course include supporting the Administration in all its war activities but which will give us something to hang party action on when the war is over."[10] In other words, the two Massachusetts senators wanted their party to unwaveringly support the cause of war while not giving an inch with regards to Wilson's prosecution of it.

"To thwart the purposes or discredit the policies of the official head of a political party is legitimate political warfare," Lodge maintained. "To discredit or break down the President of the United States upon a question of foreign policy is quite another thing, never to be undertaken except for very grave reasons."[11]

Though their objective—defeating Germany—was perfectly aligned, Lodge's persistence in opposing Wilson's tactics infuriated the president's loyalists, like George Creel. The head of CPI savaged the Massachusetts senator in his autobiography. "I was always inclined to give Senator Lodge the benefit of the doubt, crediting him with ignorance rather than dishonesty," Creel wrote.

> As someone once said, the Lodge mind was like the soil of New England—highly cultivated, but naturally sterile. An exceedingly dull man and a very vain one—a deadly combination—his vanity fosters his ignorance by persistent refusal to confess it. More than any other senator, he has the conviction of omniscience, and his solemn expression and conservative whiskers persuaded many people to accept him at his own valuation.[12]

Lodge's distinction between Wilson the Democrat and Wilson the president was fluid, and he often redrew the line between political and policy criticisms to suit his needs. His private correspondence left no doubt as to his feelings about Wilson, however. In early September 1918, Lodge wrote to Roosevelt that he hoped one of his own recent speeches would "help make it difficult for Wilson to betray the United States and the Allies by negotiating a peace with Germany with a view of the German vote in this country."[13]

Openly expressing the idea that the president might commit treason in an effort to boost the vote in an off-year election seems unthinkable, but it is the kind of hyper-partisan concept that came naturally to Lodge, who was no doubt a patriot but a Republican above nearly all else.

Despite his muscular rhetoric, Lodge understood too well the price war can extract. His son-in-law, Augustus Peabody Gardner, was a veteran of the Spanish-American War and was in his eighth term in Congress from Massachusetts when war was declared. He resigned his seat, however, and accepted an officer's commission in the U.S. Army, determined to live up to the preparedness philosophy he and his father-in-law espoused. He was originally given the rank of colonel and assigned to stateside duty in the Adjutant General's Department. But Gardner was determined to lead troops into battle, so he agreed to a demotion and was given command of an infantry battalion in training at Camp Wheeler in Georgia. After only a month in command, Gardner came down with pneumonia and died on January 14, 1918.

As September 1918 began, Lodge was basking in the reviews he was receiving for a late-August speech trying to head off any attempt by Wilson to negotiate peace terms with the Germans. "There is only one way to obtain this security of the nations, this preservation of freedom and civilization, and that is by reducing Germany to a condition where by no possibility can she precipitate another war of conquest," he declared, keeping up his familiar tough talk.[14]

Lodge was almost gleeful with the reaction. "Wilson must hate you,'" his fellow New England Republican, Connecticut Senator Frank Brandegee, told him just after Labor Day. "You have stepped in, stated the conditions of peace which he has got now to follow, because the American people won't stand for anything else."[15] Lodge felt he had successfully boxed the president in: welcoming the prospects of peace but setting an expectation that the final result of Wilson's "total war" should be nothing short of "total victory."

Weeks, too, was offering barely veiled criticism of the administration. He took to the Senate floor in mid-September and attempted to shift the focus of his "preparedness" message from readiness for war to readiness for peace, and he found Wilson's approach just as lacking for both.

"The Hun is evidently on the run; and while we may not be able to see the end of the war, the end is coming," he told his fellow senators. "It may come sooner than we anticipate; and when it does come, we should be prepared for the conditions we shall have to face. In one day, the whole world scene will change."

Weeks, who had a son serving in the military, pretended to give Wilson and the Democrats the benefit of the doubt for the approach they took in the years before America entered the war, even as he pushed for the GOP's opposing view of a post-war world. "There might have been some excuse from the viewpoint of many people for not making ample preparations to fight," he half-heartedly allowed, "but with that failure before our eyes, the example of the failures of other nations, and, more important, the provisions these nations are making for peace, there is no excuse for our country not preparing itself to meet the great after-war problems."[16]

Lodge was not on the ballot in 1918, but that did not mean he wasn't intimately involved in home state politics. In a letter to the chairman of the state Republican Party shortly after Labor Day, he inquired about the political mood in Massachusetts, particularly as it related to support for Wilson. Even while professing not to be worried, Lodge was concerned that some Republicans might support Democratic congressional candidates out of a sense of patriotism. "I should like to know whether you have any information that leads you to think that there is any danger of a Republican defection this year toward the Democratic candidates on the theory of supporting Wilson by voting for Democrats," he asked.[17] Assured by Chairman George Bacon that there were very few such signs except among the "goody-goody long-haired gentry, largely in Boston, who consider themselves too intelligent to vote as party men,"[18] Lodge was not completely comforted and urged the chairman not to be complacent. "I really believe that a strong fight in some of the Congressional districts would be very desirable," he answered. "They ought really to be well fought whether they are safe or not."[19]

The political veteran's fears would prove well founded in November, though the surprise would not come from Republicans compelled to support a wartime president in House races, but from a new political force determined to swing the state's Senate contest.

On September 15, the Austrian government broke from its German allies and reached out to President Wilson, seeking an informal peace conference to discuss terms for the end of hostilities. The president's response was swift and unequivocal: no deal.

"The Government of the United States feels that there is only one reply which it can make to the suggestion of the Imperial Austro-Hungarian Government," Wilson wrote. "It has repeatedly, and with entire candor, stated terms upon which the United States would consider peace, and can and will entertain no proposal for a conference upon a matter concerning which it has made its position and purpose so plain."[20]

Lodge saw in the Austrian peace initiative a two-for-one opportunity—to give the appearance of a statesman rising above partisan politics to support his president's war policy and at the same time to paint Wilson further into a corner by pressing for Germany's unconditional surrender while making it seem like Wilson's own stated policy. He went to the Senate floor and first presented the carrot.

"The President's reply to this stupid note," he said, "will meet, I am sure, with universal approval. His prompt and curt refusal of the Austro-Hungarian offer was not only right but wise, for it will, I believe, put an end to loose and feeble talk about these Austro-Hungarian offers—a kind of talk which is not only debilitating and confusing, but distinctly helpful to Germany."

Then came the stick.

When Prussian militarism is crushed and the Germans throw up their hands, then the United States and her allies will tell them the terms of peace which they are to accept. In no other way can the world be made safe against German wars of conquest. In no other way can we justify our entrance into the war and our sacrifice of our best and bravest. Until complete victory

is reached on German soil any negotiations or discussion with
our enemies would mean that the war was lost, our sacrifices
in vain and our high purposes defeated.

Lodge believed himself to be the preeminent foreign policy mind in
Washington—or more accurately, the preeminent mind, period—and
the architect of his party's political strategy. Here was a chance to push
back at Wilson's weakness, as Lodge saw it, and to vent his frustration
with the president's academic fantasy of world peace as laid out in the
Fourteen Points speech at the start of 1918.

"Germany has brought unnumbered woes upon an innocent world,"
Lodge railed. "She must be put in a position where she cannot strike
again. She has appealed to the lust of conquest, the dread arbitrament of
arms. By that she must abide. She shall not now resort to talk and bargain
for the decision."

"We mean to put her in physical bonds," Lodge urged. "We mean
to make the world safe for all free, law-abiding, decent people, so that
they may live their lives in peace, unthreatened and unalarmed. For this
we fight. We shall not ask more. We shall never accept less."[21]

CHAPTER 5

THE BABE

SEPTEMBER 4–7

Dawn did not break in Chicago on September 4 so much as it slipped in unnoticed. It was rainy and blustery in the Windy City on what was scheduled to be the first day of the 1918 World Series. At Comiskey Park, as they had all season, fifteen sheep were grazing in the outfield, more available and economical than human grass cutters.

During the night, notices had been slipped under the hotel room doors of the Red Sox players at the Hotel Metropole. The paper outlined the arithmetic that would divide the 55.5 percent of gate receipts from World Series games one through four, which would be shared by the owners with the players. If any of them read the notices, or paid attention to what they said, or comprehended the ramifications, it would not be apparent over the days that immediately followed. But these notices might as well have been time bombs deposited in the players' hotel rooms.

Garry Herrmann, owner of the Cincinnati Reds and one-third of baseball's National Commission, had arrived in Chicago for the World Series bearing his customary trunk full of deli meat and everything necessary to outfit a well-stocked bar in his hotel room.[1] As legendary sportswriter Damon Runyon once said of Herrmann, "his face reflected his manner of living. His nose was bulbous, his complexion at all times was as red as the sunset. He loved to eat, and he loved to drink."[2] Herrmann had boldly predicted that the 1918 series would generate more money than the financially successful 1917 World Series had brought in. Herrmann was confident, in fact, that gate receipts would top $200,000, a one-third increase from the year before. The Cubs let it be known that they expected 15,000 day-of-game tickets to be sold for the opener.

Not everyone was buying the hype. "Under the circumstances, it appears certain that while the games may be well attended, there will be nothing like the great outpouring of fans which have each year filled the parks to capacity and swelled the coffers of the clubs and players," predicted one Boston newspaper.[3]

Sure enough, at 6:00 a.m. on the morning of Game One, there were fewer than fifty people in line at Comiskey Park seeking general admission tickets. At 10:20 a.m. local time, with sleet falling at the Chicago lakefront, the game was postponed.

Babe Ruth, the center of attention, was unfazed. "It only postpones the killing for another day," he told the *Boston Record*.[4]

Red Sox manager Ed Barrow was relieved at the postponement. In the past five days, his team had played six games and traveled halfway across the continent. They could use another day to rest. When the weather improved in the late afternoon, several Red Sox players used the unexpected downtime to visit the huge War Exposition in Grant Park, where mock soldiers were digging trenches and fighting simulated battles. Another brainchild of George Creel's Committee on Public Information, the massive battlefield re-creation, designed to give the general public a sanitized look at the war, complete with heaping helpings of patriotic slogans and music, drew two million spectators during its run in the Windy City.

"I feel confident that the Sox will win," Barrow told reporters. "The Cubs may be a great ball team, but I figure that the Sox are the better aggregation." His confidence was no doubt boosted by news that third baseman Fred Thomas, who had left the team earlier in the season and enlisted in the Navy, would be back to play in the World Series. He had received a furlough from his post at the Great Lakes Naval Station in Chicago and would be able to play the entire series for Boston. Thomas had gained weight during his service, and it was evident that he was in top physical shape. His return solved a problem for Barrow, who had struggled to find a suitable replacement during the latter part of the regular season.

"Now that Thomas is back it means a restoration of the conditions that existed before the best club in the American League by far was shot to pieces," Barrow said. "Thomas strengthens the one weak spot on our team and makes the infield complete."[5]

Barrow's best player, and certainly his most impatient, was ready to go. "I hope I don't have to sit on the bench a single inning of the series," Ruth told a reporter. "Why, I'd pitch the whole series, every game, if they'd let me. Do it? Of course I can do it. Why, I used to pitch three games in one day when I was in school, and didn't I pitch a 13-inning game one Saturday while I was with Baltimore and then pitch a double-header the next day, Sunday, with the second game another 12-inning one?"[6]

While the Red Sox and Cubs were enjoying their day off, drama was unfolding in downtown Chicago. Someone walked into the Federal Building on Adams Street in the middle of the busy afternoon and left a suitcase behind a radiator near the first floor entrance. Inside the suitcase was a time bomb. A little after 3:00 p.m., it went off. The radiator was blown out the front door and killed a horse standing on the street. Every window on the lower three floors of the two buildings across the street were shattered. Inside the building, four people were killed, and another seventy-five were injured.

As with so much that transpired in September 1918, this too had a tangential connection to Massachusetts. The Federal Building was the site of a just-concluded trial in which ninety-three members of the International Workers of the World union had been found guilty of violating the Espionage Act, after dramatic charges that anti-war demonstrations and publications by the union's management had sabotaged the war effort, hindered the draft, and favored a worker uprising that would ultimately overthrow the government. The judge in the widely publicized trail, Kenesaw Mountain Landis, soon to become baseball's first all-powerful commissioner in the wake of the 1919 Black Sox scandal, was in his chambers on the sixth floor. The union's president, "Big Bill" Haywood, was two floors above that, awaiting transport to Leavenworth prison with his fellow defendants. Haywood had first become famous for organizing a textile mill strike in Lawrence, Massachusetts, in 1912, where he sought public support through a stunt in which the children of striking workers were put on trains and shipped off to New York to be cared for by other union members' families during the strike.

Within fifteen minutes of the explosion, Chicago police conducted raids on two local headquarters of the IWW and arrested nine people. Over 1,500 government agents, and the entire Chicago police department, spread out around the city in search of those behind the bombing, the general identity of whom they seemed to have little doubt.

"This outrage, in my opinion, was inevitable as an act of reprisal on the part of the IWW following the sentencing of nearly a hundred of their members," claimed Phillip Barry of the U.S. Justice Department's Chicago office in the aftermath of the blast. "We are certain that the IWW committed this deed. Several arrests have been made, and we are questioning the prisoners as fast as we can."[7]

In 1918, America was enduring an era of frequent bombings, most of them at the hands of radical unions or avowed anarchists. An Italian immigrant based in Lynn, Massachusetts, named Luigi Galleani was the most famous instigator of bombings in the country. Galleani and his followers—who became known as "galleanists"—believed that capitalism and organized government itself were oppressing poor workers. These anarchists began a bombing campaign in Massachusetts in 1916, blowing up a police station in Boston's North End and planting a suitcase bomb in the Massachusetts State House. When the United States entered World War I, the anarchists upped the ante and bombings spread across the country. Already in 1918, there had been serious, deadly bombings in Milwaukee, New York, San Francisco, and Washington, along with countless smaller bombings in other cities.

On the south side of Chicago, baseball's National Commission, the three-man committee that ran the sport and was made up of Cincinnati Reds owner Herrmann, American league President Johnson, and acting National League president John Heydler, was alarmed less by the bombing than by the seemingly low interest in the World Series. The lack of demand for tickets should not have been a surprise. In 1917, the first season after America declared war, attendance at big league games went down. During the 1918 regular season, it went down again—by 40 percent.

What was keeping fans from buying tickets? On this day, perhaps it was the gray weather. But certainly the circumstances were not helped by the huge number of young adult men—baseball's target market—who were serving in the military or war-related industries. The tight wartime economy was also a factor. Few had enough leisure time and spare cash to catch an afternoon baseball game. The government had dictated that the demographic most likely to buy tickets was required to either work or fight. Showing up at the ballpark might arouse official suspicion as to why one was not doing one or the other.

So that afternoon, in an effort to boost attendance, the National Commission decided to cut ticket prices to match the cost of attending regular season games. Reserved seats at Comiskey Park that had cost $15 for the 1917 World Series were cut to $9. Grandstand seat prices were dropped to $1.50, and tickets for the bleachers were slashed to 50 cents.

In Boston, meanwhile, the same 50 cents bought admission to a gathering at the Boston Arena on St. Botolph Street where a scoreboard had been erected to follow the action. Information about the game, relayed pitch-by-pitch via telegraph, was displayed. Babe Ruth's wife, Helen, decided to watch the details of Game One unfold there herself. At Braves Field, home of the city's National League franchise, games were scheduled between the baseball teams from the Bumkin Island and Deer Island naval squads. They began at 3:00 p.m., when the World

Series was due to commence in Chicago. For the 25-cent admission, patrons were treated to the game between the sailors, a performance by the Bumkin Island naval band, and up-to-the-minute, pitch-by-pitch reports by wire on the World Series game, posted on the scoreboard and announced to the crowd by megaphone. Other locations around Boston also displayed the results of the World Series games as they happened. Newspaper offices and bars were among the locations keeping tabs. Inevitably, these were also gathering places for those with something tangible riding on the outcome.

Gambling on baseball was open and commonplace in 1918 and perhaps in no place more blatantly than Boston. Bettors of all kinds regularly congregated along the first-base pavilion at Fenway Park when the Red Sox played at home. With the team on the road for the World Series, the "sharps" needed places to meet and trade wagers. Because the gambling culture was so ingrained in baseball, no one raised an eyebrow when Philadelphia Phillies manager Pat Moran boasted to reporters on the day of the Game One rainout that he had placed a $500 bet on the Cubs to win the Series.[8] Today, that simple admission could get a person banned from the game for life.

While players from both teams relaxed on the unexpected day off, none likely took their leisure time to the extreme that Babe Ruth did. Sportswriter Gene Fowler later recalled a party that Wednesday night where he ran across his friend, *Chicago Journal* reporter Harry Hochstadter.

"There I saw a galvanized metal washtub in the middle of the floor, and in it a mound of cracked ice and an ammunition dump of wine bottles," Fowler wrote. "Sports writers, gamblers and other students of human nature were gathered about the tub, some of them drinking wine, others the stronger stuff. Mr. Hochstadter was addressing the guests, few of whom paid attention to his speech. The orator leaned over too far, then collapsed. Babe Ruth lifted Mr. Hochstadter to a couch, and advised him to switch to beer."[9]

Fowler noticed "Ruth seemed fresh as a cornflower, although he had taken aboard many helpings of the sauce." So he asked the star pitcher if he would be in shape to pitch the next day.

"The hale young man gave me a bone-rattling slap on the back," Fowler said. "'I'll pitch 'em all if they say the word!' The Babe then announced that he was leaving us to keep a date with someone who wore skirts. On his way out he urged that Mr. Hochstadter be given a Christian burial."[10]

It was cloudy and wet again on Thursday morning in Chicago, as the Red Sox and the Cubs tried again to get the World Series underway. "Naturally, I feel confident the Cubs will win the series," Chicago manager Fred Mitchell said, with a simple rationale. "I base my conclusion on the fact that we have the better ball club."[11]

Tickets went on sale at 9:00 a.m. and even at new, reduced prices, demand was anything but overwhelming. Fans planning to attend the game were bundled up in heavy coats, many brought blankets to stave off the unseasonably cold weather. The weather did not bode well for the pair of pilots who had set out that morning from New York, bound for Chicago, in the first-ever flight of the Post Office Department's new Airmail Service. One of the two, Max Miller, was forced to put his plane down, roughly and unexpectedly, outside Cleveland, causing some damage.[12]

Players were hoping for another postponement. Pushing the Series back an extra day would require that the first three games be played on Friday, Saturday, and Sunday. The two weekend games would likely translate to greater ticket sales, higher gate receipts, and a larger revenue share for the players. Many of them grumbled that the National Commission had initially scheduled both Saturday and Sunday for travel in its effort to ensure that the Series would be completed by the government's September 15 "work or fight" exemption deadline. Weekday games were less lucrative.

Skies cleared by the afternoon game-time, however. A contingent of Boston's Royal Rooter fan club was in attendance, as was its counterpart, the Cubs' Claws—complete with a band. Comiskey Park remained one-third empty, though. Official attendance was just 19,274 in a ballpark with a capacity above 32,000.

Always the strategist, Red Sox manager Barrow, who had refused to reveal his starting pitcher for Game One, had Joe Bush warm up prior to the game. Shortly before the scheduled start time, however, the crowd—what there was of one—stirred when Ruth trotted out to warm up as well. He seemed none the worse for wear following his eventful night at Hochstadter's party. When the lineup cards were exchanged at home plate with the umpires, Barrow had Ruth penciled in as his starter.

Ruth took the mound, looking to extend his World Series pitching brilliance. In his last postseason start, during the 1916 Series against Brooklyn, he had pitched a fourteen-inning shutout for the win.

The young left-hander would be just as dominant against the Cubs.

In the first inning, one of the many Ruthian legends was born. Leading up to the series, while discussing the game plan for the Cubs, Barrow had repeatedly reinforced in Ruth the strategy for pitching to one Chicago hitter, left fielder Les Mann. "Never let up on that Mann," the manager drilled into his young pitcher. "Keep bearing down on him all the time. And loosen Leslie up the first time you face him." Barrow wanted Ruth to pitch Mann inside, to back him off the plate and keep him from digging into the batter's box.

The lead-off batter for the Cubs was right fielder Max Flack, who was destined to play a pivotal role in the Series. He was about Mann's height but thinner and, quite noticeably, batted from the other side of the plate. Ruth threw three, high fastballs in a row and struck Flack out to start the game.

As legendary sportswriter Fred Lieb spun the tale, "Grinning from ear to ear and quite pleased with himself, Babe yelled over to Barrow, 'Well, I guess I took care of that guy Mann for you.'"[13]

The Red Sox strung together a walk and a pair of singles in the fourth inning off Chicago starter Jim "Hippo" Vaughn to scratch out a run. In a portent of things to come, however, Barrow was so intent on having Ruth concentrate solely on pitching rather than hitting, he batted the game's most fearsome slugger last in the lineup. It turned out not to matter. Ruth made the single run stand up. He completely shut down the Cubs and pitched his team to a 1–0 win, extending his World Series scoreless streak to twenty-two innings. He was now within striking distance of the all-time record, held by the legendary Christy Mathewson.

"Ruth pitched great ball," Barrow said. "I certainly will start him back at the Cubs when we play in Boston. We got the jump on them today and the Reds Sox are confident of repeating tomorrow."[14] Chicago manager Mitchell had to agree. "Credit is due to Ruth for his wonderful pitching," he said. "It was the first test of strength and the breaks were against us. The Cubs have ferreted out the weak spots of the Red Sox and the score will tell a different story tomorrow."[15]

Despite the stakes of the series and Ruth's brilliant performance, for most of the game the small crowd was lifeless. With the two pitchers dominating and little action to get excited about, the spectators just sat quietly and watched.

"The effect of the war was everywhere, especially in the temper of the crowd," sportswriter Ed Martin of the *Boston Globe* noted. "There was no cheering during the contest, nor was there anything like the usual umpire baiting. War taxes, the high cost of living, the curtailed season and the shadow of war all account for the indifference of the public. The dyed-in-the-wool fans were there, but not the general public."[16]

In the middle of the seventh inning, the band at Comiskey Park struck up a rendition of "The Star-Spangled Banner," which proved to be the most memorable moment of the day.

In 1916, President Wilson had issued an executive order naming Francis Scott Key's song as the national anthem, though Congress would not officially follow suit until 1931. Wilson hoped the song would serve to stir patriotic fervor among Americans in the face of world conflict, even as he campaigned to keep the country out of the Great War. It was not unheard of for "The Star-Spangled Banner" to be played at a baseball game. A band had played the patriotic number more than fifty years earlier at the opening of the Brooklyn Union Grounds in 1862. It was also fairly common for the song to be played on Opening Day in some ballparks, as that was a day when there was most likely a band on hand to perform. In the days before pre-recorded music and public address systems, music was not automatically offered at every baseball game.

Red Sox third baseman Fred Thomas, on leave but still on active military duty, snapped to attention on hearing the opening strains of the anthem, turned to center field, and saluted the flag. Other players followed suit, stopping where they stood while the song was played. Fans in the stands rose as well.

"Heads were bared as the ball players quickly turned about and faced the music," the *New York Times* reported. "First the song was taken up by a few, then others joined, and when the final notes came, a great volume of melody rolled across the field. It was at the very end that the onlookers exploded into thunderous applause and rent the air with a cheer that marked the highest point of the day's enthusiasm."[17]

Given that unexpected response, the playing of "The Star-Spangled Banner" was repeated at every game in Chicago and then in Boston as well, and the song became a tradition at every World Series game after that. A generation later, by the onset of World War II and the widespread adoption of public address systems, playing the national anthem became a standard pre-game ritual at every Major League Baseball game.

When the tickets and the money were counted up after the game, the totals were shockingly disappointing. Between the sparse crowd and the hastily lowered ticket prices, gate receipts totaled just above $30,000. This was well short of half the $74,000 total from the 1917 World Series opener at Comiskey Park. It already seemed all but certain that the four-game gate would fall short of the $150,000 generated the year before, and National League president Garry Herrmann's boastful prediction of $200,000 seemed absurd.

The first game of the World Series had barely ended and, already, serious money trouble was brewing between the players and the owners. One thing baseball owners could do well was count money. With the disappointing gate receipts from Game One in their pockets, the three National Commission members met and made some quick decisions. Herrmann, Johnson, and Heydler decided that every player on each World Series team would get the same share, regardless of how long they had played with their team during the season. If they were on the World Series roster, they got the same as every other man on the squad. To see that this decree was followed, they announced that the National Commission would mail World Series checks directly to players rather than let the Cubs and the Red Sox disperse the shares themselves. Players, especially veterans, were furious.

By Friday, September 6, the cold spell was over, and it was a 65-degree, late-summer day in Chicago for Game Two. Hopes were high, especially among the players whose financial fortunes were riding on ticket sales, that the crowd would be significantly larger than it had been in the dreary weather of the previous day.

Barrow once again sent pitcher Joe Bush out to warm up before the game, and this time actually allowed him to start. Barrow still had a surprise up his sleeve when it came to Ruth, however. Based on the young slugger's two strikeouts against a left-handed pitcher in Game One, Barrow decided to leave Ruth out of the starting lineup in Game Two against another southpaw, George "Lefty" Tyler, rather than play him in left field.

This was a stunning decision. Ruth was the most fearsome hitter in the game, and these were the most critical contests of the season. Everyone had assumed that Barrow would find a way to get him into every game, even against Chicago's left-handed pitchers. "Ruth has no fear of portside pitching," the *Globe*'s Ed Martin had written in his series preview. "He has punished forkhand service, and facing 'Hippo' Vaughn and George Tyler will not jar him one iota."[18]

The Babe certainly saw it that way. "I've been just as sure against left handers after the first few months of the season as I have against right handers," he maintained. "I can see one just as well as the other now."[19]

True, Ruth had gone hitless in Game One, but so had a number of players on both teams in a game featuring dominant pitching performances. Even so, Barrow, revisiting his reluctance earlier in the season to use Ruth in the field between starts, began the game with his best hitter sitting on the bench.

The second inning brought an example of how different the game was in that era. It was common then for coaches and players to mercilessly ride opponents with a nearly constant stream of insults and verbal challenges. Every club had an expert at getting under the skin of the other team. Chicago coach Otto Knabe had been working on Red Sox pitcher Joe Bush in the early going, trying to distract or rattle him. After Chicago scored three runs in the bottom of the second inning, during which Knabe continually urged Bush to "duck before you get killed out there," Boston coach Heinie Wagner had had enough.

"He and Otto Knabe, the official barker of the Cubs, had been squawking at each other since the start of the gentle pastime," wrote Charley Dryden in the *Boston American*. "At the close of the second round Knabe invited Wagner under the stands. Wagner not only went, he grabbed Otto by the arm and dragged him along the dugout. A guy might as well try to wrestle a depth bomb. The chunky Knabe upset Wagner and mopped up considerable dirt with the back of the Boston coach."[20]

Chicago players pulled the coaches apart, and several Red Sox players, who had rushed across the field to the rescue, took a bloodied Wagner away.

"Heinie was calling Tyler yellow as is the custom," reported legendary sportswriter Ring Lardner in the next day's *Chicago Tribune*, "and Knabe yelled at Wagner that he had a fine license to call anybody yellow because he was yellow himself. So Heinie says I'll come down there and show you who is yellow. As far as I can see, the argument about who is yellow and vice versa is just where it was before the bloody brawl."[21]

The fistfight and the empty benches would make national headlines today and be shown from multiple camera angles on twenty-four-hour sports networks for days on end. In 1918, it was not a big deal. "The umpires paid no attention to the fracas," Dryden told his readers, framing the issue in contemporary political terms. "Let the boys fight. This is what they've got to do, or work, as soon as the series ends."[22]

In the second inning, Tyler showed that Babe Ruth was not the only pitcher in the series who could also handle a bat. After Boston's Joe Bush gave up a walk and a pair of hits, Tyler drove a single to centerfield to drive in a pair of runners and give the Cubs a 3–0 lead. The left-hander, who had pitched an amazing, twenty-one-inning, complete game for the Cubs in July, then held the Red Sox at bay into the ninth inning. With Chicago clinging to a 3–1 lead, Boston put a pair of runners on base with one out. Barrow now faced a situation right out of the mythical baseball textbook. The game was in the balance: it was potentially the last inning and the tying run was on base. A double by the next batter would likely tie the game. A home run would give the Red Sox the lead, and Barrow had the greatest power hitter in the game on the bench and available to pinch hit.

Even though Ruth had played in just ninety-five games during the 1918 season, he had led the American League with eleven home runs. It was the beginning of a stretch of fourteen years during which Ruth would lead the league in homers twelve times on his way to becoming the greatest power hitter of all time. In 1918, despite playing in just two-thirds of his team's games, he finished third in the league with sixty-six runs batted in while posting a .300 batting average.

Though Barrow valued Ruth as a pitcher, apparently, he was still not enamored of his hitting skills. The two had clashed in June and July as the manager tried to force Ruth to pitch while the kid bucked authority and found excuses to stay in the outfield. Barrow hated that the undisciplined Ruth had led the league in strikeouts as well as home runs. Now there were two runners on in the ninth inning of a World Series game. A win would give the Red Sox a commanding lead in the best-of-seven series. A loss would even the series at one win for each team, essentially spoiling Boston's Game One road win. Ruth stood in the dugout with a bat in his hand, ready to head to the plate as a pinch hitter.

Barrow left Ruth on the bench.

Twice.

Instead he chose to have a pair of right-handed hitters face the lefty Tyler. The first struck out; the second lifted an easy pop fly to second base. The Cubs won Game Two by a 3–1 score.

"When Tyler slipped a bit I was thinking of changing, but I couldn't," Cubs manager Fred Mitchell said afterward of the decision that resulted in baseball's best hitter watching from the dugout as his team's best chance to win a World Series game slipped away. "I had to go through with the left hander. A right hander would have had Ruth coming up to hit, and if he got a hold of one, good night. He is a wonderful natural player, and nobody I've ever seen takes the cut at a ball he does. He is liable to knock any kind of a pitch anywhere."[23]

Ruth couldn't hit anything without getting in the game, though, so Barrow's determination to play the percentages and stick with less-talented, right-handed hitters would long be second-guessed.

"Every player of the team expected Ruth to get the assignment," wrote Eddie Hurley in the next afternoon's *Boston Record*. "The big fellow must have been boiling on the bench when his services were spurned. Sending Jean Dubuc or any other hitter to bat with such a tremendous swatter as Babe Ruth kicking around on the bench is nothing but criminal in baseball. It was Ed Barrow's hunch and it flivvered."[24]

Afterward, the manager seemed to attribute the loss to nothing more than bad luck. "Today's game was a tough one to lose, especially as we nearly broke it up in the ninth inning," he said. "The Cubs had the better of the breaks, I think, and piled up a lead in the second inning too great for us to overcome."[25]

Ed Martin, the beat writer for the *Boston Globe*, placed the blame on Bush and the beautiful weather rather than on the manager's decision. "It was not the right kind of day for Joe," he told his readers. "When sunlight is being tossed around, ad lib, the Bullet is easy to crack. The overhead has to be draped in mourning for Joe to show the class that he actually possesses. Joe closed up like a morning glory, the Cubs banging his offerings at will in the second stanza, pushing over all their tallies."[26]

In the offseason, Cubs manager Fred Mitchell owned an apple orchard in the central Massachusetts town of Stow, just fifteen miles from Camp Devens, where he lived with his wife and three-year-old daughter. As a married forty-year-old father and a farmer, Mitchell was almost surely exempt from military service and highly unlikely to be drafted into the military. Ballplayers and their managers were under tremendous public pressure to show that they were doing their part in the war effort, however. This was especially true in the wake of the "work or fight" order that was bringing the baseball season to a premature close. After his team's Game Two victory, Mitchell announced that he would not be going home to his Massachusetts orchard after the World Series. He had enlisted in the Army Quartermaster Corps.

Immediately after the game, attention turned to dollars and cents once again. What were the gate receipts? How much did the owners and the players stand to make? On this sunny Friday afternoon in September, big crowds were gathered all around the city. An estimated 96,000 people attended the War Exposition at Grant Park in downtown Chicago, just as Red Sox players had done on their rainy off-day two days earlier. Thousands more gathered in the downtown park in the evening to see pilot Max Miller arrive with the first delivery of mail transported by airplane, following his thirty-six-hour and fifty-six-minute journey from New York City. Though flares would burn until 10:00 p.m., the second of the two airmail pilots, Edward Gardner, would not arrive until the next day, having been forced down in Indiana due to darkness. On the north side of the city at Weeghman Park, the home field the Cubs had vacated for the World Series in favor of Comiskey Park and its ability to hold more ticket-buying fans, 20,000 more people, had gathered in the afternoon for a political rally in support of Republican Senate candidate Medill McCormick, who was facing Chicago mayor William Hale Thompson in a hotly contested primary race.

On the south side of Chicago, however, fewer people had taken in Game Two of the World Series than had come out for the candidate. Almost 12,000 of the 31,000 seats remained empty. Worse, most of the tickets purchased had been for cheap grandstand and bleacher seats. Actual revenue was dismal at under $30,000, even lower than for Game One. This was not good for anyone, player or owner, anticipating a big post-season payoff.

The next day, despite publicly claiming that he would go with pitcher Claude Hendrix, Mitchell decided to send his Game One starter, Hippo Vaughn, to the mound again in Game Three after just one day of rest. The Cubs' strategy continued to be minimizing the impact of Boston's top three hitters—Ruth, Harry Hooper, and Amos Strunk—who all batted left-handed, by sending as many left-handed pitchers to the mound as possible. Red Sox manager Ed Barrow seemed content to play along, as he once again left the Babe, the game's best slugger, on the bench for Game Three.

"It was a rather punk afternoon for G. Babe Ruth," reported Ed Martin. "Orders to intern him in the dugout are always given when a southpaw goes to the hill. Babe is apt to go stale."[27]

It's hard to argue with the results of Barrow's decision in Game Three, however. Journeyman George Whiteman, Ruth's replacement in left field, was hit by a Vaughn pitch in the top of the fourth inning. Then four straight right-handed batters each singled, giving the Red Sox a 2–0 lead. That was enough for Boston starter Carl Mays, who went the distance in a 2–1 win, putting his team up two games to one and sending them back home with a series lead.

"Vaughn got the worst of the breaks today, although he was not in good form as the opening day," Mitchell admitted, while remaining confident. "The Cubs will balance the scales again by taking the fourth [game]."

Barrow stuck to his guns. "When I said last night that the Red Sox were determined to return to Boston with a two-to-one advantage in the series, I was not boasting," he said. "We are in the lead and intend to remain there. I think we shall win the series because I believe we have the better ball club."[28]

The game ended at 4:30 p.m. local time, which gave players from both teams three-and-a-half hours to catch the 8:00 p.m. Michigan Central train at the LaSalle Street Station in Chicago's downtown Loop. Money was tight, so the National Commission decided to take a regularly scheduled train rather than using a charter to transport the traveling World Series entourage to Boston. Five cars were added to the train: one for the Red Sox, one for the Cubs, one for the press, one for Red Sox owner Harry Frazee, and one for the three-member National Commission. The trip was scheduled to take until around 11:00 p.m. on Sunday night, twenty-six hours after it began.

It was a train ride unlike any the ballplayers had experienced in the past.

Conditions were ripe for trouble. Here were the two teams, forced by circumstances to share a train rather than travel separately.

The trouble started early, when several of the Boston players discovered that some of their teammates were to be paid all the way through September 15 under special deals with Frazee. Now the rest of the Red Sox wanted the extra two weeks' pay, on top of whatever World Series share they would earn. Unlike the rest of the major league players, they were still under contract, after all.

"The players on both teams are very keen to get all that is coming to them in the way of the old kale," Ed Martin wrote in his distinctive style. "Before the Sox left home a committee waited on President Frazee and induced him to pay their salaries up to September 15. Word had slipped out that certain players on the club had been guaranteed their salaries at least up to that date, and when the others heard of it they got busy."[29] Chicago players also caught wind of the under-the-table agreements for Boston players and went to team president Charlie Weeghman to demand the same treatment. He reluctantly agreed.[30]

Ever the rambunctious kid, Babe Ruth could not be bothered with all the talk about money. He recruited teammate Walt Kinney to run through the train cars stealing other peoples' straw hats and punching the tops out. It was past Labor Day, the thinking went, and fashion dictated that straw hats were strictly for summer wear. It was not the last of the roughhousing Ruth would engage in on the trip, but it was the least consequential.

The evening newspapers in Chicago listed the attendance and gate receipts for the first three games of the Series, and players had picked up those papers before they departed. Red Sox outfielder Harry Hooper, the leader of the Boston "Strategy Board" that had met throughout the summer to discuss war news, did the arithmetic on the train, and, despite the uptick in attendance for Game Three to over 27,000, the figures didn't look good.

The players' share of World Series revenue had traditionally come from the gate receipts of the first four games played. This was to discourage the players from artificially extending the series to more games—essentially, losing on purpose—in an effort to make more money. In the recent past, the payoff for members of the team who won the World Series had been as much as $3,000 to $4,000.

Owners were already bothered by how much players were getting paid, and they were always looking for ways to reduce player earnings and, therefore, increase their dependency on the owners. Prior to the 1918 season, for the first time, baseball officials decided to reduce individual players' World Series shares by splitting the gate receipts amongst the top four teams in each league, rather than just the league champions. Now there were eight teams getting a slice of the revenue pie rather than two.

The notice slipped under the hotel doors of the Red Sox players earlier in the week had outlined the formula. The Red Sox and Cubs would be splitting 55.5 percent of the players' share, with the winning team getting 60 percent of that pot and the losing team getting 40 percent. The second-, third- and fourth-place teams in the American and National Leagues would be dividing the remaining 44.5 percent that had traditionally gone solely to the pennant-winning teams.

Players had been under the impression that there was a guarantee of at least $2,000 apiece for members of the winning team and $1,400 for the losing team, up somewhat from the $1,835 and $1,215 that had gone to the 1917 World Series team members, and that the payout to the also-rans in each league would be reduced in order to ensure those guarantees. The Red Sox had been in New York wrapping up the regular season when the details of the payment plan were spelled out seemingly clearly in one Boston newspaper. "As adopted last winter by the two leagues and the National Commission, the amended regulations provide that each member of the winning club shall receive $2,000 as his share of the world's series proceeds, while the loser's individual end will amount to $1,400," it reported, noting how odd it was that this number was fixed and not tied to gate receipts, as had been the case in the past.[31]

The National Commission was making no effort to disabuse anyone of that notion.

As the train headed east, Hooper was reading through the notice and running the numbers. He discovered that the $2,000 and $1,400 figures were not guarantees. In fact, they were caps. He also discovered that the difference was largely irrelevant, however, as the split was in fact based on gate receipts. Given the money totals from the first three games, and with just one game left to add to the pot, it looked like the players' share was likely to be just $900 to the winners and $600 to the losers. First the players had been pressured into donating 10 percent of their winnings to the war effort. Now it appeared that they stood to make less than half what players from the 1917 World Series had earned.

Hooper decided to share his discovery not only with his teammates but also with his opponents. Into the night, players from both teams groused to each other about what they saw as the deceitful actions of the National Commission, on top of what they saw as double-dealing by the two owners that had been revealed earlier in the trip. These men were losing their livelihood as baseball shut down for the duration of the war, and they faced uncertain financial futures. Many were convinced they were within days of being drafted into military service and rushed off to war. They had families to consider.

"It was not the series itself or its outcome that occupied the attention of the Red Sox and Cubs on their eastward journey," Martin wrote in the *Globe*, "but the amount of swag they are going to receive for taking part in the classic."[32]

As the train continued east, the players knew they were headed into a confrontation with baseball owners. They did not know that they also were headed directly into a maelstrom of disease and death that was just about to explode.

CHAPTER 6

SPANISH FLU

SEPTEMBER 4–7

At Camp Devens, Major General McCain was planning ahead, as usual. He issued an order that banned any World Series information from the camp until after six o'clock in the evening. He knew interest would be high, but he was determined that his men would finish their drilling and their dinner without any distractions from the outside world.

In Boston, the options for a man seeking a distraction were narrowing. The War Department announced that twenty-five saloons within a half mile of the Wentworth Institute in Roxbury must close. Hundreds of recently drafted young men were undergoing training at the location, and the elimination of temptation was deemed the prudent course. Rumors filled Boston about which neighborhoods might be targeted next.

On the Wednesday following Labor Day in the Boston suburb of Dorchester, seven-year-old Francis Russell and his third-grade friends were back at the Martha Baker School on Walk Hill Street for the first day of the new school year with their teacher, Miss Sykes. As it did for their parents and other adults, the war permeated nearly every aspect of the children's daily lives.

"For the victory of our boys, we ate peaches and baked the stones dry to be used for gas masks," Russell said of that memorable school year. "On Boston Common, there were peach-stone collection barrels. How they were used we didn't know, but the newspapers showed a boy in Roxbury who had saved 2,000."[1]

Peach stones contain carbon, and 200 of them were enough to provide the necessary carbon to manufacture one gas mask. So, citizens from coast to coast felt the pressure to collect as many as they could. As one publication unsubtly put it, "Every American man, woman or child who has a relative or friend in the army should consider it a matter of personal obligation to provide enough carbon making material for his gas mask."[2]

Lieutenant Mark King, home on leave from the 101st Regiment of the Yankee Division, offered his support for this endeavor based on first-hand experience. "The gas mask is the best friend a soldier has," he told a reporter. "That little bit of carbon in the respirator is a bigger life saver than any other single thing in a soldier's kit. Save peach stones by all means. Pile 'em up! Keep your mind on it."[3]

At Jordan Marsh, the department store in downtown Boston, they were filling six barrels with donated peach pits every day, including the ones brought in by thirteen-year-old Samuel Borstel of Roxbury, which he had picked up out of the streets. "Every time I think that 200 no-good peach stones saves a soldier's life and remember that my four older brothers are fighting in the trenches, I just beat it down to the Crossing with this market basket over my arm and go hunting for peach stones," young Sammy said in his newspaper profile.[4]

The war effort was as much a part of the kids' daily routine as academics. "We joined the Junior Red Cross and wore rectangular celluloid pins in our buttonholes," Russell recalled. "Then there were the Thrift Stamps at 25 cents each for us to buy from Mr. Gibney the postman. Mr. Gibney gave us a little book to paste the stamps in. Each space to be filled had a motto like 'A Penny Saved is a Penny Earned' or 'Great Oaks from

Little Acorns Grow.' When we had 20 stamps we exchanged them with Mr. Gibney for a War Savings Certificate."[5]

Across the Charles River from Boston, on the campus of Harvard College in Cambridge, 5,000 men were enrolled at the Naval Radio School, learning the intricacies of a new technology that promised to revolutionize communication, with immediate and particular application in the conduct of war. A few cases of influenza were reported at the school, though the illnesses barely registered there. Plans were moving forward for the weekend dedication of a new building on campus, for which a large crowd was expected.

When the night arrived, thousands of invited guests packed into the school's drill hall to hear a speech by Rear Admiral Spencer S. Wood, watch drill team and calisthenics exhibitions, and dance until midnight in celebration of the opening of the new building.[6] Unfortunately, the revelers provided an optimum breeding ground for the influenza virus, right at the geographic center of the gestating epidemic.

Almost a year earlier, Navy Surgeon General William C. Braisted had delivered a speech before the American Public Health Association in Washington in which he had boldly proclaimed that "infectious diseases that formerly carried off their thousands, such as yellow fever, typhus, cholera, and typhoid, have all yielded to our modern knowledge of their causes and our consequent logical measures taken for their prevention."[7]

Dr. William Welch knew better. Welch was the pre-eminent American medical scientist of the day—past president of the American Medical Association and the National Academy of Sciences, currently the president of the Rockefeller Institute of Medical Research, and about to become the first dean of the Johns Hopkins School of Hygiene and Public Health. He was already considered "the father of American medicine" for his staggering accomplishments. When America entered the Great War, sixty-seven-year-old Welch entered the military because he understood that through the ages men at war had always died in greater numbers from disease rather than from wounds. As the foremost medical expert in the country and the man almost single-handedly responsible for dragging American medicine out of the dark ages and into the scientific age, he felt it was his patriotic duty to serve. Welch knew that the biggest impact he could have on the war effort was to prepare the military to prevent, if possible—but more likely respond to—an epidemic of infectious disease among the troops.

In 1916, with the likelihood of American involvement in the war increasing, Welch directed the establishment of the National Research Council, for the purpose of "encouraging the employment of scientific methods in strengthening the national defense, and such other applications of science as will promote the national security."[8] Even as President Wilson campaigned on a platform of staying out of the war, Welch saw the need to prepare for the worst. By the time war was declared a year later, Welch had built a team of the most knowledgeable infectious disease specialists from around the country, most of whom had studied or served directly under him and had already begun to prepare the Army and the Navy for the immense challenge of caring for millions of soldiers and sailors and keeping them as healthy as possible. As the ranks of the military began to swell, Welch and his team communicated best practices to the medical teams at bases and camps across the country, and they personally traveled to oversee those facilities.

Welch and two of his colleagues—Dr. Victor Vaughan, dean of the University of Michigan School of Medicine, and Dr. Rufus Cole, the leading respiratory disease expert at the Rockefeller Institute and the first director of the institute's hospital—headed out from Washington on one of those inspection tours of southern military camps early in September, anxious to see that the precautionary medical efforts they deemed so critical were being put in place.[9] Little did they know that their grave concerns of an epidemic ravaging military installations, feeding on thousands of men in cramped quarters and close physical contact, were already being realized—except to the north rather than the south. Soon, they would come face-to-face with the reality of their fear and find it almost beyond even their most-learned comprehension.

When death came to the Chelsea Naval Hospital, across the river from Boston and hard by the Boston Navy Yard, it came all at once. On

September 5, six of the influenza patients being cared for there died in one day, the first victims of a tide that would rise up and sweep across America. Five of them were sailors but one, in a sign of a critical complication yet to come, was a hospital apprentice.

Two of those initial victims were local area natives. Joseph Lonergan was a twenty-four-year-old seaman from Dorchester. James Shaughnessy was twenty-three, from West Roxbury, and had fallen ill aboard the USS *Aztec*, the flagship of the First Naval District, headquartered at Boston.

Dr. Milton Rosenau and Dr. John Keegan knew they had a crisis on their hands in the hospital. Experienced infectious disease specialists, they could do the math in their heads and predict where these early cases could lead. So, from the time of the very first patients, they had tried to contain the disease. They were looking at an epidemic in its embryonic stage and needed to act quickly if they were to have any hope of containing it. But the arithmetic overwhelmed the science. In less than ten days after the first influenza cases appeared on the receiving ship at Commonwealth Pier, hundreds of naval personnel had become ill. The doctors could not keep up.

"The onset is very sudden," Keegan reported, "the patient sometimes passing from an apparently well condition to almost prostration within one or two hours. The fever rises rapidly from 101 to 105 F., the patient usually complaining of severe headache, weakness, general malaise and pains of varying severity in the muscles and joints, especially in the back. As frequently described, the patient feels as though he has been beaten all over with a club."[10]

Rosenau had met with Welch, as well as Army Surgeon General William Gorgas, during the summer as part of the efforts at preparedness and prevention. Earlier in the year he had been at Camp Devens to consult on an outbreak of meningitis that threatened to spread through the cantonment. Almost his entire career had been spent studying infectious disease. Now, he was right in the middle of a virulent storm that was growing in ferocity faster than he and the Chelsea Naval Hospital staff could manage. Here was exactly the right doctor in precisely the right place, yet he was proving helpless to stop the disease's relentless march.

Despite the confident claims by Rosenau and others in the preceding years that science had learned enough about influenza to be able to control it and prevent its spread, medical knowledge about the disease was still spotty. Scientists knew that there were microbes, tinier than normal bacteria, that could cause disease. They called these "filterable viruses" because they were small enough to pass through filters used in research to capture and isolate bacteria. That was quite advanced for its time but far from the whole story.

Rosenau and Keegan, convinced that a filterable virus was causing the strain of influenza ripping through the ranks of military and civilian personnel in and around the Navy Yard, were already conducting tests to prove that such a virus was responsible. The hope was to find it, isolate it, and produce a serum to fight it. As the numbers of sick men increased, the pressure mounted to find the cause.

With all of the daily news from the war and the World Series to follow, hardly any Boston civilians paid note of the isolated illnesses and resulting deaths. But a select few were not only battling the disease, they were trying to sound the alarm as well. Dr. John S. Hitchcock, who headed the communicable disease section of the Massachusetts State Department of Health, sent a notice to local health officials across Massachusetts that spelled out the situation among the civilian population. "The malady appears to be in the nature of old-fashioned grippe," he explained, noting that, so far at least, "no deaths have occurred." He also referred to the efforts of Rosenau and Keegan at Chelsea. "The Naval medical authorities who have the matter in charge are doing everything humanly possible to control the outbreak," he noted before adding an inexplicable claim that flew in the face of the reality on Commonwealth Pier. "Now the daily list of cases appears to be diminishing."

If Hitchcock was trying to put the best possible spin on the news from the Navy Yard for the sake of public morale in his statewide notice, he also hit upon a hard truth. "Unless precautions are taken, the disease in all probability will spread to the civilian population of the city," he predicted.[11]

He was right.

If Hitchcock's civilian warning reached military commanders via official channels or passed along by local authorities, it was ignored. There were already eighty-four soldiers in the Camp Devens hospital suffering from influenza and subsequent pneumonia. The outbreak had military doctors there confused. On Saturday, September 7, a soldier was admitted to the camp hospital and diagnosed with meningitis. By Sunday, twelve more men from his same unit, D Company, Forty-Second Infantry, were admitted with what doctors also believed was meningitis.[12] Was this related to the pneumonia cases from earlier in the week? Was it a recurrence of the meningitis outbreak from earlier in the year? Finally, through a process of elimination, the doctors reached the conclusion that this was influenza.

One Boston paper reported on Hitchcock's warning but buried it on page seven next to an article warning of "Housewives Cheated by Ice Men." Still, the state health department doctor did his best to prepare the public. "With a focus of infection of this size, it seems probable that the disease will escape into the civil community in spite of all efforts at control," Hitchcock predicted. "People should be reminded that under these conditions persons with coughs and colds are not choice companions, and that a good doctor is a friend. It should also be remembered that our past experience with this disease has shown the danger of persons suffering from it continuing at work or trying to return to their occupation sooner than safety dictates."[13]

No one seemed to take notice.

The next day, even as a new rash of influenza cases was reported at a Navy training camp on Bumkin Island in Boston Harbor, 300 servicemen traveled by ship from Boston to Philadelphia. They quickly integrated with troops from other parts of the country, and they were almost immediately shipped out again to destinations such as the massive Great Lakes Naval Training Center north of Chicago, or all the way to the west and the facility at Puget Sound in Seattle.[14]

The virus had escaped.

CHAPTER 7

FENWAY PARK

SEPTEMBER 8–11

U naware that an epidemic was germinating in Boston, the World Series players headed there had decidedly different matters on their minds. "There is plenty of grumbling on the part of the players about the splitting of the series cash," Nick Flatley wrote in the *Boston American*.[1] In the *Globe*, however, sportswriter Ed Martin confidently reported that "there is nothing approaching a strike or a walk out."[2] On the train from Chicago, some Red Sox and Cubs players were, in fact, advocating a boycott, suggesting that both teams refuse to finish the World Series. Others, more realistically, figured out how little power or leverage they really had. Public opinion certainly wasn't on their side. Thanks in part to George Creel's CPI and its constant stoking of patriotic fervor, they were widely seen as overpaid slackers using baseball to avoid their civic, patriotic, and moral duty to contribute to America's war effort.

For the moment, cooler heads prevailed. As the train moved eastward, the players decided to approach the National Commission with two proposals. First, they would ask that the new system for dividing and distributing World Series shares be postponed until baseball restarted after the war, however long that might be. Second, they would request that winning and losing team members be guaranteed $1,500 and $1,000, respectively. That would be significantly lower than the $2,000 and $1,400 they believed they had been promised and also lower than what had been shared with the World Series players in 1917. They proposed that the money come from the amounts due to be paid to the second-, third- and fourth-place finishers in each league. After all, those teams had never received anything before, so even a smaller-than-planned payout would be an unexpected bonus for them.

The players chose two representatives—outfielders Harry Hooper for the Red Sox and Les Mann from the Cubs—to go meet with Garry Herrmann in the National Commission's car of the train and make the pitch. But Herrmann told Hooper and Mann he wouldn't meet with them without American League president Ban Johnson being present. Johnson, conveniently, was not on the train. Herrmann did promise Hooper, however, that he would arrange a private, three-way meeting on the morning after the train arrived in Boston

Not all the players were focused on the issue of money, though. Outside Springfield, Massachusetts, as teammates Babe Ruth and Walt Kinney continued to horse around like adolescents, the train suddenly lurched. Ruth, who was standing in the aisle, was thrown into a window, breaking the glass. Or something to that effect. The Babe's own recollection didn't exactly match up with those of others, though it was close enough.

"We had a second-string left-hander on our club by the name of Kenny," Ruth wrote in his autobiography, characteristically butchering his teammate's real name. "He and I used to go in for a lot of roughhousing. We'd grapple and box and roll all over the floor. On the train ride back to Boston for the fourth game we started at it again. I took a swing at Kenny, but he ducked and I hit the knuckles of my left hand on the steel wall of the car. The middle finger of my left had become swollen to three times its normal size."[3]

Held out of games as a hitter because his manager was relying on him as the team's best pitcher, the injury to Ruth's pitching hand had put the Red Sox World Series prospects in jeopardy.

"You damned fool," Barrow barked at Ruth when the train pulled into Boston. "You know I've picked you to pitch tomorrow and you go and bust up your hand that way. What the hell is wrong with you?"

"Don't worry Ed," a sheepish Ruth replied. "It's okay. I'll be in there pitching for you, if you still want me."[4]

The following morning, the appointed player representatives went to the Hotel Touraine, but Hooper and Mann did not get the meeting with the National Commission that Herrmann had promised the day before. Instead, Herrmann informed the players that he, Johnson, and acting National League president John Heydler needed to see the actual revenue totals from each of the first four games before they could have any kind of discussion about changing the players' shares.

Hooper and Mann returned to brief their teammates, and the players' anger level rose once again. Many of the players threatened to walk away that morning and leave the World Series unfinished. At the very least, they reasoned, they could deny the owners the proceeds from any additional games. Others were willing to play Game Four, see what the reaction of the National Commission would be to the players' proposal, and walk away at that point if they weren't happy with the results.

On a positive note, interest in the World Series had picked up considerably now that the games had moved to Boston. These were to be the first World Series games played at Fenway Park since the year it opened in 1912. The Red Sox home games in the 1915 and 1916 World Series had been played at nearby Braves Field, home of the city's National League team, where capacity was higher and there were more tickets to be sold. Just 1,500 reserved seats remained unsold for the four possible games to be played at Fenway Park, priced at $1.65 each. Bleacher seats cost 55 cents.

Now, the Red Sox held the city's attention. Governor Samuel McCall closed his office in the State House on Beacon Hill, dismissed the office staff for the day, and headed to the game himself. Players allowed themselves a bit of hope that all this excitement would translate into brisk day-of-game sales for grandstand and bleacher seats, and just maybe the revenue would be enough to get the players the newly contemplated $1,500 and $1,000 figures after all.

Because more than an inch of rain had fallen during an overnight storm in Boston, the grounds crew at Fenway Park prepared the playing field for Game Four of the World Series by pouring oil on the infield dirt and lighting it on fire. The flames from the burning oil also removed the standing water.

Just before game time, fifty-four soldiers from City Hospital, freshly returned from France, arrived at the park in cars supplied by the Red Cross. Among them was Jimmy Coughlin, who had led the Royal Rooters marching band in support of the Red Sox during previous World Series. Some of the men were on crutches, others missing limbs; all were guests of the *Boston Globe* newspaper. Injured members of the Yankee Division's 101st Infantry, mostly local men, were featured in a newspaper photo the next day, sitting together in the grandstand. The doughboys received a huge ovation when they entered the park and took their seats, a tangible symbol of the local heroes in the Yankee Division, who were at the front. "Veterans in every sense of the word and in the United States only because their days of usefulness in France are ended, they made the most stirring picture that Boston has seen since the war began," crowed the *Globe* of its own publicity stunt.[5]

Ruth was back on the mound for the Red Sox. As the game opened, he was in the midst of a string of twenty-two and one-third scoreless World Series innings, dating back to the 1916 series. In this game, he would have a chance to break the great Christy Mathewson's record of twenty-eight straight shutout innings. When Ruth took the field, there were iodine stains visible on his pitching hand, evidence of the medical treatment he had been receiving since the mishap on the train the night before. In the early going, it was clear that the hand was bothering him. He allowed men on base in each of the first three innings.

"All the world should know, Babe said, that it was not the finger that was troubling him, but the stuff that was on it, and the stuff that was on it was putting too much stuff on the ball," went Ed Martin's overstuffed explanation afterward.[6]

Ruth ran into some unusual luck, however, when Chicago outfielder Max Flack ran into the record books. In the first inning, Flack was picked off of first base on a throw from Ruth to Stuffy McInnis. Then in the third inning, it happened again when an inattentive Flack was picked off second base. These were rare mental mistakes by the veteran Flack. Never before, nor in the nearly one hundred years since, had a runner gotten himself picked off twice in a single World Series game.

The Babe had another streak going at the plate, and it was not one he wanted to continue. He was mired in a 0-for-10 World Series hitting slump, also dating back to the 1916 series against Brooklyn. That cold spell was the justification manager Ed Barrow had used for not having Ruth pinch-hit in the ninth inning of Game Two. As he headed for the plate in the fourth inning for his first at bat, his manager spoke to him briefly. "I don't know if they'll let you hit or not," Barrow said, thinking the Cubs might walk Ruth, even if it meant loading the bases. "But if they pitch to you, you can win your own game. I know you can do it."[7]

As the Babe strode to the plate, Cubs pitcher Lefty Tyler noticed that Flack was playing far more shallowly in right field than he had during Ruth's at bats in Game One, so he motioned for Flack to back up and play deeper. Flack barely moved. Again Tyler waved Flack back, and again the right fielder ignored him.

Predictably, perhaps, Ruth ripped a line drive over Flack's head for a triple and gave the Red Sox a 2–0 lead. "Giving Babe Ruth a fast straight ball, letter high and exactly over the plate is not a mite more dangerous than tickling the roof of a man-eating tiger's mouth with your little finger," Burt Whitman colorfully recounted in the next day's paper.[8]

"That was a fastball Tyler fed me," Ruth told the scribes after the game. "I put plenty of beef behind that swing and gave it a good healthy wallop."[9] In the stands, Governor McCall stood and cheered as Ruth slid into third base and, as cheerfully reported by one paper, actually pinched his lieutenant governor, sitting beside him, in his excitement.

There was no doubt that Ruth had put a charge into the ball, but what was the matter with Flack? He was generally regarded as one of the headiest players in the game. Now he had made three uncharacteristically boneheaded plays in a single game. Was this a coincidence? Was he distracted? Was this a symptom of his unhappiness over the paycheck controversy?

Or was Flack trying to "throw" the game and ensure a Boston win? Flack's lackadaisical actions were almost too much to ignore.

Baseball was still a year away from its worst-ever scandal, when the Chicago White Sox conspired to purposely lose the 1919 World Series. But the "Black Sox" episode was more a product of its time than an aberration. Baseball gambling grew rapidly during the war, in large measure because horseracing tracks were closed and gamblers had no other daily action on which to wager.

In August, Hal Chase of the Reds had been suspended for throwing games after years of living under a cloud of suspicion. Owners, including National Commission member Garry Herrmann, who owned Chase's Cincinnati Reds, tolerated gambling up to a point. Much like pro football enjoys the attention of fantasy players or office Super Bowl pools today, baseball executives saw a low level of gambling as maintaining interest in the game.

If Flack was looking to cash in on his ability to affect the outcome of games, he would easily have found plenty of takers in and around Fenway Park. "The worst city of all for baseball gambling was Boston," sports betting historian Daniel Ginsburg writes. "Boston gamblers essentially 'took over' the Boston American and National League parks as bases of operations."[10] In fact, at one point in the ongoing feud between Harry Frazee and American League president Ban Johnson, Johnson threatened to simply revoke Frazee's ownership, using the pervasiveness of Fenway Park gambling as the excuse. "This thing has gone far enough," he huffed. "It has had its swing for several years. I am going after it strong."[11] Predictably, nothing happened.

It was just an accepted fact that big-time, Boston bookmakers like Sport Sullivan, who would be at the center of the 1919 Black Sox fixing scandal a year later, made a living taking bets inside both of the city's ballparks. Sullivan and his like would raise a big pot of money—at times from shady, crime-connected figures—and use it to fund all kinds of bets from all comers, often wagering money on either side of a given outcome. The Boston gamblers had every incentive to seek a sure payday. The 1918 season had been rough for them, as one sportswriter noted. "Most of the pessimist talk on the Red Sox chances comes from the gambling element, which has been hit hard this year," Francis Eaton had noted before the series. "The professional calculators of chances have overplayed the Boston team on past reputation, and by making them 100-to-60 favorites every day have virtually gone broke."[12]

On the mound, Ruth labored. It seemed clear that the finger he had injured on the train was bothering him. He was helped by sparkling Boston defense, especially from second baseman Dave Shean and short-stop Everett Scott, and managed to keep the Cubs off the scoreboard.

"The way that Stuffy McInnis, Scott and Shean prevented scoring was a picture Mike Angelo would have been crazy to paint," Martin told his readers.[13]

When he finished the sixth inning, Ruth had broken Mathewson's World Series scoreless innings record. "I still don't know how I got as far as I did," Ruth admitted. "I was lucky to get that far."[14]

Obviously fatigued, Ruth got wild but stayed on the mound into the eighth inning, when he finally allowed a run on a grounder to second base. His new record of twenty-nine and two-thirds straight scoreless innings pitched in the World Series lasted for forty-four years. "I'm still prouder of my achievement of pitching 29 consecutive World Series score-less innings than I am of my subsequent home-run records with the Yankees," he wrote shortly before his death.[15]

But the game was tied 2–2 as the Red Sox came to bat in the bottom half of the eighth inning. Boston scored when McInnis bunted, and the throw to first was wild. Flack—again—was so slow tracking down the errant ball in the outfield that McInnis, who had failed to touch first base as he rounded the bag, was nevertheless able to go back, tag the base, and still make it into second safely. The error allowed the winning run to score, and the Red Sox were a win away from another World Series title.

"Today's game gives us a big edge in the series," said a confident Barrow. "I expect one more game will finish it up and that Boston will come through the winner tomorrow."[16]

Despite high hopes, attendance for the game was just 22,183, and now the final figures on gate receipts and players' shares were clear. The first four games had generated a total of $69,000 in revenue. This was far below the $150,000 spent on tickets in the 1917 World Series, and it was even further from the $200,000 that Herrmann had widely predicted at the start of the series.

After the game, the players' discontent could no longer be contained. Members of both teams were openly discussing their anger with any sportswriter who would listen. "The Chicago Cubs were not only a disconsolate but a highly disgruntled force last night," the Boston Post noted. "The subject of a much-depleted monetary reward for engaging in the classic disturbs them mightily. Threats to strike and refuse to play today's game were uttered—and uttered freely."[17] Some Cubs players were publicly demanding the $1,000 per player guarantee that was in the as-yet-not-delivered proposal to the National Commission. Curiously, this was the losers' share, and Chicago was still alive in the series, though they now trailed three games to one.

The players' anger likely rang hollow with many in the general public, however. That same day, the Boston and Middlesex railmen's strike was settled, and management granted the workers a two-cent-per-hour raise, bringing their wages to 35 cents an hour. For them, $1,000 represented about a year's pay.

The players also had to compete with the image of former players who were on active military duty rather than enjoying the chance to play a boy's game for money. One newspaper account told of the 150,000 rounds of live ammunition used by new recruits during the day's target practice at Camp Devens. "I'd like to see the game today, but I wouldn't give this up to go," the story quoted Second Lieutenant Jimmy Corey, a Worcester native and former Red Sox second baseman. "This is a bigger game, with Uncle Sam and the rest of the world in the grandstand."[18] It was a story with all the hallmarks of George Creel's government propaganda machine.

That evening, players from both teams were invited to a performance of the stage play *Experience* at the Shubert-Majestic Theater. It was not one that Red Sox owner and theater impresario Harry Frazee had produced, but it was another unusual opportunity for players from the two clubs to mingle and talk. Pay, not the play, was the dominant topic of conversation.

Hooper and three other players, one from Boston and two from Chicago, skipped the show and went instead to the Copley Plaza Hotel for their promised meeting with the National Commission. Gate receipts from the first four games were in and accounted for, and all the necessary figures for determining players' revenue shares were known. When they arrived, there was no one at the hotel to meet them. The delegation waited until 1:00 a.m., but Herrmann, Johnson, and Heydler never showed up.

Boston's newspapers were covering almost every possible angle of the World Series story. The *Boston Post* offered perhaps the most offbeat perspective. "Mme. Lora, who is giving a demonstration of mental telepathy at the Bowdoin Square theatre, and tells the audience all about their business and love affairs, has predicted the results of the four World Series games so far," the paper assured Red Sox fans, "and today she says Jones will pitch and Boston will win."[19]

Yet, up to this point, the one compelling baseball storyline the press had only touched upon lightly was the growing divide between players and owners over money. Now, however, the rift was out in the open, and the writers could no longer ignore the players' unhappiness. Several stories in that morning's papers mentioned the seemingly sudden possibility that the series might end prematurely.

Nick Flatley, in the *Boston American*, noted how unhappy the players were, but his story missed the main point of contention—low payouts—and instead focused on the provision that every player on each team would receive an equal share. Using the example of a pitcher who had ridden the Red Sox bench during the season, he pointed out, "The athletes' money will be passed out individually by the illustrious Commish. Every eligible player will get an equal share. Thus Pertica, who has never pitched a ball in a big league contest, is awarded what Babe Ruth, Harry Hooper, et al. collect."[20]

Later in the morning, Hooper and the player delegation finally got their "private" meeting with the National Commission, but Johnson invited the press. He saw it as an opportunity to paint the players as greedy. Ignoring Johnson's ambush, Hooper made an impassioned appeal to the National Commission, making the case for his fellow players. "We do not think we have been treated fairly," he began.

> We believe we were promised $2,000 and $1,400. We are asking that the other first division clubs not receive any series money this year. The players have made baseball the national game and it's the players that have made the World Series the sporting attraction it is. The crowds come out to see us, and we're getting a lousy return for our efforts. We didn't have a voice in making the rule that took away a big portion of our money, which was all wrong. We earn it, and the earner should be considered. We aren't a bunch of burglars. Baseball is our business and a man can't be blamed for looking after his business.[21]

Herrmann tried to appear sympathetic without conceding any ground to the players' demands. "I understand your concern, Harry," he told Hooper, "but to change these rules, it would be necessary to get the consent of both leagues. Unfortunately the game receipts were much less than anticipated. The Commission is sorry, gentleman, but what can it do?"[22]

This line of reasoning was absurd on its face. The very rules in question had been established during the offseason without a vote of the owners. If the National Commission could unilaterally make the rules, couldn't they also change them? Once again, it seemed that the players had not carefully studied the paperwork they had been given regarding the allocation of World Series shares; the document actually went to some length to point out why the National Commission was justified in making these rules *without* a vote of owners. But these were ballplayers, not lawyers or businessmen. The fine points were lost in the blizzard of obfuscation that the shrewd members of the National Commission were throwing at them.

For his part, Johnson was far less conciliatory. "It's too late now," he scolded the players in front of the sportswriters. "It's all been decided. Nothing you can do about it. You'll have to go out and play."[23]

Herrmann tried to diffuse the tension a little by telling the players that the Commission would regroup and issue a final decision after Game Five, probably at about 5:30 p.m. that afternoon. But what was left to decide? Herrmann was adamant that no rule changes could be made without the consent of the owners. Plus, Herrmann had a clear conflict of interest. Any move to rescind the rule would take money out of the pockets of his own Cincinnati Reds players, who had finished third in the National League and were in line for an unexpected bonus.

Boston's afternoon paper reported on the meeting but was not sympathetic to either side. "The little matter of the division of the series money has almost caused a revolution," it said, "While the affair will not occasion a strike or anything of the kind, it is a very interesting sidelight to the series. It is one more example of the way the powers that be in the dying national pastime do things."[24]

The game was scheduled to start at 2:30 p.m. At noon, in keeping with the unusual joint approach they had taken since boarding the train from Chicago, the two teams met together in the Red Sox clubhouse. "They want to put us off until the series is over," Hooper reported. "We've tried to meet with them since Sunday, and every time we do they have a new excuse."

Then Hooper said something very interesting; something that cast the game ultimately played later that day in a disturbing shadow.

"If the Red Sox win the fifth game," he explained, "the series will be over. And what power will we have then? The Commission would simply say 'tough luck.' They told us they would give us an answer today. I think we should sit here until we get it."[25]

So Hooper had laid down a marker of sorts. If the players didn't get their way, they would hurt their own cause if they played and Boston won the game. Given the way the game eventually unfolded, it raised serious questions as to the effort the Red Sox may, or may not, have expended in trying to win.

The leader of the Cubs, outfielder Les Mann, decided he wasn't going to wait for an answer from the Commission and got on the telephone with Herrmann. The conversation quickly became heated when Herrmann wouldn't budge from his 5:30 p.m. timetable for an answer.

"So that's it?" Mann persisted, "Is that the Commission's final word? You'd better decide right now if that's it, because I've got 40 players here who aren't putting on their uniforms until we get a satisfactory agreement."

"If the players intend to strike, you'd better go out in front of the park and tell them to stop selling tickets and letting fans through the gates," Herrmann shot back.

"We're waiting for you and your decision," Mann was yelling. "As far as the fans go, they'll wait just like us until the Commission shows up and tells us its decision face to face. If that takes until 5:30, so be it." Mann slammed down the phone.[26]

A crowd of over 20,000 was waiting in the stands at Fenway Park, and it was clear that something odd was happening. There were no players on the field warming up. Some were actually walking through the stands in street clothes. As game-time grew near, mounted Boston police officers took up positions in the Fenway Park outfield. The gathered spectators grew restless. A group of war veterans arrived, as had been the case the day before, and when the band played "Over There," the fans stood and removed their hats. But the distraction was temporary.

"While these murmurings were going on at the park, Ban Johnson, the American League member of the Commission, was at a convivial drinking party at the Copley Plaza," recalled sportswriter Fred Lieb. "In high good humor and about three sheets to the wind, Ban reached the park about five minutes before scheduled game time to learn the entire park was waiting for him."[27]

Again the members of the National Commission refused to meet with players. Instead, Red Sox owner Harry Frazee talked to some of them, trying to find a compromise.

"If Frazee and Weeghman have conceded anything to those bastards, I'm through with baseball," Johnson told everyone within earshot, which at that volume was a considerable distance. "I'm through. I'm through."[28]

The players were effectively on strike, with no intention of playing the game before confronting the National Commission over how much they were to be paid. After a half hour of stalling, when it became apparent that neither the Cubs nor the Red Sox would take the field unless their grievances were heard and resolved, a meeting was arranged in the umpires' dressing room under the stands, a tiny space.

It was a chaotic scene. Hooper and Mann attended as the chosen representatives of the two teams, but a handful of additional players crowded into the room as well, as did a knot of sportswriters. Former Boston Mayor John "Honey Fitz" Fitzgerald, whose grandson and namesake, John Fitzgerald Kennedy, was fifteen months old at the time, was there. There were even some fans packed into the cramped little room.

Finally, Herrmann and Johnson showed up. They were clearly and seriously drunk.

Herrmann clung to Johnson, who was himself propped up in the middle, with acting National League president John Heydler trying to steady them both. Hooper was once again prepared to speak for the players on both teams. Johnson got in the first words, straightening up, puffing out his chest, and launching into a self-serving sermon.

"I went to Washington and had the stamp of approval put on this series," he boasted, at one point actually pounding his own chest. "I made it possible. I did. No one else could have got it but me, Harry. If I hadn't gone..." Johnson trailed off. Suddenly his demeanor changed, and he began to cry and beg Hooper to play.

"Harry old boy, whyn't you stop all this and play ball? Huh?" Now the words were stringing together in weepy slur. "Harry, you know I love you. I want you to go out there on the field because there's 25,000 people waiting. Harry, go out and play the game. You'll win easier than yesterday. The crowd is waiting for you."

Johnson was on a roll and kept up his blubbery speech.

"Harry, do you realize you're a member of one of the greatest organizations in the world, the American League? Do you realize what you will do to its good name if you don't play? I love you, Harry. Go out there for the honor and glory of the American League. Go out and play."[29]

Hooper then suggested that the World Series money go to charity. The Commission liked that idea, until they understood that Hooper was talking about the owners' share as well as the players' portion.

This was going nowhere, and Hooper knew it.

"You can see our predicament gentlemen," he said, turning to the press and expressing his frustration over the inebriated state of the Commission members. "These men are not in any condition to hear our arguments. We have nobody we can talk to. Nobody who can talk."[30]

Reluctantly, Hooper reported back to the players gathered in the Boston clubhouse. It appeared they had no choice but to delay a decision yet again and discuss the matter further once Herrmann and Johnson sobered up. Here is where his earlier comments took on a more immediate meaning. If the game were played, and the Red Sox won, there would be no more negotiating. The matter would be settled. Hooper had already made it clear. If the game were played, it would not be in the players' collective best interests for the Red Sox to win.

Hooper returned to the claustrophobic little room beneath the stands to see Herrmann and Johnson one more time. In front of the assembled witnesses, Hooper asked for assurances that there would be no retaliation taken against the players for their temporary walkout.

"That's right Harry," Johnson gushed. "Do that for me. Go out and play. Everything will be all right. For the honor and glory of the American League, go out and play. No action will be taken."[31]

Like so many others, it was a promise the baseball executives would not keep.

Herrmann also came over to shake Hooper's hand on the deal and was about to break into a new speech when Barrow cut him off. "We've wasted enough time," the no-nonsense manager butted in. "To the field everybody."[32]

Stunned at the sudden turn of events, Johnson was nonetheless quick to claim credit. "By Jolly. I did it. I did it," he told all who would listen and those who couldn't help do so.[33]

At 3:15 p.m. "Honey Fitz," like any good politician, grabbed center stage. He got on a megaphone and read a statement to the crowd announcing that the players had decided to play after all, then basked in the resulting applause. It was the kind of populist move to which the reserved and aloof Senator John Weeks, sitting in the stands, would never have stooped. Under the stadium, Herrmann and Johnson toasted their success at delaying any decision for another day.

At 3:30 p.m., an hour later than planned, Game Five got underway. Why did the players give in? It may have been the realization that nothing Herrmann or Johnson might promise could be trusted, even if they were sober, and any apparent victory could not be counted on. It may have been the knowledge that players had no real leverage and ran the risk of being further portrayed as greedy and unpatriotic at a time when society had little tolerance for either. Perhaps it was as simple as feeling they had no choice. But it is also quite possible that Hooper's decision was the result of his weeks of studying and debating war news with his "Strategy Board" of teammates throughout the summer. He might well have been making a tactical retreat.

The Cubs sent left-hander Hippo Vaughn to the mound for the third time in five games. Barrow countered by benching the left-handed hitting Ruth yet again. Vaughn turned in his best performance of the series, and Chicago breezed to 3–0 win. The Red Sox seemed to sleepwalk through the game, which moved at a brisk and uneventful pace. Boston never mounted a serious challenge. They managed just five hits, four of them singles, and never advanced a runner past second base.

Barrow wasn't happy. "I don't care to talk about it," he told the expectant writers afterward. "The Cubs win today merely prolongs the series. We expected to end it today but things broke too well for Chicago."[34]

After the game, Red Sox owner Harry Frazee, seemingly seeing some writing on the wall, ordered the team's employees to stop selling tickets for Game Six.

Most of the Boston press was brutal in its criticism of both the players and baseball management for the brief strike. Arthur Duffy's column in the *Boston Post* seemed to sum up the prevailing opinion, not just about the holdout but about baseball in general in a time of war.

"It's a mighty good thing that baseball is dead," he wrote. "The game has been dying for two years, killed by the greed of the players and owners. Professional baseball in the past four years has only been a mad scramble for money. The wrangling of the players and magnates yesterday over the spoils furnishes a disgusting spectacle. All decent sporting spirit has long ago fled and the game just reeks with scandal after scandal."[35]

Fed up with the delays, angry about their pay, pilloried in the press, and facing uncertain financial and personal futures, the Chicago Cubs players refused to leave their hotel the next morning to go to Fenway Park in anticipation of Game Six of the World Series.

Having been repeatedly stonewalled by the National Commission, Hooper, Mann, and the rest of the players' committee decided to change tactics. They headed to the Copley Plaza Hotel and met instead with team owners Harry Frazee of Boston and Charlie Weeghman of Chicago. The two men had little to offer. The National Commission held the money and was determined to distribute it directly to players. Frazee and Weeghman couldn't get their hands on it, even if they were sympathetic to the players' plight. Instead, they gave the group of players some vague assurances that they would do what they could.

Dejected and faced with few options, the players decided to go ahead and play Game Six.

What choice did they have at that point? If they refused to play, they were unlikely to receive even their reduced shares from the National Commission. They might not even succeed in keeping more money out of hands of baseball owners and management by denying them the gate receipts from one more game. The *Chicago Herald & Examiner*, though alone among newspapers covering the World Series, reported that two boxcars full of replacement players were standing by, and they were ready to don Red Sox and Cubs uniforms and play out the remaining games.

So the two teams made their way to Fenway Park for the afternoon game, but it was likely the least festive atmosphere in World Series history. Cold weather had moved back in, there had been an early autumn frost overnight, and the temperature hovered in the 40s. It was the coldest September 11 in nearly half a century. Because Boston was rife with rumors that the game would not be played at all, and because the Red Sox had cut off ticket sales the previous day, the ballpark stands were just half full. It would turn out to be the smallest crowd to see a World Series game since 1909.

Curiously, the Red Sox broke with long-standing baseball tradition and superstition and actually posed for their official World Championship photo before the game even began. Just before the picture was taken, there was another slight delay when the team noticed that pitcher Joe Bush was not lined up with them.

"He was sore because I wouldn't let him pitch that game," Barrow later recalled. "I wanted to make sure so I pitched Carl Mays. So Bush refused to sit for his picture and I had to go in and haul him out of the clubhouse."[36]

It was as if everyone involved, from players to fans, just wanted to get the 1918 baseball season behind them and go on to deal with the real issues facing America.

When the game got underway, at least one member of the Cubs once again suspiciously played as if he was doing his best to ensure that his team lost.

In Game Four, Chicago outfielder Max Flack had played a decidedly uncharacteristic sloppy game. He got picked off the bases twice. He lazily chased an errant throw. He misplayed a Babe Ruth line drive into a triple. Now, two days later and no closer to the payoff players believed they deserved, Flack once again seemed to be going through the motions, or worse.

In the third inning, Red Sox leftfielder George Whiteman hit what appeared to be a simple looper to right field. Flack moved over in an easy, nonchalant manner to make what appeared to be a routine catch. Instead, the sinking line drive clanked off his glove, allowing two runs to score rather than ending the inning

"Honestly, I can't explain it," he said afterward. "I never felt surer of a fly ball in my life. Not that it was such an easy play, but it was a play I should have made and expected to make. I don't know why I didn't do it. It wasn't overconfidence, I'm sure of that. I butterfingered the play and am unanimously elected as the goat. Ten years from now, the scribes will write of how Flack's muff cost the series in 1918. It's the way of the old game."[37]

He was right. In the *New York Times* story about the game, Flack was the focus of ridicule for his transparent lack of effort.

"Flack made a ludicrous muff of Whitman's line drive," the story reported.

> Flack came running in to make an easy catch. He caught up to the rapidly descending ball and had it entirely surrounded by his hands. Tyler was offering thanksgiving for crawling out of a bad hole when the ball squeezed its way through Flack's buttered digits. As the ball spilled in a puddle at Flack's feet both Mays and Shean were well along on their way home before Flack's alarm clock went off and woke him up.[38]

As the game moved along, three soldiers released a carrier pigeon at the end of every half inning to make the half-hour flight to Camp Devens with updates on the action and the score. "The one that was released at the end of the fifth inning evidently did not have its mind on its work," Ed Martin noted with amusement, "for it started downtown, but must have realized that it was in the Army now, for it turned about suddenly and decided to go back to Devens."[39]

In keeping with the mood of players on both teams, the game plodded along uneventfully following Flack's big error. Carl Mays held the Cubs to just three hits, and when Les Mann hit a simple ground ball to second in the ninth inning, it was over. The pair of runs that scored on Flack's miscue was all the Red Sox needed for a 2–1 win and yet another World Series title.

"Only 15,238 saw the farewell battle," Martin's game story in the *Boston Globe* recounted. "Of course, the weather was far from ideal, but the disagreement between the National Commission and the contesting payers, which held up the starting of Tuesday's game, was the thing that kept the public away. With minds wandering in serious channels, it can plainly be seen that it was a fatal mistake for baseball men to argue over dollars, creating a situation that should have been diplomatically squelched in its infancy."[40]

There was no celebration by the Red Sox players. They walked off the field and headed to the clubhouse, where first baseman McInnis had his teammates sign the ball from the final out of the series and presented it to Massachusetts Governor Samuel McCall.

It was as if the players had been asked to do a dirty job under miserable circumstances and had gotten it over with, however unwillingly. They seemed almost relieved that it was over and fatigued by the losing fight over money with the powers that be in the game. That's certainly the way this final game of the 1918 season, perhaps the final season of big league baseball as it was then known, was portrayed in the press.

"It may be a long time before there is another world's series, and this finish, the all-important, which hinged on a life-sized laughable muff, closes a topsy-turvy season," summed up the *New York Times*, but not before taking a thinly veiled shot at the players' demands for more pay and at Flack in particular. "The players are unanimous in the belief that if Whiteman had hit a silver dollar out to Flack instead of a baseball Boston would never have won the championship today."[41]

The *Boston American*'s Nick Flatley called his account of the aborted strike and the Red Sox victory that followed "Funeral Ceremonies for the Once Great Game of Baseball and the Once Powerful Commission."[42]

Even Martin bemoaned the way in which the home town team's victory was dampened by controversy. "What a great opportunity was lost to send the old pastime back into the wings in a blaze of glory," he wrote with regret. "Baseball should have gone out with a farewell that had all the stuff on it that a New Year receives."[43]

The Boston Red Sox were now unquestionably the dominant team of the age, having won four out of the last seven World Series. "During the interregnum of our national game—between the time Dave Shean of Arlington tossed out Les Mann at first base for the last put out of yesterday's contest and until universal peace shall have been imposed on the world and the unspeakable Hun put down where he belongs—the Red Sox will be titlists," Burt Whitman wrote in the *Herald*. "Surely nothing could be fairer. Never has Boston lost a World Series in which either of its big league teams has participated, and the almost annual success of the Hub Hose in the Big Money tilts bespeaks much for the quality of ability, gameness and support the [managers] Stahl, Carrigan and Barrow teams have brought to the supreme test."[44]

While Harry Frazee may have owned the Red Sox, the Red Sox owned big league baseball. "The championship deserves to remain here until the war is won," he boasted.[45]

There was no joyous outburst in the stands at Fenway Park when the game ended, however. What few spectators were there had an entirely unenthusiastic response to their team's world championship triumph. They simply got up and went home. They had no way of knowing, of course, that it would be eighty-six years before the Boston Red Sox would once again win a World Series, and ninety-five years before they would do so on their home field at Fenway Park. Winning would never again be as commonplace.

In retrospect, given the decades of frustration that followed for the team and its fans, with nearly impossible misfortune befalling them time and again, it is hard to comprehend that a Red Sox World Series win seemed almost inevitable to just about every baseball fan at the time. "Down came the curtain," Martin wrote in the aftermath of the victory, "and from out of the stillness that swept over the battleground came a lone voice piping up, 'Those Red Sox were always a lucky bunch.'"[46]

So baseball was over and everyone, from players to owners, now had to face the stark reality of war. Late in the afternoon, Cubs' president Charlie Weeghman registered at the Boston draft board and then caught a train at South Station to return to Chicago.

CHAPTER 8

THE BATTLE OF ST. MIHIEL

SEPTEMBER 6–12

After nearly a week of night marching since being mobilized from their training locations around Châtillon-sur-Seine, France, the U.S. Army's Twenty-Sixth Division had reached its destination near the town of St. Mihiel.

"We finally arrived at our pre-determined position, directly in the rear of the front-line trenches," remembered Private Connell Albertine of Somerville. "From all indications this was supposed to be a very secret concentration. It was said that General Edwards had given orders that no soldier was to occupy the front-line trenches, for fear that one or more might be captured in a surprise attack and the Boches might get the information they were looking for."[1]

There was a great deal of work yet to be done before the planned American offensive could begin. Again, the men of the Yankee Division, like Edward Sirois of Lawrence in artillery Battery C, did most of their work under cover of darkness. "During the long hours of the night, the boys worked diligently, constructing gun platforms and trail holes, laying telephone lines and establishing communication, bringing up ammunition and supplies; in general, getting everything in readiness for the opening day," he later wrote. "Always, as daybreak peeped through the clouds, all work would be concealed, and all men would return again into the woods, awaiting darkness to go on with their labor."[2]

Amidst the work, some of the men, like Frank Sibley, the *Boston Globe* reporter, got a look at the landscape that sat between them and the Germans. "Out in the plain lay a second rank, so to speak, of little towns," Sibley wrote. "Champion, Sauk, and Wadonville were the nearest, and back of them Riaville, Marchéville and Saint-Hilaire. These were the towns which came to interest the Yankees most. But from the crest of the hill it was possible on a clear day to see eighty-two towns, many of them busy factory towns, with their chimneys smoking away as peacefully as if there weren't any war. They were all in the hands of the Germans."[3]

This piece of ground had been held by Germany since 1914, despite several attempts by French troops to retake it. In that time, through the repeated assaults, the Germans had reinforced their position until it became a nearly impenetrable labyrinth of trenches, berms, and barbed wire, with hardened front line defensive positions and a series of fortified fallback points.

"The German trenches were well out in the plain," Sibley recalled.

> Nowhere else in our experience did we see so much wire as there was in this sector. Elsewhere there had been belts, anywhere up to thirty yards across; here belt followed belt, and there were literally miles of wire entanglements. At the No Man's Land area, the woods were, of course, blown to bits. Gaunt skeleton tree trunks stood here and there, but the position had remained as it was for so long that thick underbrush had grown up round the trees, and travel was almost impossible even for unburdened, free-going foot-passengers, in peace. It was awful country.[4]

Yet it was the country the men of the Yankee Division would have to cross when the order came to attack.

September 5 marked the first anniversary of when the 101st shipped out for Europe. In Boston, to much fanfare, the 101st Infantry Auxiliary Association kicked off a drive to raise $100,000 to replenish a fund used by the regiment's commanding officer, Colonel Edward Logan, "in providing comforts for the boys in the trenches." These wives and mothers and family members of the unit, who were primarily from Boston and the surrounding towns, had a host of events planned. A flyover of the city included what the auxiliary promoted as "a bombardment of literature from airships" intended to flutter down on the city's pedestrians.[5] Nearly one thousand young women took to the streets selling more than a quarter of a million daisies from locations around downtown. When they ran out of paper flowers, simple cards were hastily printed with a picture of a daisy, and 150,000 more were sold. By nightfall, nine out of every ten people on the city's streets were said to be wearing a paper daisy, and the auxiliary was struggling to count what one person described as "a literal avalanche of money."[6] The desire to support any war effort, or at least the pressure to be seen as supporting a war effort, remained at a feverish level.

The next day was Lafayette Day, still celebrated every September 6 in Massachusetts on the birthday of the French hero of the Revolutionary War era, and observances were held across the state, with speeches and parades in many communities. None failed to note the apt nature of America now coming to the aid of the French in their hour of great need, just as Lafayette had done for the American colonists in their struggle for freedom nearly 150 years before. The story of Lafayette and the bond between the United States and France were very much on the minds of Americans as a result of the war. It is no coincidence that a top aide to General Pershing, speaking at a July 4 commemoration in France in 1917, had famously marked the arrival of American doughboys by proclaiming, "Lafayette, we are here."

The Yankee Division—including the men of the 101st—were in place and making final preparations for a major offensive. Among them was

Captain Joseph McConnell, a well-known Boston lawyer in peacetime but now in command of Company A of that same 101st Infantry the ladies were rallying to support.

McConnell was a native of western Massachusetts, born in North Adams, and a graduate of Williams College and Boston University Law School. For three years he was a sportswriter and the baseball editor of the *Boston Post*, where he covered the Red Sox in the first-ever World Series in 1903. Once he passed the bar, he joined his older brother, John, and opened the Boston law firm of McConnell & McConnell.

In 1912, he joined the state's militia and moved up to second lieutenant and then first lieutenant in 1916. He served under Pershing along the Rio Grande in the Border War that year, when U.S. forces invaded Mexico to capture Pancho Villa. When America declared war in 1917, McConnell and his unit of guardsmen became part of the Twenty-Sixth Division.

In August 1917, the forty-year-old lawyer married Mary Clexton, thirteen years his junior, and shortly after that shipped out for France, where he was commissioned a captain. He had turned down an opportunity to leave the front and join the Department of Judge Advocate General, the military's legal branch. Like all soldiers, from draftees and enlisted men to officers, he longed for home. However, McConnell felt a duty to remain on the front lines with his fellow Massachusetts men, who affectionately referred to him as "The Skipper."

"Gosh, how he looked forward to letters from his bride," Major William McCarthy remembered. "When he answered them I noticed that he blew a puff of cigarette smoke into the envelope before he sealed it. He said his wife had written that when she detected the odor of cigarette smoke in his letter it seemed to bring them closer."[7]

It was raining again in France, and the men of the Twenty-Sixth Division were drenched as they waited in position for their orders. "I don't know whether you can read this or not," one doughboy wrote home, "but I'm balancing myself on my tin helmet. It has been raining hard and the tin hat is the only water proof thing I've got."[8] McConnell and McCarthy shared a late-night meal together in the middle of the driving rain, waiting for the signal to go over the top. "We had a bang-up feed at midnight and we kidded each other about it," McCarthy remembered. "We said we'd have one good banquet before Fritz got us."[9]

The Twenty-Sixth was in the midst of a massive buildup of men and arms. The pressure was building behind the Allied lines, and the inevitable explosion of force was drawing very near. "There was an amazing amount of artillery in position," noted Sibley. "When General Edwards was consulted by the Corps as to what artillery he wanted for the coming push, he answered, 'All I can get.' And for once he got plenty."[10]

The men of the division's Artillery Battery C, primarily from Lawrence, had never seen anything like it. "The guns were hauled into position, by hand, placed on the platforms, put into position and all final preparations made for the opening of fire," one of them wrote. "By this time every place one went, there were guns and guns and guns. There seemed to be no end of them. We never before had seen so many guns of such different calibres and styles and never dreamed even that there was so much ammunition in the world as there was around here. During all this time the Infantry patiently waited in the woods for the order to go in."[11]

One man was not nearly as patient. John Singer Sargent was an artist in search of a subject, and he was prowling the front lines looking for inspiration. He had been commissioned by the British government's Ministry of Information to create a large work depicting the cooperation of the Allies in the cause of war, and he had been given three months of access to troops and battlefields he could observe up close and search for a scene to capture and memorialize. On this day before the St. Mihiel offensive began, however, he was discouraged. His time was running out, and he still hadn't figured out what he would paint. "The weather is breaking and rain and mud have set in for good, I fear, and I hate to consider my campaign over before my harvest of sketches has grown to something more presentable in quality and quantity," he wrote to a friend. "The program of 'British and American Troops Working Together' has set heavily upon me, for though historically or sentimentally the thing happens, the naked eye cannot catch it in the act."[12]

Sargent was sixty-two and a member of one of the most prominent families in Gloucester, Massachusetts, a working class fishing port north of Boston and home to generations of men who made their living on the sea. Sargent's life had little in common with that hardscrabble existence, however. He was born in Florence, Italy, after his parents traveled to Europe to escape their grief at the death of an older child, and he grew up an expatriate. He had no formal early schooling, as his mother believed that a life spent visiting Europe's bulging museum collections and majestic cathedrals provided an education all its own. At eighteen he enrolled in the prestigious École des Beaux-Arts in Paris and quickly garnered attention. By his early twenties, he discovered that, while landscapes might be his preference, portraits paid the bills. He quickly became the foremost portrait artist in the world, making a living from commissions to paint grand images of European nobility.

Despite his deep connections to the European art world—Sargent was an acquaintance of artists who are now considered the giants of late nineteenth and early twentieth century art, men like Monet and Degas—he retained his American citizenship and a lifelong connection to Boston. He spent long stretches of time in Boston over a twenty-five-year period leading up to the war. He was a trusted friend and advisor to Isabella Stewart Gardner, the preeminent art patron in the city and adoptive mother of Augustus Peabody Gardner (who married the daughter of Senator Henry Cabot Lodge, spent a dozen years in Congress himself, and resigned to take a commission during the War). It was Sargent who convinced Mrs. Gardner to purchase many of the pieces in her stunning collection, and who painted a famous full-length portrait of her, which still hangs in the museum that was once her home in Boston's Fenway neighborhood.

As America became involved in the war, Sargent was working on a massive project in Boston. He had made some efforts to quit the portrait business and was working on a series of murals in the Special Libraries Hall of the Boston Public Library recounting the history of religion. He was also making plans for another upcoming Boston project, his painting inside the rotunda of the new Museum of Fine Arts, just a five-minute walk down the Fenway from Gardner's home.

Between his portraits and now-familiar paintings such as *Carnation, Lily, Lily, Rose*, Sargent's work hung in museums from the Tate Gallery in London to the Uffizi Gallery in Florence. He was famous around the world. By September 1918, however, he was frustrated. On the front lines working on his new project, he was finding that men in war were often quite removed from the enemy, firing artillery shells from a distance or hunkered down fighting fear and hunger and boredom more often than the Germans. "How can there be anything flagrant enough for a picture when Mars and Venus are miles apart whether in camps or in the front trenches? And the further forward one goes, the more scattered and meager everything is. The nearer to danger the fewer and more hidden the men—the more chaotic the situation the more it becomes an empty landscape. The Ministry of Information expects an epic—and how can one do an epic without masses of men?"[13]

With a personal Army escort supplied by his British patrons, Sargent continued to look for a scene that captured his attention. As September wore on, he grew more despondent. "I have wasted lots of time going to the front trenches. There is nothing to paint there. It is ugly and meager and there one only sees one or two men." What's more, he could not seem to find British and American soldiers actually working together. "They do this in the abstract, but not in any particular space within the limits of a picture."[14]

On the night of September 11, the men of the Yankee Division got word that they would be on the attack before dawn. "Except the men who were actually going over in the attack and the artillerymen, who somehow got a little sleep in the early part of that night, everybody was busy in the region," remembered Sibley.

> Officers, their orders all given, were out reconnoitering; captains sedulously went through their outfits to make sure that everything was understood and no equipment missing. From the rear the horses and mules went on straining their hearts out, bringing up material and ever more material. They were not in the best of shape to begin with; there had been a great

deal of hauling in the recent weeks, and fodder had been short. They died by the dozens Wednesday night and Thursday, falling down by the roadsides from overwork and giving up the ghost with a patient sigh. Some teams tried and then simply refused to try again to haul their wagons.[15]

There was debate among American commanders as to the artillery plan. Some argued for a sustained fourteen-hour barrage that would clear the miles of barbed wire strung by the Germans over the years in front of their positions. One tank commander, thirty-three-year-old Lieutenant Colonel George Patton, argued that such a move would make the ground so soft that tanks would have difficulty maneuvering. Others argued for no artillery support at all, so as to catch the Germans by surprise. In the end, a compromise plan was conceived that called for three hours of bombardment on the southern side of the salient and seven hours on the western side, where the Twenty-Sixth Division was prepared to take the lead.

"Without any warning, at one A.M., our artillery opened up with such a terrific bombardment that we all thought the end of the world was at hand," recalled Private Albertine. "The earth shook and trembled, making the animals that were tied to a simple corral line neigh, and two horses broke away and ran wild, never to be seen again. The flashes from the muzzles of the guns lighted up the heavens so that we could see they were very close together; at times it looked like daylight. We must have had all the American Artillery in France assembled here for this drive."[16]

The first American offensive of World War I had begun. For General "Black Jack" Pershing, months of preparation were about to be put to the test, and the stakes were enormous. "The sky over the battlefield, both before and after dawn, aflame with exploding shells, star signals, burning supply dumps and villages, presented a scene at once picturesque and terrible," he wrote after the war. "The exultation in our minds that here, at last, after 17 months of effort, an American army was fighting under its own flag was tempered by the realization of the sacrifice of life on both sides, and yet fate had willed it thus and we must carry through."[17]

There was no time for introspection on the battlefield, however, as the bombardment began. "Promptly at one o'clock there turned loose such an inferno of sound as we had never before heard," Sibley later wrote.

> The whole top of the earth seemed to burst into flame. From right and left and rear, from every hilltop and from every valley, the cannon began to bang, and the echoes ran round and round until the whole sky was roaring continuously. It seemed as if those guns must be firing indiscriminately in the direction of Germany and letting it go at that. Yet we knew that every gun had its carefully selected and ranged target, and that the shells jumping out of that hell of noise were being scientifically planted on the enemy's front trenches and his wire, on support trenches and his strong points.[18]

Another reporter, Don Martin of the *New York Herald*, marveled, "I have seen many bombardments and barrages, but I never saw any which for intensity and destructiveness equaled these. They were gorgeous, if such an adjective may be used to describe such a grand horror and destruction."[19]

Even Ed Sirois and his fellow artillerymen from Lawrence in Battery C were overwhelmed by the firepower and caught up in the patriotic fervor of war. "It was as if all HELL itself had been let loose," he gushed.

> My God! What a sight! What a thundering noise! What a picture it all presented! What a scare it must have put into the unsuspecting Germans! Oh! What wouldn't we have given to have been there and to have seen the look on their faces as that deluge came pouring down upon them. It was raining in torrents, but what cared the American Army for rain, when they were driving against the barbarians of civilization.[20]

Despite the massive barrage, German guns returned fire, and shells began to fall on the American lines as well.

"It was the most terrifying bombardment I had ever witnessed or been in," thought Albertine as he waited with the 104th to advance toward those German guns and the men firing them.

> The Boches were not taking this lying down, but were retaliating with a counter bombardment. It was real dark, even though the flashes lit up the surroundings. One shell landed only a few yards away, causing me to drop flat on my stomach and crawl into a nearby shell hole half filled with water. Staying in this shell hole was nauseating, for the water was stagnant and there was a dead body floating around. I decided I would be safer up front than here, so I started groping my way back through ankle-deep sticky mud. I finally arrived at the Second Battalion Headquarters, in what resembled a tool shed. No protection from a direct hit, but safe from shrapnel and from the rain that had started again. Protection now was something we gave little thought to, because soon we would be going over the top and after them.[21]

Despite Albertine's fear, the Germans were, in fact, offering only a cursory response. The order had gone out by 3:30 a.m. to retreat to defensive positions closer to the base of the salient, leaving token opposition in place and a half-hearted artillery barrage. One veteran American officer noticed almost immediately and correctly noted "the Germans are pulling out."[22]

Nonetheless, for four brutal hours the Allied bombardment lit up the night, pounding the German positions along the entire salient front lines. Then the guns fell silent.

"At 5 A.M., the fire ceased abruptly for five minutes," according to Sibley. But the cessation was brief. "Prisoners afterwards told us that they expected the attack then, and lots of them came out of shelter when the sound stopped, only to get caught in the renewal. That renewal came in gas shells, too. At seven o'clock there was a ten-minute let-up in the firing; both these silences were to permit the sound-ranging, which we were just installing, to be done."[23]

Not all the Germans were fooled. The men around Battery C came under fire themselves from the remaining German guns.

"About five o'clock in the morning, while the artillery preparation was still in progress, a German sacrifice battery opened up and began to shell the town of Mouilly, all the shorts (shells dropping short of their intended mark) landing on our position," recounted Sirois.

> One of these burst in front of some empty ammunition boxes. Sgt. William Hart, who was on duty at the switchboard at the time, was also there, sitting on one of these empty boxes. The boxes were riddled with the splinters from the shell; the head of the shell crashed through the box on which Bill Hart was sitting, whistled between his legs and finally stopped. Hart was dumbfounded. He had just returned to the battery from the hospital, having just recovered from wounds received at Chateau-Thierry. He simply said, "Well I suppose they'll get me good one of these days."[24]

Through the night, the American artillery barrage roared on. "Cold rain poured down on us," artilleryman George Higginson recalled, while "we poured the hot steel into them."[25] Then the weather turned.

"The past two weeks, while we were concentrating and massing and welcoming the rain and wanting it, because it prevented the Boche from getting a line on what was going on, it had fallen in torrents," noted one artilleryman. "Now, when the drive was on and we were attacking and wanted good weather, it came. For, at daybreak the rain ceased and the sun shone brightly and soon all the mud had dried up. It seems as though even the elements were out to beat the Hun."[26]

Even as the sun rose through the smoke and haze, the relentless Allied bombardment of the German positions continued. "I wish you could have seen the show," Captain Charles Coulter of Maynard, Massachusetts, wrote to his mother. "What with the roar of the cannon and the bursting of shells and the colored lights and the low-hanging rain-filled clouds. I had a picture that will long live in my memory."[27]

Pershing had nearly half a million men under his command, and now he threw them into action. The plan was deceptively simple. An attack would begin from the southern side of the salient, led by the First Division. Three hours later—enough time for German attention and reinforcements to concentrate their efforts in one direction—the Yankee Division would engage from the west, on the left flank of the Allied lines, just northeast of St. Mihiel, where the bubble-like salient rejoined the straight part of the German lines. The plan was to advance one hundred yards every four minutes, with a goal of reaching a road between the tiny towns of Lamarche and Nonsard by the end of the first day and then meeting up with the First Division, attacking from the right flank in a pincer move at the town of Vigneulles on day two, encircling German forces, and cutting them off from any means of retreat.

The southern attack began during the 5:00 a.m. lull in artillery bombardment. After three more hours of artillery pounding, the Twenty-Sixth began its advance from the west. Captain Joe McConnell and the Boston men of the 101st Infantry took the lead across hundreds of yards of remaining barbed-wire coils then a complex series of trenches which the Americans did not yet know were largely abandoned. The 102nd Regiment followed close behind.

"We climbed a hillside in a trench, and went along to the elbow," Sibley wrote for the *Globe* from his place among the Yankee Division soldiers. "It was eight o'clock. Across the ravine, the patient little bushes had clothed the hillside, though the earth showed brown and torn between them, in stripes. Suddenly one noticed that some of the brown stripes seemed to be moving. It was the attack."[28]

Albertine and the men of the Yankee Division were those stripes. The American Army, under American command, had taken center stage in the war.

"At eight A.M. the barrage lifted and the command was 'Over and at them,'" he recalled.

We crossed a very muddy cow path into a trench partly filled with water. This trench led into a communication trench and then into a ravine. This was supposed to be No-Man's Land. We climbed a good-sized hill. Up to now we had met no resistance and seen no Boche soldiers, only plenty of dead ones. Upon reaching the top of this hill we came into the Boche trenches. They were made of cement and had drainage. The walls, from quick observation, were at least five feet in thickness and over six feet high. We entered some of their dugouts and were amazed to see how nicely they were fitted out. All the comforts of life—wooden beds with mattresses, electric lights, stoves, beautiful kitchens, rugs on the floor, running water, even pool tables and graphophones. There were oil paintings of the Kaiser and Von Hindenburg on the walls. They even had a small narrow-gauge railroad to bring up supplies and ammunition. Apparently they had left these dugouts in great haste, for they had left their soup and coffee steaming on the kitchen ranges, all cooked and ready to eat.[29]

"Would you believe it," marine Private Frederick Crowther marveled in a letter, "they had built a bowling alley. It was a pretty good one at that. It was only one alley, but it was covered over by a roof to keep the rain out."[30]

For the first half mile or so of their advance the men of the Yankee Division met little resistance and made better-than-expected time. But the reprieve did not last long. German artillery resumed. The men crawled and clawed their way forward, taking back ground that the Germans had held for nearly four years, since long before America declared war.

McConnell, the Boston lawyer, spotted his chaplain, Father Michal O'Connor, in the early hours of the morning and joked with the priest that he had put on a brand new set of underwear for the attack. "If the Huns get me today, Father, they'll get me clean."[31] Humor was one of the ways he set an example for his men. "Joe was always smiling and cracking jokes to brace up his men," according to O'Connor.

As the battle continued, McConnell and Company A moved up the Vaux-Saint-Remy road toward the German lines.

"He was taking his men through a wooded stretch, when artillery fire came down on them," Sibley reported. "At the first explosion he ordered his men to jump into a trench near by, but he was too late himself; a second shell fell near him, and the up-driving fragments killed him. The company was obliged to move on, and the captain's body was left lying in the edge of the woods, near the road, until Father O'Connor found it next morning."[32]

"He died a soldier's death, leading his company," the priest remembered later. "A fragment of shell pierced his neck. There actually was the trace of a smile on his lips, death came so suddenly."

McConnell's death was not as quick and merciful as the priest would have liked to believe, however. "As we approached the end of the woods there was a seriously wounded captain from the 101st U.S. Infantry lying on his back," is how Private Albertine remembered it.

> His identification tag read, "Captain McConnell, U.S.A." and a serial number. A piece of shrapnel had hit him in the neck and he was bleeding very badly. I took his first-aid pack and took the bandage out and gently placed it around the large gap in his neck. He was in great pain but still conscious. One of the boys ran back to the first-aid station that we had passed en route, and two Medical Corps men with a litter came up and took him away. By the looks of the wound, and from his losing so much blood, if we hadn't come along there was no question but that he would have died right there. Before we left he asked for a cigarette, and someone lit one for him and put it in his mouth, and we left him with a smile on his face.[33]

None of the smoke from the cigarette would find its way into an envelope with a letter home to McConnell's wife. The smile, at least, was consistent to both recollections.

The Americans and their allies continued to push through the heavily fortified and entrenched German lines. On the western side of the salient, Sibley watched as engineers used a mix of mechanized technology and old-fashioned muscle to break through the lines.

> Back in the ravine, the engineers were tearing at their task. How they accomplished it nobody can say, for the very lieutenants don't know it all. The men clawed stone out of the overhanging banks with their hands, and fetched it in the skirts of their slickers when they could find nothing else. They chopped down trees and filled trenches and emplacements with the thick trunks. They blew up the wire, and then rolled the wicked barbed stuff out of the way. They picked a possible grade up that terrible ravine and through No Man's Land. At first the way was winding, but loop by loop they straightened out the road. And at 3 P.M., they got two guns up the road.
>
> Before the second wave had been in the German trenches thirty minutes the first of the German prisoners came back. The stream of prisoners never did stop flowing after that for twenty-four hours. Once we were through the ring of machine guns, they quit fighting.[34]

At the same time, not far away along the curved lines that formed the salient, protruding like a bubble in the front, Albertine and the 104th Infantry reached a position from which they witnessed the enemy in full flight. "When we arrived at the top of the last hill we came to the very dense woods of Les Éparges," he later wrote.

> We arrived at three P.M. and here we rested. In front and sloping down from these woods was the plateau of Woëvre. Because of the over-all swiftness of our advance we captured many prisoners, hundreds of guns of all sizes, and stacks and stacks of ammunition. As we lay on our stomachs on the edge

of these woods overlooking this vast plateau, we could see the Boches pulling out on trains. Farther in the distance the small villages nestled in this plateau were being set afire by the retreating Boches.[35]

Into the late afternoon the battle continued. Around four o'clock, the 101st faltered temporarily in the face of continued artillery fire, and the 102nd Infantry, held in reserve, stepped through their lines to take up the fight. Fresh men were more than the remaining Germans could handle.

The outcome was no longer in doubt, but the fighting was still not over. Colonel Billy Mitchell had been given command of the largest force of aircraft ever assembled: almost 1,500 planes from several countries, flying out of fourteen separate air bases. As the afternoon skies cleared, the Allies took command of the air.

America's "Ace of Aces," Lieutenant David Putnam of Newton, Massachusetts, was aching for a fight, but the weather had not been cooperating. He was temporarily in command of the 139th Aero Squadron of the U.S. Air Service based in Toul. For days, Putnam and his fellow fighter pilots had been relegated to periodic reconnaissance flights due to the rainy weather. His single-wing French Spad could fly when the traditional biplanes could not, but he longed to get the red-painted aircraft he had nicknamed "Putnam's Red Devil" back in action, bringing down German planes in dogfights above the front.

By midafternoon, American pilots got back to the sky to recommence the ground strafing of enemy troops in support of Putnam's fellow Massachusetts men in the Twenty-Sixth Division. From the air, the planes could drop small bombs or use their mounted machine guns to attack German ground troops.

Around 4:30 p.m., Putnam spotted enemy troops, transport vehicles, and guns retreating from the salient on the road between Vigneulles and St. Benoit, at a choke point on the only escape route from St. Mihiel. It was the point the Yankee Division was racing for in an attempt to cut off that retreat. So Putnam attacked in a strafing run.

Suddenly, eight German planes descended from the clouds in a surprise attack from above. They were quickly joined by nearly as many more. Putnam, true to his nature, stayed and fought. He brought down one of the German Fokkers, drove off more, and then headed back to base. On the way, he spotted an Allied biplane that was under attack by eight German aircraft, and he went to the rescue. The biplane got away. Putnam did not.

German Lieutenant Georg von Hantelman, who had already shot down an American pilot that day and who would go on to score twenty-five victories, including bringing down three separate Allied aces, brought Putnam into range with his Fokker and fired. Two bullets pierced Putnam's heart. The bright red SPAD crashed southwest of Lomay, France. The title of American "Ace of Aces" would pass on to another.

"Thus died a glorious American boy and a brilliant fighter," wrote Eddie Rickenbacker, who would become the most celebrated American ace of the war, in his memoir.[36]

Putnam was awarded the *Croix de Guerre* and the *Legion d'Honneur* by the French and the Distinguished Service Cross by the U.S. Army. General Pershing recommended him for the Congressional Medal of Honor. Among his personal effects, a letter from Putnam to his mother was discovered after his death. "There is no question about the hereafter of men who give themselves in such a cause," he wrote. "If I am called upon to make it, I shall go with a grin of satisfaction and a smile."[37]

Lieutenant David E. Putnam, America's "Ace of Aces," was nineteen years old.

America's first unified action of the Great War was already an unqualified victory, but a new opportunity presented itself. The Yankee Division had reached its second-day objective in less than a single day, and if the advancing units from the south and west could meet up, they could encircle the Germans and cut off any retreat. "Using the telephone myself, I directed the commander of V Corps to send at least one regiment of the 26th Division toward Vigneulles with all possible speed," Pershing recalled.[38]

Major General George H. Cameron, the V Corps commander, passed the order on to General Edwards and the Twenty-Sixth. "This is your chance, old man," he told Edwards. "Go do it. Try to beat the 1st Division in the race and clean up."[39]

Edwards was at divisional headquarters in Rupt-en-Woevre, so he picked up a phone to relay the new orders to General Shelton, in command of the Yankee Division. Lieutenant Frederick Linton of Roslindale answered, and informed Edwards that his CO was at the front. Could Linton get a message to Shelton quickly? Absolutely, he answered. So Edwards explained the new plan, and Linton set out to deliver it.

As night was falling, he made his way across the battlefield and through the trenches, traveling nearly ten miles to reach Shelton on the front lines and successfully passing on the updated orders. Thanks to Linton's daring trip, Pershing's orders were implemented in less than two hours, a remarkable feat given the unreliable field telephone system and the nearly impassable roads hindering direct message delivery. From the left flank, the 102nd Infantry was sent on a brazen, five-mile, overnight race for Vigneulles, where they were to meet up with elements of the First Division, pinching in from the right. The objective was to cut off all remaining German troops within what used to be the St. Mihiel salient.

Under Colonel Hiram Bearss, the 102nd moved straight down the Grande Tranchée de Calonne road totally unprotected, with thick forests close by on either side. They moved quickly, deep into German territory. Their orders were to be in Vigneulles by dawn.

"We advanced steadily," Captain Francis Clyde Lee of Company F remembered, "through burning villages where we captured prisoners, etc., until we arrived at our objective, which was a large village already in flames, set fire by retreating Boche, of course."[40]

Remarkably, "Hiking Hiram" and the 102nd made it to their target by 2:30 a.m., hours ahead of schedule and well before Pershing's favorites from the First Division. The Battle of St. Mihiel was won.

"This is my birthday," Pershing jotted in his diary, "and a very happy one."[41]

In the aftermath of the victory, the men of the Yankee Division could take stock of what they had accomplished and appreciate the reaction of the newly freed French residents.

"The 26th Division had liberated over a dozen French towns, and thousands of French citizens who had been held prisoners for four long years," artilleryman Ed Sirois recalled.

> When the Infantry went through these towns, the civilians did not know what to make of them, as they had never seen the Americans before and did not know that we were in the war as the Germans authorities kept all this from them. When we told them that we were Americans and that we were in it 2,500,000 strong, they were overcome. The girls threw their arms around our boys, the older people rejoiced and the citizens and soldiers together celebrated. Everything that we wanted was ours for the asking. They invited us into their homes and nothing was too good for us. One of the best captures for the tired thirsty Americans was a German Brewery near St. Maurice that was well supplied with good German beer. There was also a large amount of cigars taken here and almost every man in the division smoked for the next week on the Boche.[42]

In the afternoon of September 13, French units relieved their American allies, and orders came down for the men of the Twenty-Sixth to take up new positions further north.

"The boys weren't in any too great a rush to go," reporter Frank Sibley noticed.

> Not only had they been fighting twenty-four hours, but it was discovered that in the hurry of his retreat Fritz had been unable to destroy his stores. There was a fine large depot at the foot of the hill, at Vieuxville, full of beer and mineral water, of canned provisions and brand new trench helmets,

of all sorts of thing interesting and attractive. Word was somehow passed round, and companies somehow spared their ration carts for a few minutes, and that depot somehow never did get reported thoroughly, — until it was mostly too late.[43]

Beyond the supplies, the Yankee Division had captured over 2,200 German soldiers and untold quantities of ammunition. The impact of America's smashing success would reverberate militarily and psychologically through the German command. It was clear on both sides that the war had suddenly entered a new, and potentially final, phase.

"The first ALL AMERICAN OFFENSIVE planned and carried out solely by American officers and men had been a wonderful success," marveled an effusive Sirois after the war. "In two days the 1st American Army, in their first drive, had made a wonderful record and won a glorious victory. For four long years the St. Mihiel salient had jutted into the Allied lines and been a great menace. Several times the French had tried to reduce this salient and straighten out the line, but had failed. In less than two days the American had completed an enormous task, that no one thought possible."[44]

Pershing, who had insisted on assembling dispersed American units into a single army, was proven correct. The doughboys had won the day and, in a significant way, turned the tide of the war. "This striking victory completely demonstrated the wisdom of building up a distinct American army," Pershing boasted. "No form of propaganda could overcome the depressing effect on the enemy's morale of the fact that a new adversary had been able to put a formidable army in the field against him which, in its first offensive, could win such an important engagement. The St. Mihiel victory probably did more than any single operation of the war to encourage the tired Allies. After years of doubt and despair, of suffering and loss, it brought them assurance of the final defeat of the enemy whose armies had seemed well-nigh invincible."[45]

CHAPTER 9

EPIDEMIC

SEPTEMBER 8–16

September's drenching rain continued. Despite the downpours, servicemen were on the move. As the second week of the month began, almost 200 wounded soldiers arrived in Boston Harbor aboard a Hamburg-American liner, a German passenger ship confiscated at the outbreak of war and pressed into service as a troop transport vessel. These men were coming directly from the front line of both the war and the European flu epidemic.

In an ill-timed essay—undoubtedly distributed to newspapers around the country by CPI, the government's civilian propaganda arm—which ran in Boston on Sunday, September 8, Army Surgeon General William Gorgas detailed all the measures the military had taken to prepare for the medical challenges of war, with particular emphasis on advances in sanitation that would be critical in preventing diseases. "At present, the wards of our base hospitals are in a position to handle the new draft of enlisted men from depot brigade to port of embarkation, with enlarged experience and every possible improvement of ways and means."[1]

Careful readers were also getting the first hints that trouble might be brewing locally, even if it still seemed isolated to military facilities. Several Boston newspaper accounts reported "all the hospital beds at the forts at Boston harbor are occupied by influenza patients."[2]

The state government had issued no public warnings in the week since a health commission doctor had notified local health boards of the looming probability of widespread civilian infection, and people continued to unknowingly engage in activities that were near perfect for feeding an epidemic. At the Mission Church in Roxbury, a crowd estimated at 25,000 gathered for a flag-raising ceremony on September 8. Some 4,000 people marched in a parade to the local Catholic church, where a flag containing 937 stars—one for each of the parish's servicemen, including eight gold stars for parishioners who had given their lives in the war effort and five crosses for the church's priests serving as chaplains—was hoisted. Clergy and politicians, including Cardinal William O'Connell, Mayor Andrew Peters, and Admiral Spencer Wood, gave speeches. It was exactly the kind of mass gathering in which the influenza virus could be easily transmitted to unsuspecting victims.

Boston, like the rest of America, was ill-equipped to handle a public health crisis.

William C. Woodward was both a doctor and a lawyer, with degrees from Georgetown University. In actuality, though, he practiced neither. "My particular forte is administrative, coordinating the work and directing," he said. "I have been offered opportunities to specialize, but my experience for twenty-four years has been administrative, and I prefer it." He was, in other words, a bureaucrat.

Woodward was health commissioner of Washington, D.C., for almost a quarter century before accepting an offer to nearly double his salary and take on the same role in Boston. At age fifty, he had been on the job for five weeks, and he had already identified his biggest challenge. "We haven't been able to keep our public health service forces intact," he admitted. "All the best doctors and nurses, veterinarians and women in the health lines are wanted by the army, the navy, and the Red Cross, and efficient help to carry on the work of the department is unobtainable."[3] Still, he insisted, he was on the job and ready for emergencies.

President Wilson's all-encompassing demands in support of the war effort had profoundly changed life on the home front all across the country, not just in Boston. Among the effects of the war effort was a severe stateside shortage of young doctors trained in the modern practices of the twentieth century. As Woodward noted, they were nearly all serving in the armed forces. At the urging of Dr. William Welch and others, the number of military doctors had risen from around 800 at the start of the war to nearly 38,000. That left the civilian population virtually defenseless, under the care of older, less-skilled physicians, typically small-town practitioners unaccustomed to treating patients with anything but run-of-the-mill maladies. Even more critical was the shortage of nurses.

"The demand for one thousand nurses a week by the Surgeon General has made it necessary for everyone to buckle down to work from one end of the United States to the other in order to rout out every possible nurse from her hiding place," Red Cross nurse Clare Dutton Morse wrote to a counterpart in Italy during the first week of September. "There will be no nurses left in civil life if we keep on at this rate."[4]

The country's military and civilian infrastructures were also woefully lacking when Wilson committed the United States to the fight, despite three years on the sidelines watching the country be drawn inexorably toward the war. Now, virtually every aspect of American life was touched by the need to put the country on a war footing. Ford Motor Company announced that it had entirely suspended the production of motorcars so as to utilize all of its facilities for government manufacturing. Sunday, September 8 was proclaimed another Gasless Sunday, and driving, except in instances of emergency or war-related need, was all but banned. Newspapers were filled with reports of empty streets, tallies of the number of cars counted, and stories of local police forces stopping motorists for real or imagined offenses and, ominously, "recording tags" of cars seen on the streets. Driving was not strictly illegal, but societal pressure against it was stiflingly oppressive.

"From all parts of the East come indications that any automobile owners using cars tomorrow, except for necessary trips, will brave the condemnation or worse of the whole population," weekend newspaper stories warned.[5] *Or worse.* There, in the open, was a barely contained exhortation in favor of violent confrontation in the cause of victory. *Do your part or else.* It was the constant, audible hum beneath so many aspects of American life in September 1918.

A critical aspect of the war effort was the government's perceived need to control the press and to direct as much news coverage as possible toward the goal of boosting morale among the civilian population and the millions of young men about to enter military service.

The Wilson administration had taken drastic measures—likely the most extreme in American history—to control what was written about the government, the war, and the war effort, both by the press and by individual citizens. In 1917, the Espionage Act gave the postmaster general the power to refuse to allow any periodical he alone decided was insufficiently pro-war or overtly critical of the government to be delivered. In an age before radio or television, when much of the information circulating in the country came from magazines or leaflets sent through the mail, this was extraordinary power. In 1918, Wilson went even further, pushing through Congress amendments to the Espionage Act, which became known on their own as the Sedition Act. Under that law it became illegal for any American to "utter, print, write or publish any disloyal, profane, scurrilous or abusive language about the government of the United States."[6] Anyone convicted of criticizing the Wilson administration faced a fine of $10,000 and imprisonment for twenty years—even if their statements turned out to be true.

The president wanted to go further still. He had pushed for full press censorship when advocating for the Espionage Act, and his attorney general wanted the government to keep track of individuals and the things they said publicly or privately.

The tendency towards censorship during wartime was typical in Europe too. The reason influenza was coming to be known in America as "the Spanish flu" was that Spain was neutral in the war and alone among European nations in its lack of press censorship. As a result, newspapers were free to report on the widespread outbreak of influenza and the toll it was taking in the country. The lack of coverage in other countries of the same wave of illness, where public acknowledgement might hurt morale or prove a key strategic misstep, made it seem like the disease was only prevalent in Spain. But a version of this influenza epidemic had already ravaged much of Europe in 1918.

Researchers now believe the deadliest strain started in the United States, at Camp Funston in Kansas in February, then spread with the deployment of American troops to Europe. It began to appear in France, where U.S. doughboys disembarked, and had spread to German forces by late April. In May it began to infect British troops before spreading to Spain, where it was first widely reported. Even as the virus tore through the troops on each side of the front, both Allied and German leaders made every effort to hide the fact, lest the other side perceive a weakness that could be exploited.

Now, the same need for governmental control of the press in America worked against the urgent need to inform the population about the burgeoning epidemic and the possible means of prevention. After all, no editor wanted to face a charge of "scurrilous" criticism of the government for publishing news about an influenza infection being spread by soldiers and sailors.

These conflicting objectives help explain why the earliest outbreaks were being spun in newspapers as "reassuring" and reports insinuated, with no foundation whatsoever, that the worst had already passed.[7]

With beds in the Chelsea Naval Hospital overflowing with sick sailors, the Navy reached out for help. At 3:30 p.m. one afternoon, a call went out to the Massachusetts State Guard at Brookline and, by 6:00 p.m., a tent hospital with room for 200 beds had been erected "as if by magic" atop Corey Hill in the Boston suburb.[8] The site was somewhat isolated and offered open air and potential sunshine still thought to be therapeutic for influenza sufferers.

A steady stream of ambulances pulled into the temporary tent hospital. By evening, all 200 beds were filled. Under the headline "Influenza on Increase Here," one Boston paper strangely stated that "so rapidly has it spread that its presence could no longer be kept a secret."[9] Unanswered was the question of who had been keeping the extent of the illness so quiet—and why. In the story, Captain John Edgar, medical director for the Naval District, revealed for the first time that the total number of influenza cases reported in his jurisdiction had topped 1,100 in two weeks' time, with 160 new cases discovered the day before. Edgar was adamant in his assessment, however, that "it is just plain grippe, without any fancy Spanish influenza trimmings."[10]

Despite the alarming rise in cases, public denials ruled the day, both civilian and military. Massachusetts General Hospital pointedly refuted claims that "any unusual number of doctors or nurses are ill with grippe at the hospital." The commander of the Harvard Radio School insisted that influenza cases were "comparatively slight" and that "precautionary steps taken have checked it there." Commissioner Woodward and the Boston Board of Health nevertheless decided to take tentative steps toward addressing the growing influenza problem. Their solution was to issue an order prohibiting spitting in streetcars, on sidewalks, and the floors of buildings. "I have ordered my inspectors stringently to enforce the antispitting law, and persons had better be more careful about this or they will find themselves paying fines," the commissioner harrumphed.[11]

Woodward's assistant, Dr. David Broughton, had a solution of his own. "Girls should stop kissing sailors," he announced. It wasn't irrational advice, though it was followed by a wholly unfounded conclusion. "When they do, Spanish influenza will be an unknown quantity around these parts."[12] If only it were so simple.

Once again, it fell to Dr. John Hitchcock of the Massachusetts State Board of Health to be the voice of reason. Hitchcock repeated his public warning first issued nearly a week earlier and offered practical advice far more useful than Woodward's self-important proclamations against spitting. "The state department of health believes this outbreak may be most serious," Hitchcock said. "Patients should be kept isolated to protect others. Don't fail to call a good doctor. The disease is contagious. Put them in bed and keep them there until sure they are entirely well."[13]

Buried on the back page of a Boston tabloid was a small item noting that Rear Admiral Joseph Oman, at the Navy's torpedo station in Newport, Rhode Island, had banned sailors in the First Naval District from visiting Boston in light of the growing number of influenza cases. There were eighty men sick in Newport, but it was not noted whether Oman's order was designed to keep the influenza in or out—by isolating the sick or preventing even more infections from outside contact.[14]

Despite the mounting influenza death toll, contradictory messages from both the government and the media abounded. While the *Boston Herald & Journal* was running warnings from Dr. Hitchcock about the dangers to civilians, the *Boston Globe* was reporting that the spread of influenza was "pretty much in hand" on the very day Navy officials in Boston announced 163 new cases had been reported in the previous twenty-four hours.[15] Captain William Bryan, the chief sanitary officer for the Public Health Service, steadfastly insisted that "there is no cause for alarm."[16]

Among the victims was one of the doctors working with Milton Rosenau and James Keegan at Chelsea Naval Hospital to isolate and treat the disease. Assistant Surgeon Harold Porter contracted influenza from the patients he was treating. It quickly and characteristically turned into pneumonia, and Porter died. On active duty for just four months, he had been among the first to treat incoming patients at Chelsea in the initial days of the outbreak. Porter was one of seven ill doctors, along with eleven afflicted nurses, and one of the five Navy personnel to die on the same day, all of whom were stationed at Commonwealth Pier in South Boston. The death toll among sailors was now at thirty-two, but the Navy spokesman continued to downplay the threat, calling the number of dead "comparatively small" given that over 20,000 Navy men and women were on duty in and around Boston Harbor.[17]

Behind the scenes, however, the military was taking action in response to the epidemic, though it would still not let the public know the starkly serious nature of the biological threat. When 200 new enlistees in the Naval Aviation Service arrived at South Station for their expected train departure for training in Charleston, South Carolina, they

were sent home to await further orders. A decision had been made not
to send these potentially infected Boston area natives into a new camp
of men not yet exposed to the influenza virus. At the same time, 2,500
sailors from Commonwealth Pier were sent to a new tent encampment
in the suburban town of Framingham to get them out of harm's way.

Not only was the military withholding information from the public
that could have saved lives, it was actively spreading misinformation to
serve its own purposes—an endeavor it undoubtedly believed to be
patriotic. Rear Admiral Spencer Wood, commandant of the Navy's First
District, complained that the public was unfairly blaming sailors for the
spread of influenza. Making the claim again that this was "plain grippe
without any fancy names," Wood made the completely unsubstantiated
accusation that the disease began in the civilian population and the
epidemic was touched off when a worker brought it from home to Commonwealth Pier.[18] He went so far as to claim that an investigation had
proven this theory conclusively, though no serious investigation existed.

One fact was undeniable: the disease was now spreading further
outward from that initial point of origin into the wider civilian population. The virus showed no deference to social status. In Quincy, the
town's first influenza fatality occurred when a fifteen-year-old shoe
factory worker, Daniel McDougall, died less than forty-eight hours after
he became ill.[19] In Beverly, the thirty-year-old vice president of First
National Bank, Edward Winslow, succumbed as well.[20]

In Washington, D.C., Surgeon General Rupert Blue issued a statement calling attention to the nature of the influenza, admitting that it
had become an epidemic and laying out instructions for doctors and
patients alike. "The disease is characterized by sudden onset," he told
the press.

> People are stricken on the street, while at work in factories,
> shipyards, offices or elsewhere. First there is a chill, then fever
> with temperature from 101 to 103, headache, backache, red-
> dening and running of the eyes, pains and aches all over the
> body, and general prostration. Persons so attacked should go

to their homes at once, get to bed without delay and immediately call a physician. Treatment under direction of the physician is simple but important, consisting principally of rest in bed, fresh air, abundant food, with Dover's powder for the relief of pain. Every case with fever should be regarded as serious, and kept in bed at least until temperature becomes normal.[21]

The *Boston Post* ran a summary on page twelve, below a comic strip. The *Boston Globe* buried an abbreviated version of the story three-quarters of the way down on page two, under other, more optimistic stories headlined "Grippe Abating at Naval Stations," "Sees No Cause For Alarm," and one entitled "No Epidemic In Schools." In reality, however, Boston was reporting twenty-five new cases in its schools, though Dr. William Devine, director of medical inspection for the city's school district, maintained, "I don't think it's alarming when you consider the large number of children in the schools." Besides, he assured people, "I rely on my 45 doctors and 40 nurses to keep me posted daily."[22]

At Camp Devens, Major General Henry McCain had been drilling his new recruits nearly non-stop and spent significant time observing individual units and their training progress. Two days of torrential downpours dumped nearly two-and-a-half inches of rain, the heaviest September storm in eighty-five years, and forced most of the training exercises indoors. Not all, though, as McCain personally supervised 200 men undergoing gas training in atmospheric conditions considered far more realistic than could be recreated on a sunny day. Now, he wanted to see the new Twelfth Division in all of its glory, with every man in formation and drilling. As a means of boosting civilian morale he wanted the public—including the families of many of the recruits who were from Massachusetts—to see the size and projected power of the division as well. He announced a review on the parade grounds at Camp Devens for Saturday, September 14, and thousands of people showed up to see it.

The gates of Camp Devens were thrown open to the general public to witness the enormity and the training progress of the new Pilgrim

Division. General McCain and his staff expected this to be a propaganda coup, with civilians invited in to see how their home town heroes were being quickly shaped into a precision fighting force ready to head overseas to fight the Kaiser. It was certainly a spectacle, as more than 20,000 troops demonstrated drilling techniques and calisthenics and then marched by a reviewing stand in a parade of troops that took over thirty minutes to pass in its entirety.

McCain was enthusiastic about the review. "They made a remarkable showing," he said afterward. "When you consider that they are scarcely yet organized as a division the true meaning of their splendid appearance in the review this morning is brought home to you. They marched well and conducted themselves well generally. We are going to see great things when these men get across."[23]

While the day may have been a military and public relations success, it was a medical disaster.

"The mobilization of an army is a medical as well as a military problem," Dr. Victor Vaughan, one of the leading infectious disease specialists in the country, said in explaining the challenge of battling disease.

> The procedures followed in the mobilization of our soldiers in the World War brought into every cantonment every infection then existent in the areas from which the men came. Drafted men were assembled at some point in each state. They came from every community; they came in their ordinary clothing; some clean, some filthy. Each one brought many samples of the bacteria then abounding in his own neighborhood. They brought these organisms on and in their bodies and on and in their clothing. They were crowded together at the state rendezvous and held here for varying periods of time, long enough to pass through the stages of enlistment. Then they filled troop trains and were transferred to their respective cantonments. On the trains the men from the first to the last car mingled freely. These men had brought the infection from

their homes and had distributed its seeds at the state encampment and on the train. No power on earth could stop the spread.[24]

The geometric expansion of influenza at Camp Devens was no different. What was different was the deadly nature of this particular virus compared to anything ever seen before. This was the most virulent infectious disease the world had seen since the Black Death plague of medieval times.

"These men start with what appears to be an attack of la grippe or influenza, and when brought to the hospital they very rapidly develop the most viscous type of pneumonia that has ever been seen," N. R. Grist, a doctor at Camp Devens, wrote to a friend. "Two hours after admission they have the mahogany spots over the cheek bones, and a few hours later you can begin to see the cyanosis extending from their ears and spreading all over the face, until it is hard to distinguish the coloured men from the white. It is only a matter of a few hours then until death comes, and it is simply a struggle for air until they suffocate."[25]

The day before McCain's camp-wide public review was held, 350 men were admitted to the cantonment's hospital with influenza. That doubled the day after the review, and the first two deaths at Camp Devens attributable to the rampant influenza were announced. Army press reports were quick to note, however, that the rise in cases had not interfered in any way with training, and they "expected that the epidemic will spend itself without any serious results."[26]

But now the general public had been inside the Camp Devens gates. Much as the Army worked to impress them with the gigantic assembly on the parade grounds, there was no way to isolate the truth about the number of sick soldiers at the base. Word spread quickly about the apparent severity of the epidemic, and military officials did their best to suppress it. Lieutenant Colonel Condon McCornack, the Camp Devens divisional surgeon, released a statement carried by the evening papers. "There is no cause for alarm," he insisted. "We are getting our share of a disease that is going the rounds. We will probably have more of it during the coming week. It is nothing more than the grippe, unpleasant, but in no way serious if due care is exercised."[27]

The Navy was reading from the same playbook, working hard to publicly downplay the seriousness of the outbreak. "These cases are simply grippe without any fancy, high-sounding other name," insisted Admiral Wood at the Naval Radio School in Cambridge. Reluctantly, Wood bowed to some pressure, however, and agreed to issue daily reports on the number of influenza cases in the First Naval District, "in view of the publicity already given the situation, and for no other reason."[28] His first report revealed that the Navy had just under 2,000 cases already, in barely two weeks.

Then the death toll began to rise. Stephen McLaughlin died at Chelsea Naval Hospital on September 15, one of six men to succumb to influenza there on a single day. McLaughlin, a seaman, second class in the U.S. Naval Reserve Force, had enlisted in Boston during the summer of 1917. Now, at the age of nineteen, he was dead. His body was returned to the home of his parents, Stephen and Hattie, on Dudley Street in Roxbury, and he was buried in New Calvary, the Irish Catholic cemetery in Dorchester.

Francis Russell and his friends in the third grade at Martha Baker School saw McLaughlin's funeral, and countless others, pass beneath their windows.

"Our one-story stucco school building verged on Walk Hill Street, which half a mile farther on branched off on to Mount Hope and New Calvary cemeteries," Russell recalled.

> Before this we had scarcely paid any attention to the funeral processions that passed at the rate of one or two a day, as we dawdled along the footway going to and from school or played in the yard at recess. But with the spread of influenza the processions became almost continuous, and we began to notice.
>
> Most of the carriages were still horse-drawn, the familiar black hacks with black horses and solemn silk-hatted

coachmen. But now more and more high-topped limousines were appearing with their long shiny hoods and polished lamps. We could hear the carriages passing outside, the clop of horses' hooves in the wet leaves or the swish of vacuum cup tires above the rain trickling in the gutters.[29]

In suburban Framingham, eleven-year-old Kenneth Crotty had an even closer view of the process. He was an altar boy at more than thirty funeral Masses that fall. "They'd have those monstrous big candles on the first six aisles as the body was drawn down," he recalled decades later. "I remember the heartbreak I felt when I saw that person lugged down the center aisle, down the steps, packed into a small truck."

Two of Crotty's four sisters came down with influenza and survived. Five people from his small neighborhood were not as lucky. His predominant memory of the time was fear. It was a feeling that remained fresh even as Crotty approached his hundredth birthday. "People were very leery of each other," the impressionable young boy remembered as an adult. "It was scary, because every morning when you got up, you asked, 'Who died during the night?' You know, death was there all the time."[30]

In the early days of the epidemic at Chelsea Naval Hospital, the victims were disproportionately local. Many of the personnel stationed in Boston Harbor were from New England, especially Massachusetts. Plus, as the commanding officer of the hospital noted in a report to his superiors in Washington, "the congestion of the ships as well as the repeated intercourse with the civilian population is believed to be a menace to the health of the personnel and may have its influence on the present prevalence of influenza."[31]

Boston Harbor was too crowded with ships and men. Too many healthy people were coming into contact with the sick. The pattern of troop deployment and social movement of seamen stationed close to home contributed to the disproportionately high death toll among predominantly local natives in the early days of the outbreak, which leveled out as the weeks passed.

Quite by coincidence, the sick men at the Chelsea Naval Hospital were under the care of one of the country's foremost infectious disease specialists. Dr. Milton Rosenau was part of a small circle of American scientists, all familiar with each other's work and all making remarkable strides in the battle against communicable diseases. Nothing Rosenau could come up with would stem the flood of influenza cases he was seeing, however, and the death toll mounted. He and the doctors under his direction at Chelsea began conducting experiments on volunteer prisoners from the Navy brig, desperately searching for answers.

They took swabs of the mucus in the noses and throats of sailors infected with influenza and attempted to purposely transfer the virus to the volunteers. The idea was to test incubation times, isolate the virus causing the disease, and perhaps develop a serum that could be used as a vaccine. It wasn't working. None of the volunteers came down with the flu, though one of the doctors conducting the experiment fell ill and died.

Circumstances had conspired to put violently sick men precisely at the location where one of the foremost medical experts in the field was working every day. By an amazing happenstance, he cared for the very first infected patient. He had the knowledge, the assistance, and the equipment to figure out what was happening and to stop it. Nothing he tried would work.

Even as the most advanced medical techniques then known were being utilized by the military, the public at large remained uninformed. In the absence of official answers, unofficial suggestions prevailed. So, directly beneath a page-one story in the newspaper with the headline "Spanish Grip Claims Nine" ran an ad nearly indistinguishable from story content. "Avoid Spanish Grippe," read the bold print over a short paragraph that said, "The victims of Spanish grippe are those who are weak and run down. Build new strength with Father John's Medicine, the pure food tonic, free from alcohol."[32]

Invented by a pair of druggists from Lawrence, Massachusetts, Father John's had already been around for more than sixty years at the time. A version of Father John's is still sold today. Reputedly, it was a homemade concoction that had once been given to a beloved but ailing local priest, Father John Murphy. On recovering from his cough, he began to recommend the brew to his parishioners, and a business was born. The trouble was that the influenza epidemic raging through Boston was not devastating primarily the "weak and run down" but the seemingly healthy and strong. One of America's top immunologists described the terrible helplessness doctors faced in treating those previously hale and hearty people who became infected. "The husky male either made a speedy and rather rapid recovery, or was likely to die," he said bluntly. "Nature overdoes the resistance, kills the invading organisms too rapidly and sets free such an amount of poison that death occurs. Infection, like war, kills the young, vigorous, robust adults."[33] The virus was not going to be prevented or cured by spoonfuls of cod liver oil flavored with licorice.

Still, the enormous pressure on government officials, doctors, nurses—and for that matter every American—to view every aspect of life or death through the prism of the war effort was working at counterpurposes to public health. How could anyone admit there was a frighteningly deadly epidemic tearing through Boston? What would it mean for morale? How could anyone complain about illness, even some fatalities, when American boys were fighting and dying in the fields of France? Few dared speak up about bad news of any kind, afraid of somehow violating their patriotic duty. And how could they not be afraid? Fear was one of the government's key tools in shaping public support for the war, an "important element to be bred in the civilian population," according to the official newsletter directed at Four Minute Men. "It is difficult to unite a people by talking only in the highest ethical place."[34]

In such an environment, the government was now reluctant to admit, and the newspapers loath to print, any realistic assessment of the serious danger the people were facing.

At Camp Devens, the cantonment's top medical officer, Lieutenant Colonel McCornack, ordered an autopsy on the body of Private Ernest Stone of Greenfield, Massachusetts, who had fallen ill on Thursday and died on Friday. The cause of death could hardly have been a surprise at that point, however. The façade that Army officials worked so hard to maintain was beginning to crumble, especially after the large crowds entered the camp for Major General McCain's review the day before. Families had visited with their loved ones and undoubtedly heard the truth about the sheer numbers of soldiers affected by the disease. Publicly, the brass maintained its stance that all was well, but cracks in the story, and their confidence, were starting to appear. "A number of cases of Spanish influenza were admitted to the Base hospital yesterday," the *Lowell Sun* newspaper reported, "but the situation causes the medical officer no alarm. They were much more perturbed by the report published that the civil authorities had been asked to cooperate in stamping out the epidemic. No such appeal was made or contemplated, they say, and it is felt that the circulation of such reports will lead the public to believe that the epidemic is much more serious than it really is."[35]

The real fear, that public morale would somehow be dampened if the truth of the extent of the epidemic were known, outweighed concern about the rate of infection or death. While McCornack's staff took great pains to deny that *civilian* help was being sought, increasingly urgent requests *were* going out for military help. The commander of the camp's hospital, Lieutenant Colonel Channing Frothingham, telegraphed the surgeon general of the Army asking for ten additional doctors and forty more nurses. The Camp Devens medical facilities were straining under the influx of suddenly sick soldiers, and thirteen of the 109 nurses had fallen ill themselves.[36]

It was about to get much worse.

Less than forty-eight hours after the massive review of the troops, a shocking 1,189 new cases of influenza were admitted to the Camp Devens hospital in a single day, and four more soldiers died.[37] When the weekend began, before every soldier in camp had assembled to march and drill and perform for their commanding officer and the general public, about 350 soldiers were sick. Now, with astounding ferocity, the virus was cutting a swath through the camp. Two full days had yet to pass, 3,000 soldiers were now sick, and over a thousand new cases were being diagnosed every day. All this was happening in a cantonment where there were a total of only 1,800 hospital beds.

Corporal John McQueen was an orderly in one of the camp's hospital wards. "I found 181 sick men laying on straw beds," he reported. "Two blankets—no pillows—no sheets. No medical supplies."[38] McQueen did what he could for his fellow soldiers under the circumstances, working nearly non-stop. After five straight days of it, a doctor pulled him aside and ordered him to have some Old Crow whiskey and an aspirin and to do the same for the patients. "He made me take my first drink of whiskey to keep going."[39]

Still, the military would not concede that it had a crisis. "We are not alarmed over the number of cases now being attended at the base hospital," an Army official said the day after the review. "We will not say that they are 'Spanish influenza' cases. We do not know where that rumor originated. You must remember, we had a lot of rain last Sunday and Friday and some of the boys got their feet and clothing wet, with the result that they got heavy colds."[40] Ironically, the denial ran alongside a photo of the men massed for review and under a page-wide headline that shouted "2,000 Men Ill with Grip at Camp Devens."

Finally, nine days after the first diagnosis of influenza and two weeks after the initial patient was admitted to the cantonment's hospital, the camp epidemiologist, Dr. Paul Wooley, formally reported the influenza outbreak to the Army surgeon general.

All the while, Private Estlin Cummings, or "Eddie," as the few men in his unit with whom he had any social interaction called him, was bored. Everyone at Camp Devens had to deal with the rain and the drilling and the marching and the senseless discipline-for-discipline's-sake, but Cummings chafed at it more than other soldiers. For one thing, he was an intellectual—a graduate of Harvard, the son of a prominent minister in Cambridge. The military is not always meant for people with imaginations. Thinking men can die in a war, while the instinctual, the habitual, the unquestioning order-followers have a better chance to survive—at least according to the message pounded into soldiers' heads day after endless day. For another, he was an artist—a painter who was always sketching what he saw around him, a writer of journal entries and letters to friends with complex sentences describing profound ideas.

In a daily life dominated by routine and repetition, there was little to draw or describe.

Most of all, Cummings was different than the other draftees and enrollees in the Twelfth Division because he had already been to France and seen the war. On those dreary September days, Cummings was a year removed from the front.

Like most of his Harvard friends and fellow members of the school's Poet Society, Cummings was torn between his natural pacifism and his desire to experience the world. When America entered the war, he was faced with the very real prospect of being torn from his bohemian life of art and letters by the draft. A family friend, Richard Norton, was organizing an ambulance corps in France, and it offered Cummings a chance to control his fate, minimize his risk, and still fulfill his patriotic duty. His father impressed upon him the advantages of choosing his role as a volunteer rather than be subject to the vagaries of the draft and a likely assignment to the infantry. The day after President Wilson asked Congress to declare war, Cummings joined the Norton-Harjes ambulance corps and was soon headed for Europe. "I'm glad to be out of here by the 1st of May, when everybody is to be tabulated on pink, violet, yellow, (and I dare say orange) cards, for the benefit of conscription," he wrote his father. "It will mean everything to me as an experience to do something I want to, in a wholly new environment, versus being forced to do something I don't want to & unchanging scene. I only hope I can see some real service at the front."[41]

En route, he bumped into an acquaintance from home, William Slater Brown, who had also signed up, and they traveled together aboard a luxury liner to France. A mix-up on their arrival found them separated from the rest of the volunteers and in a Paris hotel awaiting specific orders. Faced with a choice of forcing the issue with their superiors to clarify their assignments or life in the magnificent city, they decided the war would find them soon enough and spent five weeks experiencing everything the City of Lights had to offer—food, wine, women. He and Brown devoured Paris—its museums, its restaurants, high and low culture from the *Ballets Russes* to the *Folies Bergère*—and took up with a pair of high-end Parisian prostitutes.

Eventually, someone noticed they were gone. Cummings and Brown were ordered to return to Norton-Harjes and were put to work. As punishment for their lack of urgency, they were mostly assigned to washing the ambulances while others handled transporting the injured. It was Cummings's first exposure to the boredom of military, even quasi-military, life. Still, he did the job. His French was fluent from his Harvard days and newly polished by his Paris nights, and he became close to the French members of the unit. In them, he found an honor and simplicity that he felt were lacking in the mostly privileged American volunteers. His letters home reflected the drudgery of his job and little of the horrors of war. He was trying to keep his head down, in military parlance. But it was never going to last. He and Brown were not cut out for the discipline of military life. Their erstwhile vacation meant they had received no real training. While ostensibly officers by virtue of their positions, they fraternized with, and were subsequently treated like, enlisted men. Their commanding officer was offended by their preference for spending time with French soldiers rather than fellow Americans, going so far as to tell them he wanted them to "show those dirty Frogs what Americans were like."[42]

While Cummings at least made an occasional effort to conform, Brown did not; his letters were filled with criticism of his officers, sarcasm about the war effort, and troubling reports about French morale. The letters caught the attention of censors, who hauled Brown in for questioning and—because everyone thought of them as a pair—brought Cummings in as well. It was clear from their interrogation (and the fact they had already read his letters and found nothing objectionable) that there was no reason to hold Cummings. They were about to release him when they asked one last, standard question: did he hate the Germans? "No. I like the French very much," he replied honestly because he truthfully harbored no ill will against the German people and this son of a minister would not lie. Having discovered his insufficient enthusiasm for hatred, officials shipped him off to detention with Brown.

For three months, he was held in a facility at La Ferté-Maceé, in the French forest, facing more boredom and more monotony. Once word of his incarceration reached home, his father began to pull strings in an effort to gain his release. Edward Cummings was a prominent man with a formidable network of friends in high places. He was the head of the World Peace Foundation and the successor to the famed Edward Everett Hale in the pulpit of the South Congregational Church in Boston. His demands that his son be released reached to the top of the government in Washington, where Secretary of State Robert Lansing began looking into the case. Finally, in December 1917, Cummings was shipped home.

He returned to New York to paint and write and reconnect with the artistic set. Then came the government's "work or fight" order the following summer and, once again, Cummings found himself exposed to the draft. His father suggested several jobs that could keep him out of military service. "I would rather die than leave New York at this moment," he wrote back angrily. "I should worry about General Crowder. Also the work-or-worry bill, which will not go into effect until July 1, anno domine, etcetera. Meanwhile my presence here on this spot and moment is requisite to my absolute and individual success in existence."[43]

Cummings's disillusioning experience in France, marked by the reality of war and the absurdity of authority, had festered, and his return to America had not helped. In fact, his cynicism had grown. "Little children mouth the bloody-thirstily-inspiring words of 'over there, over there' 'so what are you doing to win the war' etc. ad infin.," he wrote in his increasingly eccentric style.

> Moovies show reels where ex-soldiers about-to-commit-traitery are so moved by the patriotic appeal of babies in nightgowns that they weep bitter tears—and go out and kill Mexicans! A grim looking bunch of dames sits collectively in a booth on 14th shrieking faintly at everyone "buy a stamp," while o'er their sacred heads wring the printed words "Help to make the Kaiser's coffin," or some such reference to the "Baby Killer." How fierce we are.[44]

But the "work or fight" deadline passed on July 1, and a few days later Cummings was called to service. By late July he was on his way to Camp Devens as a member of the Pilgrim Division's 3rd Company, 1st Battalion, Depot Brigade. Though he had tried to avoid it, he was an infantryman after all, and, as he had feared at the outset of the war, he was "being forced to do something I don't want to & unchanging scene." Soon, he was again battling all of the internal challenges he had faced in France. He could not connect with the other men. He didn't respect them. He was at once intellectually and, he felt, morally superior to many of them, especially the officers. They were the ones barking an unending indoctrination of hate against the enemy, which may have been the element of Army life that Cummings resisted the most. He struggled to find any redemptive aspect to his training and pined for his friends and his life in New York. "Do you think that I have suffered for nothing the obligatory conscription and all the evils which accompany a complete separation from all I hold to be life?" he wrote to his mother on September 11. "Not on your tintype, as Uncle George ecstatically would remark. I say, the artist is merely the earth's most acute and wily observer of everything under the sun. The artist keeps his eyes, ears, & above all his NOSE wide open, he watches, while others merely execute orders he *does* things."[45]

Despite his best efforts to keep his brain and creativity engaged, he was mind-numbingly bored. To make matters worse, he had fallen in love, and, like the weeks-long relationship he had carried on with the prostitute in Paris, it was a complicated and conflicting situation for someone raised in such a religious family. Cummings had fallen hard for his best friend's wife.

Amidst the marching and the target practice and the gas drills, under the oppressive clouds and constant rain, even as an epidemic ravaged all around him, lovesick Private E. E. Cummings was writing poetry for Elaine Thayer, the wife of his friend Scofield Thayer, ignoring punctuation, experimenting with spacing, and concentrating on the way words looked on a page as well as the meaning they conveyed. It was a style that would later make Cummings among the best-known American poets of the twentieth century.

While Cummings was pre-occupied with his budding romance, all around him men were dying. "We did discuss the matter of placing the camp under quarantine," Lieutenant Colonel McCornack finally admitted, "but found that there were just as many cases among the civilian population, so we said what's the use."[46]

The Navy continued to be hit as well. There were now 677 cases at the receiving station at Commonwealth Pier. Nearly 700 were stricken at the Radio School in Cambridge, and a quarantine was instituted, forbidding anyone to enter the school grounds.

Away from military installations, civilian cases were exploding as well. In the towns of Milford and Sharon, with the disease spreading and absentees mounting, local officials decided not to open schools for the week on Monday morning, September 16. At Boston City Hospital, there were 200 influenza cases, and the staff had finally decided to close the hospital to visitors and start using gauze facemasks when caring for the infected. Steadfastly, Boston Health Commissioner Woodward insisted that the influenza death rate was no greater than in previous years. He also issued another of his head-scratching explanations, this time regarding the emerging realization that those over the age of fifty-five seemed to be far less affected by the epidemic. "Persons of advanced age do not get about as readily and mix in crowds," he posited with no basis in fact.[47]

And yet at Massachusetts General Hospital, the incidences of influenza were growing so rapidly the facility could not handle them all. Surgical wards were filled with flu patients. The young interns were pressed into service, with each one assigned a medical ward to oversee. The two most senior medical interns at the hospital remained in the emergency department full-time, taking turns relieving each other after twelve-hour shifts but never leaving the hospital. The building was becoming overrun.

"The morgue was completely filled, and the undertakers could not begin to keep up with the number of dead," recalled Dr. Thomas Cunningham, who was an intern at the time. "Many patients were brought to the emergency ward dead in the ambulance. Others would die an hour after admission. It was not unusual to pass two or three of your patients being carried out the back door as you were going up to make your midnight visit."[48]

Woodward still did not seem to grasp the magnitude of what was transpiring. Instead, he once again offered nothing but a slogan to his city, which was under bacteriological siege. "Keep cool, keep calm, keep cheerful."[49]

CHAPTER 10

THE HOMEFRONT

SEPTEMBER 13-28

I n Boston, the newspapers trumpeted the victory news from France that Americans had been waiting to hear. When it came, it was couched predictably in terms meant to justify societal support of the war.

"Sixteen months of vast war effort by the United States reached its first goal today when General Pershing's forces struck their first independent blows in France against the German Army," read a page-one story on the battle at St. Mihiel. "The all-American attack meant that the months of ceaseless toil and effort have now brought forth a third great organized army, backed by its own supplies and millions of soldiers if needed, which has taken its place beside the French and the British armies and is striking for decisive victory for democratic ideals."[1]

The message was unmistakable. America, this is why you stopped driving on Sundays and gave up sugar and collected peach pits and wore paper daisies. This is why you must continue to sacrifice and buy more liberty bonds and keep up your morale. Implicitly, it also underscored the need to downplay anything that might in any way undermine those sacrifices or impinge on that morale—such as, say, news of a deadly epidemic.

Stateside, the victory at St. Mihiel lifted spirits, even though loved ones at home in Massachusetts were still unaware of the key role played by the men of the Twenty-Sixth Division. "The first step on the road to Berlin," one local headline called it.[2]

"Overseas, the great attack on the Hindenburg Line had begun," and the news rippled through seven-year-old Francis Russell's school.

> Our own Yankee Division was at St. Mihiel. Eliot Dodds came to school with a pin that said "To H-LL with the KAI-SER" but Miss Sykes made him take it off. The Lynch boys' father, who was in the Navy, was torpedoed and rescued.
>
> Always, when the time came for singing, Miss Sykes would step forward on the platform and sound the pitch for us to begin. But now, instead of "The Harp that Once" and "Loch Lomand [sic]" we sang "Pack up your Troubles," "Keep the Home Fires Burning" and "Over There."[3]

Just as President Wilson had hoped, all Americans—down to the youngsters in grade school—were infected with war fever. Credit goes to George Creel and CPI. He and his staff had blanketed the country with patriotic and pro-war propaganda, and it had worked.

"There was no part of the great war machinery that we did not touch, no medium of appeal that we did not employ," Creel claimed. "The printed word, the spoken word, the motion picture, the telegraph, the cable, the wireless, the poster, the sign-board—all these were used in our campaign to make our own people and all other peoples understand the causes that compelled America to take arms."[4]

The stateside army of speakers known as the Four Minute Men was a highly organized example of the depths to which the effort to deliver constant, targeted messages to the American people extended. The organization was built with a military-style chain of command, where orders emanated from the top, filtered down through geographic units, and were carried out by the foot soldiers—prominent, trusted local men. For the first half of September 1918, for example, the benign-sounding topic chosen by CPI for all Four Minute Men was "rumors." In reality, the speakers were instructed to convince their audiences that it was unpatriotic to believe any information that was not being delivered to them by the government directly. Anything heard from friends, relatives, even the newspapers, should be viewed with skepticism.

"We are all so keenly interested in the war that we greedily take everything said about it with too unquestioning faith in sources of information," said George U. Crocker, a well-known Boston lawyer, former city treasurer, and chairman of the Boston contingent of Four Minute Men, in announcing the latest theme. "The lies and the damaging statements are always started by people who are actually in the employ of Germany or are active sympathizers, and who whisper to their unsuspecting friends that are loyal to our cause. Active propagandists are easily reached and caught in the finespun net of the government intelligence services, with the prompt cooperation of loyal people everywhere."[5] Crocker went on to urge the public to report to authorities any person or publication voicing doubts or criticism of the war effort.

In point of fact, the Four Minute Men were themselves a vast force of "active propagandists" more successful than any the United States has seen it its history. "The Four Minute Men were as effective in the battle at home as was the onward rush of Pershing's heroes at St[.] Mihiel," Creel claimed.[6] And yet, some of their messages, like the one for September urging citizens to question everything they heard from anyone other than the government, had unforeseen tragic results.

Among those coming to the aid of Creel and CPI was a financial expert from Wellesley, Massachusetts, named Roger Babson.

Babson was a dyed-in-the-wool Yankee, a tenth-generation native of Massachusetts, practical, deeply religious, and fiercely bright. He graduated from the Massachusetts Institute of Technology in Cambridge with an engineering degree, but his no-nonsense father advised him to get into a business where he could find repeat customers. Babson decided that, with his head for figures, he would pursue finance. He might have ended up a wealthy Wall Street financier, but a bout of tuberculosis left him frail, and he decided to stay close to home and away from the pressure of New York. That did not stop him from becoming wealthy; he just did it from his own street instead. In 1904 he started the Babson Statistical Organization, used his own proprietary methods to analyze stocks and markets, and began selling a newsletter of financial advice to subscribers.

By the time the United States formally declared war, Babson was famous—first for the innovative statistical calculations he used to predict financial trends but mostly as a widely read business pundit of a sort. Aside from his main business offering advice to subscribers, he was making a significant amount of money writing freelance and syndicated articles and columns for publications such as the *New York Times* and *Saturday Evening Post*. The press nicknamed him "The Wizard of Wellesley."

"When our country entered the first World War, I had a certain background which I knew would be helpful to President Wilson," Babson recalled in his autobiography. "I felt that, with this background, I could bridge the chasm between captains of industry, who were making huge profits, and wage-workers who were engaged in the manufacture of munitions."[7]

Babson volunteered to help the war effort and moved his family from Massachusetts to Washington for a post in the Labor Department. In short order, Creel recruited him to head CPI's Division of Industrial Relations but quickly thereafter arranged for his transfer directly to the newly created Labor Administration. "As I have explained to Mr. Babson, there is nothing that he wishes me to do that I will not attempt to do," Creel wrote to Labor Secretary Baker, "and this applies to the use of the Four Minute Men, the Speaking Division and the publication of printed matter that you may not be able to issue."[8]

But what was this background Babson felt could be so beneficial to the cause? "I could use my knowledge of publicity methods to the mutual benefit of the nation," he believed. "My work primarily was to 'sell the war' both to employers and to their wage-workers. Employers were urged to be reasonable as to profits, and wage-workers were urged to give the best they had in time and energy."[9]

The government had clear leverage in getting industry to see things its way; nationalizing companies it felt were vital to war interests. In Springfield, Massachusetts, that September, the War Department took over operation of the Smith & Wesson Company after the gun manufacturer refused to abandon its practice of forcing employees to sign contracts promising not to join a union. The move was necessary, the government said, to ensure the "maintenance of industrial peace."[10] And, they neglected to mention, to keep the production of guns moving.

On the other hand, efforts to co-opt labor to the cause of war were less straightforward and more layered. As evidenced by the Bolshevik revolution in Russia and the growing radicalism of American labor organizations such as the IWW, employers and the government were both concerned about a potential workers' uprising. "We are sitting on a volcano and that war might cause an eruption," the head of General Motors told an advisor to President Wilson.[11] For once, management and unions had similar concerns. Industry feared that a shortage of manpower resulting from massive military enlistment might create pressure leading to higher wages and better benefits. Some union leaders, especially American Federation of Labor founder and president Samuel Gompers, feared a workers' rights movement might tip toward socialism. The government just wanted productivity. Creel was determined to bring both sides together to work toward that goal, couched as always in patriotic slogans. Babson and Gompers, as one historian put it, were "charged with the special responsibility of keeping labor industrious, patriotic and quiet."[12]

Among Babson's projects was a massive poster campaign, topping out at nearly 650,000 printed and distributed per month, with messages promoting vigilance and self-sacrifice. Posters were among the most effective tools at CPI's disposal. "I had the conviction that the poster must play a great part in the fight for public opinion," Creel said. "The printed word might not be read, people might not choose to attend meetings or to watch motion pictures, but the billboard was something that caught even the most indifferent eye. What we wanted—what we had to have—was posters that represented the best work of the best artists; posters into which the masters of the pen and brush had poured heart and soul as well as genius."[13] CPI's Division of Pictorial Publicity produced some of the most memorable images of all time, including the iconic Uncle Sam by James Montgomery Flagg, beckoning recruits to join the U.S. Army.

Babson sent these and other posters to factories and offices across the country for prominent display to workers. Along with the posters were "confidential" bulletins intended for employers, keeping up the constant drumbeat of the need for productivity and stability in the cause of victory. In addition to the poster campaign, Babson instituted a program whereby small cards were inserted into the paychecks of workers. These 3-inch-by-3-inch cards included what were intended to be inspirational messages on the need for efficiency, productivity, and patriotism. The approach was simple. "The war taught us the power of propaganda," Babson stated matter-of-factly.[14]

It was a single-minded effort designed to keep factory owners and their workers focused on a single goal: winning the war. "I know nothing of labor and capital," Babson claimed, referring to a well-known quote from Kaiser Wilhelm. "I know only honest Americans, who all want to help in this great fight of the people against Kaiserism. In wartime we lay our family quarrels aside. We don't want the Kaiser to settle them for us."[15]

Beyond the propaganda campaign, real-life effects of the war continued to seep into every imaginable aspect of life in Massachusetts, as they did across the country. From Washington, the War Industries Board issued a request, as these directives were always characterized, that all non-essential building construction be halted for the duration of the war. Massachusetts appointed a Committee on Curtailed Nonwar Construction with the authority to approve or reject any home renovation or new construction expected to cost more than $2,500. "We are living in a time when every pound of material and every ounce of energy must be used in the successful prosecution of the war," rationalized Henry Endicott, executive manager of the state's Committee on Public Safety.[16]

At the Capitol, Senator Lodge, like any good politician, was looking ahead. For years, he and former President Theodore Roosevelt had advocated for "preparedness" in anticipation of war. Now Lodge strategized with his friend about how to bring to an end a war they had both agitated to join.

"We ought not to discuss anything with the Germans at present," he wrote in a September letter to Roosevelt. "Not a thing. The moment we begin to discuss negotiations the war will be over and we shall have a German compromise peace."[17] It seemed premature to be thinking about the terms of a peace that was not yet assured, but Lodge had long been suspicious of President Wilson's resolve when it came to Germany. Just weeks before committing the U.S. to war, Wilson had appealed to the two sides in the conflict to end hostilities and pursue a strategy of "peace without victory." To Lodge, any negotiated resolution of the conflict was unacceptable. He felt the stakes were too high.

"We have no territory to gain and seek no conquests," he maintained, "but I think the American people are determined on placing Germany in the position where she can never again menace the peace, liberty and civilization of the world or the independence of other nations."[18]

Lodge's distrust of Wilson, and his qualms about the president's willingness to wield America's military might in the cause of freedom and democracy, had grown increasingly personal. It was partly partisanship and partly principle, but Lodge did little to conceal his contempt for the man. "I never expected to hate anyone in politics with the hatred I feel toward Wilson," he said in one of his frequent letters to Roosevelt.[19]

Across the United States, some 13 million American men reported to their local draft boards on September 12 to register for induction into the military. The Wilson administration had pushed a Selective Service bill through Congress shortly after the declaration of war in 1917, instituting a draft of men between the ages of twenty-one and thirty to build up the woefully undermanned U.S. Army. A second round of registration had just taken place during the summer, with two phases to sign up those who had turned twenty-one since the draft began.

Now, however, Secretary of War Newton Baker and Provost Marshall General Enoch Crowder, the pair responsible for the "work or fight" order that curtailed the baseball season, had decided that even more men were needed. The age range of the draft was expanded significantly to include every man between the ages of eighteen and forty-five, and they were all required to report to their local draft board to add their names to the rolls on September 12. This day might have been the greatest triumph of Creel, Babson, and CPI. They had created such unanimity of purpose in America that millions trudged to their local draft boards and willingly—unquestioningly—signed up for service. There were none of the widespread draft riots that had marked similar efforts during the Civil War. Apparently, it did not cross the collective American mind to oppose the idea.

"Now that it is all over, the nation must surely be rubbing its eyes and marveling that a people with so little military tradition, with so little interest in wars and armaments as such, was able within a day's time to enroll the man power out of which will be developed an army destined by all present indications to seal the defeat of the greatest military autocracy the world has ever seen," observed the *New York Times*.

> Only two years ago it would have been unbelievable. There were army officers who then held that it could never be done in a country that had not made a habit of militarism. And yet without a military tradition, with no other magic to evoke it than a vital faith in a great cause, the manhood of this country from coast to coast—peaceful citizens engaged in peaceful pursuits—stepped before their draft boards and registered themselves for service as the Government shall deem them fit; and having done so without any noise or fuss, they went back to their shops, their offices, and their desks to continue their

peaceful pursuits as peacefully as ever until such times as the Government will need them for the serious tasks of war.[20]

With the influenza virus already hopping rapidly from one person to another, nearly 100,000 young Boston-area men went out in torrential rains and dutifully descended on registration locations across the city. Among them were five Massachusetts congressmen and former Governor David Walsh, who was running for the U.S. Senate. In long lines, infected men mixed with those who had thus far avoided the virus. They stood, shoulder to shoulder, exhaling and inhaling the deadly germs. Then, they too went home to their families, unaware that they might be bringing death home with them.

Captain John Edgar, the naval medical officer who just two days earlier had dismissed the epidemic as "just plain grippe," issued an update. There had now been 1,331 cases and twenty-six deaths among naval personnel in and around the Boston waterfront. It was getting more and more difficult to dismiss the outbreak. Efforts to downplay the growing crisis were running smack into deadly reality.

Also on September 12, the day after their World Series victory, the Red Sox players arrived at Fenway Park to get their paychecks. "Money talked at Fenway Park," Ed Martin wrote in the *Globe*, "and had the floor all day."[21] The National Commission made one concession after all, agreeing to allow the teams to pay the players in person rather than have the Commission mail them their shares. Team owner Harry Frazee honored his promise to pay the players their full salary through the fifteenth of the month, and he personally wrote out checks. For the winning Red Sox, the final share of World Series revenue ended up being $1,108. Members of the Chicago Cubs received $671 as the losers' share. They were the lowest payouts in World Series history. Just as the players claimed they could, the National Commission made unilateral policy changes. Each player was given a separate check for $154.50, which was deducted from his total bonus. This represented the ten percent portion of receipts pledged to charity, and, rather than baseball making a single large donation on behalf of all players, each was encouraged to divide the money as they saw fit between war-related causes in their home towns. In another change from the Commission's original plan, some players received only partial shares of the pool. Third baseman Fred Thomas, headed back to his post at Great Lakes Naval Station following his World Series furlough, received $750. Eight players, including Dick Hoblitzell and Dutch Leonard, who departed during the season to join the war effort, were given $500.

Boston outfielder Harry Hooper, who had convinced his manager to convert Babe Ruth into an everyday player, had spent long summer train rides studying and discussing war news, and had battled baseball hierarchy on behalf of his fellow players, was less than sanguine about the series and the sport itself.

"I've been with the Red Sox for ten years, and yesterday I felt that I was playing in my last big game," he mused before heading home to California. "I'm getting old for big league ball, and the outlook for the sport seems so dark. I don't anticipate there'll be any baseball next year. Then when the game is resumed, salaries will be low and I may not be able to afford to come across the continent."[22]

Most players left the park later in the day to catch trains home to their families and their draft boards. Babe Ruth headed to nearby Revere Beach, where he served as the official starter for a bike and motorcycle race.

Martin dutifully recounted the individual payoffs and reported on the impending plans of players now subject to the "work or fight" rules. Some had shipyard jobs lined up; others were expecting a call from their local draft boards. A few figured to be exempt. When Martin finished his story for that day's *Boston Globe*, he was justifiably uncertain about the future of baseball. He was also unaware of the uncertainty in his own life. Before the end of the month, influenza would visit the Martin household.

With primary elections in both parties fast approaching, Massachusetts politics was on full unseemly display. In the Sixteenth Congressional District race, Congressman Peter Teague used a tried-and-true strategy, claiming his opponent, fellow Democrat and former Boston

Mayor John "Honey Fitz" Fitzgerald, wouldn't bring home enough bacon. "Mr. Fitzgerald does little but talks much," Teague said on the campaign trail. "He was in Congress for six years. If he can point to one single dollar of a federal appropriation that he ever brought to this city during his entire six years in Congress, I will cheerfully withdraw in his favor."[23]

In the nearby Twelfth Congressional District race, the tactics were far more personal. Incumbent James Gallivan loudly and unapologetically accused his Democratic opponent, another former Boston mayor, James Curley, of being a suspected German spy. "If I am to be defeated," Gallivan told supporters, "I want it to be by a loyal citizen of the United States."[24] A day later, Curley would respond by calling Gallivan "a cowardly liar."[25]

In Washington, Massachusetts Congressman Frederick Gillett of Springfield was the leader of House Republicans. Whereas Lodge headed a GOP majority in the Senate, his fellow Bay State legislator was in the minority. Gillett saw himself as spokesman for his party colleagues and was already outlining themes ahead of the November elections. "It is a piece of effrontery for the Democrats to contend, as they have, that the Democratic Congress before the war showed greater foresight and was more liberal in military preparation than Republican Congresses," he said in a speech on the floor of the House, making a demonstrably valid point. "You Democrats are trying to frighten the country into belief that the kaiser will think the election of a Republican House will indicate that the nation is half-hearted about the war. Do you think that the kaiser is as ignorant as that?"[26] Gillett's efforts would pay off, as Republicans would win a majority in November and he would rise to be speaker of the House, giving Massachusetts men control over both houses of Congress.

Not every congressman from the state was focused on geo-political matters, however. Republican Joseph Walsh, representing Cape Cod and the state's southeastern coastal area, was concerned with somewhat more mundane matters. "The United States, through its officials and departments, should set an example of economy and conservation," he declared from the well of the House chamber. "On the contrary, however, we have a deluge of bulletins, reports, surveys, magazines and various other publications which are choking the government printing office, clogging the mails and which clutter up many an office in business houses. The shipping board has broken out with printers' inkolitis."[27] Perhaps unsurprisingly, the former reporter did not believe that paper conservation should extend to newspapers, which he maintained were "patriotic," apparently unlike the government itself.

Undoubtedly thrilled with news of the victory at St. Mihiel, the Putnam family gathered on Saturday, September 14, for the wedding of Dorothy, a nurse in training at Children's Hospital, to Lieutenant Harold Hayes at the Newton Highlands Congregational Church. Those assembled for the celebration were as yet unaware that the bride's brother, Lieutenant David Putnam, had been shot down and killed in the battle, though he was very much in their thoughts.

"From time to time letters arrived from him but they were all modest and contained little news of the details of his doing in the air," the groom told a reporter. "The last batch of letters received from him was on or about August 18. In it he said he was very, very busy. He was never showy. It would not be surprising if there was further promotion for him as his letters have ceased since August and I presume he is still busy downing them."[28]

Far from the emerging horror in his home state, Charley Crowley was in his first days of college. The Cambridge, Massachusetts, native was fresh out of high school and had traveled all the way to the Midwest to attend college, where he expected to play football for a small school that was just starting to make a name for itself on the gridiron. In the East, universities like Yale and Cornell and his home town school, Harvard, already had long and proud football traditions dating back to the last century. Despite having played for just as many years, schools beyond the Appalachians, like Michigan and the colleges in the brand new Western Conference already being referred to as the "Big Ten," were seen as second rate. This included Crowley's new school, the University of Notre Dame.

The newspapers were saying that there might not be a college football season in 1918 because of the war. "Football undoubtedly is a splendid game for preparing boys for the service," said Major Fred Moore, who was at once a military intelligence officer and the graduate treasurer of athletics at Harvard, "but it is not the quickest way of making a soldier or an officer. It does not seem to me that it would be possible to carry on organized football activities as a university proposition under the present conditions."[29]

Like most colleges of consequential size across the country, both Notre Dame and Harvard had all but turned over administration of their institutions to the U.S. government as part of the pervasive societal obsession with the war effort. The War Department controlled curriculum, mandated military training for students, and saw universities as another key factor in the war effort—the place where future military officers would be identified and trained. There seemed to be little room in all of that for something as relatively trivial as football. The same congressional act that established the military draft also created the Students' Army Training Corps, "to utilize effectively the plant, equipment, and organization of colleges for selecting and training officer candidates and technical experts for service in the existing emergency."[30] Young men enrolled in SATC were technically on duty in the Army and subject to activation. As a practical matter, however, the program was seen as a way of delaying, if not avoiding, being shipped to the European front. The students were required to spend forty-two hours per week in the study of "military subjects" and fields deemed critical to the war effort, such as engineering, arithmetic, and sciences. In addition, at least eleven hours of physical training, primarily military drills and physical conditioning, were mandatory.

Some schools, especially in the East, had found these military obligations, on top of travel difficulties and a shortage of young men to play, to be insurmountable obstacles that required cancellation of the football season. Others disagreed, using the argument Boston Red Sox owner Harry Frazee had earlier made regarding baseball—that sports were critical outlets for a stressed and war-weary populace. "The addition of military courses at the colleges will necessarily take up most of the time which the squads in the past have given over to football practice," the *New York Times* reported. "It is believed that the military officers will see the necessity of football as a diversion."[31]

The chairman of the Department of War's committee on education and special training, Colonel R. I. Rees, sent a letter to college presidents during the second week of September informing them that sports requiring extended trips or specialized training would not be permitted. While the government encouraged athletics in general, they could not be allowed to interfere with academic pursuits or military training schedules, and competitions must therefore be staged only with nearby schools.[32]

Many college presidents were vehemently opposed to the idea of a shutdown. Sports, even then, meant significant revenue for some schools. Schedules had been set, travel plans booked, and ticket sale receipts anticipated. University officials quickly got in touch with their senators to voice their opposition to the War Department's decision.

It was early in the academic year, and the Notre Dame football team was holding its first practice of the season on its campus in South Bend, Indiana. It was scheduled to do so, anyway. Heavy rain had turned the field to mud and the first day was more of a meeting than a practice. Also, since only twenty students showed up, the team didn't have enough players to stage a full scrimmage. At least Charley Crowley thought he might get a chance to play. It was a big reason he had made the trip west from his home in Cambridge.

Under six feet tall and only 185 pounds, Crowley was an interior lineman and small for that position even for the era. Players remained in the game for both offense and defense in those days. Any player who came off the field for a substitute could not return to the game until the next quarter. As the 1918 Notre Dame squad gathered for the first time, however, Crowley didn't have to worry about his size. No one on the team seemed appreciably bigger than he was.

None of this deterred the man in charge. He seemed enthusiastic and unfazed by the small turnout of small players. After several years as a successful assistant, it was Knute Rockne's first day running the Notre Dame football program as head coach. Rockne had graduated from Notre Dame and played on the football team, where he and quarterback Gus Dorais were credited with an innovation in 1913 that changed the game for good: the forward pass. After getting his degree, Rockne stayed on at the school as a chemistry teacher, track coach, and assistant to head football coach Jess Harper. Early in 1918, Harper decided to leave coaching and return to his cattle ranch. He believed the war would curtail the sport, as it had for big league baseball. He also struggled with the rising backlash against the growing success and popularity of the game. Many felt that it was getting too big, focusing too much on the money it could generate and losing its sense of sportsmanship and amateurism. In short, Harper didn't think the game had much of a future.

Following the 1917 season, Rockne had verbally agreed to accept the head coaching position at Michigan State. With Harper's resignation, however, the way was clear for him to remain at his alma mater. He might have had second thoughts given the grim state of the program at the time. Harper's inattention, the roadblocks of wartime society, and the shortage of healthy young men posed serious challenges to Rockne as he took over. Yet he took it all in stride and was confident he would prevail if only by virtue of his focus and relentless drive. There simply was no question about it in his mind.

To Charles Crowley, however, things looked pretty shaky on September 18, the first day the team got on the field for a practice. A handful more of students showed up this day, as opposed to the previous one, so at least they had enough warm bodies to scrimmage. But Rockne was working alone. Budget cuts meant that, in addition to earning just $3,500, some $1,500 less than Harper had received, he had no assistant coach, not even a trainer. Rockne himself was taping up the players. Also, there seemed to be a shortage of uniforms and equipment.

Rockne gathered his men around at the start of practice and spoke to them in his clipped, rapid delivery. His point was simple. Since they were all of draft age, these Notre Dame students were lucky to be here, on this muddy field, at a time when other Americans their age were fighting and dying on the fields of France. Crowley and the others listened in rapt silence. Already it was clear that this man, about to conduct the very first practice of his head-coaching career, was an inspirational leader. Now, it remained to be seen if he knew anything about football.

The Notre Dame squad had lost nearly all of the players from 1917 to graduation or the draft. Wartime regulations severely limited the amount of time that could be spent practicing. The schedule was in shambles as schools canceled their entire seasons or severely curtailed them to save on travel costs. But it was already clear to Crowley that they had two very important things going for them: their charismatic new coach and returning halfback George Gipp.

Crowley played right tackle on the team's front line, opening running lanes for Gipp and a freshman that shared the backfield duties, Earl "Curly" Lambeau, from a town in Wisconsin named Green Bay.

Gipp came to Notre Dame from Laurium, Michigan, intent on playing baseball. Legend has it he was drop-kicking a football 60 or 70 yards across the campus one day just for fun when Rockne saw him and convinced him to play football. He did a little of everything during his first year on the team as a sophomore. He ran, he threw, he punted, he returned punts. He was the undisputed star of the team. While Gipp supplied the versatility and finesse, Lambeau gave the Fighting Irish their muscle. In its season review, the *Notre Dame Scholastic* called him, "a line-plunger of terrific power, he was also wonderful in off-tackle drives."[33] In other words, Lambeau did much of his running right behind the kid from Cambridge.

The backlash over the government's announcement regarding the cancelation of most schools' games led to immediate action in Washington, D.C. The controversy grew so quickly that, just a day later, the War Department issued a statement denying the idea completely once congressmen started to relay the concerns of colleges and their constituent football fans. Still, curtailing college football during wartime appealed to some. Similar to the criticism of baseball players and owners, there was a significant faction in America who believed that the war would succeed in returning a purer form of amateurism to a sport they felt had begun to focus far more on financial issues than on athletics and competition as simple measures of a man. "The game will be more in the nature of a recreation for the entire student body rather than a spectacle in which only a limited number of players are trained to a high standard of playing skill by specialists," predicted the *New York Times*, reflecting an opinion widely held by its eastern, more educated, and well-heeled readers. "This is the state of affairs that college athletic directors have been seeking for a long time, and now the opportunity is at hand to put it into practice, and they will undoubtedly grasp the opportunity."[34]

As Notre Dame prepared for their opening game against Case Tech in Cleveland, expectations were muted. No one knew what to make of these raw recruits and their first-time head coach. "Green is the word to describe the material for the gold and blue," the local South Bend newspaper said. "Not that the youngsters do not know any football at all, or that they are an awkward squad. Some of them look promising, but they have a long way to go to measure up to traditional varsity standards."[35]

Even Crowley had noticed that his teammates were on the small side. Of the twenty-nine players that eventually made up the squad, twenty-eight weighed less than 200 pounds. Rockne did not share in the skepticism. "This team, despite its light weight, has all the spirit and fight that any of the older and heavier teams had," he maintained.[36]

So, on September 28, the young coach and his young players faced their first test. The first quarter, at least, lived down to the low expectations surrounding the team, as Case jumped out to a 6–0 lead. Then, with Crowley and the other undersized front linemen leading the way, Notre Dame's backs began to dominate the game. Lambeau scored a touchdown to tie the game in the second quarter, and then Gipp scored two more. He also threw for over 100 yards and handled all of the Notre Dame punts. The Irish scored twenty-six unanswered points and made a winner of Rockne in his first game, twenty-six to six. Charley Crowley's decision to leave Massachusetts for Indiana was looking better. "Crowley from Boston played his part with honor," the Notre Dame school newspaper said of him. "A shifty man on defense, he was hard to put out of a play, and when called upon to clear the way for the backfield the men carrying the ball never failed to find an opening."[37]

George Gipp and Curly Lambeau's paths crossed at Notre Dame during just the 1918 season and then again in football history books. Gipp, of course, became famous as the best football player in the country in the following two seasons, but he died of pneumonia shortly after being named the school's first All-American in 1920. His legend was burnished eight years later when, during half-time of a tough game against Army at Yankee Stadium, Rockne quoted him asking on his deathbed for a future Fighting Irish team to "win one for the Gipper." His place in American culture was assured when an actor named Ronald Reagan played Gipp in the movie *Knute Rockne, All American.*

Lambeau went home for the holidays after the 1918 season but contracted an infection. By the time he was healthy, it was six weeks later and too late to return to Notre Dame for the second semester. So he got a job at the Indian Packing Company, a meatpacker in his home town of Green Bay. The next summer, he decided to organize his own team and asked his company to sponsor their uniforms. Over the next two years, Lambeau turned the team into a professional club. In the process, he founded what became known as the Green Bay Packers and helped turn the association in which they played into the National Football League.

Back home in New England, amidst all the sadness and fear in September 1918, it must have seemed jarring when baseball talk briefly resurfaced in the papers, with two familiar rivals staking out positions and offering very different assessments of the state of the game in wartime.

"I do not believe that the national authorities and the people of the United States will permit the great game of baseball to be thrown aside," outspoken Red Sox owner Harry Frazee once again predicted. "I am confident that both the American League and the National League will play championship baseball next year. I base my belief upon my knowledge of the American people and their desire for healthful relaxation. I think there will be strong popular demand that the great national game be continued."

Cincinnati Reds owner and National Commission member Gus Herrmann was more cautious. "Major league ball for 1919 now depends entirely on the authorities at Washington," he deferred. "Measures will soon be taken to ascertain the opinion of those in control. If it seems best to the government that baseball should stay dormant for another season, the magnates will cheerfully obey. But if the government wishes baseball to be resumed as a tonic for the public's nerves, the magnates will go ahead."[38]

To people in Boston, the mere idea of a baseball season must have seemed remote, and the World Series a distant memory, in the face of so much death. Baseball, too, seemed to face a bleak future. While Babe Ruth was in Hartford, Connecticut, pitching in a 1–0 win with a barnstorming team on what was, one might have technically argued, the last day before World Series players were subject to the government's "work or fight" ruling, organized professional baseball was literally being shuttered. Red Sox management was locking up the ballpark. "Fenway Park will be barred and closed until happier times arrive and baseball comes back into its own," the *Boston Post* reported, though no one knew when, or if, that would actually happen.[39]

In the two weeks since the Boston Red Sox had won the World Series, Babe Ruth had been enjoying the sweet life. He had played in a couple of exhibition games, reportedly earning $300 per appearance—meaning he had made two-thirds as much in those games as he had for the entire World Series. He had also been contemplating offers to work and play for industrial companies in Quincy, Massachusetts, and Providence, Rhode Island.

Lebanon, Pennsylvania, was closer to his home town of Baltimore, so Ruth worked out a deal with "Pop" Kelcher, the physical director of the plant there, and reported to work at Bethlehem Steel. While technically satisfying the "work or fight" order, Ruth's primary role at the plant would be as a baseball player. There he would join his former teammate and catcher Sam Agnew and fall into the ranks of ballplayers trying to get through the war doing what they did best.

In his first game for the Bethlehem Steel factory team, Ruth went hitless in three at bats and was intentionally walked once. The weather dictated that the season was winding down, however, and Ruth missed a couple of games taking care of unspecified "personal business" in Baltimore, including one against his Red Sox teammates, who were on a barnstorming tour. The first game would turn out to be the only game in which Ruth played for Bethlehem Steel, as fall and the armistice brought his short-lived industrial career to a close.

Back in Boston, Henri Rabaud was chosen as the new conductor of the Boston Symphony Orchestra in the last week of September, though he was still abroad and would not take over the role until the following month. The circumstances that led to Rabaud's appointment served as a stark indicator of the extent to which patriotic fervor had been whipped up by President Wilson, George Creel, and their public relations campaign.

Karl Muck was the conductor of the symphony from 1906–1908 and again from 1912 until earlier in 1918. A concert pianist with a doctorate from the University of Leipzig and its highly respected music conservatory, Muck was born in Germany, moved with his family to Switzerland as a child, and was therefore a Swiss citizen. Nearly every native German was viewed with suspicion in America at the time, however, especially after Wilson's proclamation in November 1917 that they could all be considered "enemy aliens" and were therefore subject to restrictions on travel and assembly. As war fever spiked, Muck was the subject of near constant rumor and innuendo, stemming in part from his friendship with Kaiser Wilhelm during his years at the Berlin National Opera. It was the Kaiser himself who reportedly gave his consent for Muck to leave Berlin for Boston, though that was years before the start of the war.

Muck understood the sensitivity of his situation and offered to resign as conductor after the United States declared war in 1917, but the orchestra's founder, Henry Higginson, would have none of it. Muck stayed on at Higginson's insistence, even in the face of public criticism when the orchestra continued to play works by German composers. Anti-German sentiment continued to rise, fueled so expertly by Creel's ubiquitous and polarizing campaign, and ostentatious displays of patriotism became all the rage. Giant flags were hung in symphony halls. New York Symphony Orchestra conductor Walter Damrosch, ironically a native of Germany himself, began the practice of playing "The Star-Spangled Banner" at all performances. Rumors flew that any orchestra not adding the number to their program might lose their license to perform. Pressure mounted for the Boston Symphony to do the same. In October 1917, the orchestra played one of its regular dates in Providence, Rhode Island, where the editor and publisher of the *Providence Journal* saw an opportunity to live up to his motto to "raise hell and sell newspapers." The paper ran an editorial objecting to the program of German music, criticizing Muck's ties to the Kaiser and insisting that he conduct the orchestra in playing "The Star-Spangled Banner" as some sort of test of his loyalties.

Muck never knew about the demand. Higginson and symphony manager Charles Ellis were aware but made the decision their orchestra would not be bullied into altering its program, and the performance went on without any added numbers—patriotic or otherwise. That simply bolstered the newspaper's cause and fueled a controversy that spread across the country. Again the conductor offered to resign, and again Higginson refused. Three days later, at a performance back in Boston, the Boston Symphony Orchestra performed the song under Muck's baton. Higginson announced to the audience that it was his decision not to play it in Providence and that the conductor had never had any objection to its performance. It was too late. Muck was denounced coast-to-coast as the German conductor who refused to play "The Star-Spangled Banner."

"Any man who refuses to play 'The Star Spangled Banner' in this time of national crisis should be forced to pack up and return to the country he came from," spouted former President Theodore Roosevelt.[40]

"If Dr. Muck had spoken up like an honest man and said: 'How can you expect me, as a loyal citizen of Germany, to conduct 'The Star

Spangled Banner' when you know that my sentiments in this war are in sympathy with my own country?' fair minded Americans would have accepted this attitude," claimed Damrosch, getting every detail exactly wrong.[41] Muck was not a German citizen and had not been a vocal supporter of the German cause. Plus, the very existence of the controversy belied the notion the public would be understanding or accepting.

Following Wilson's "enemy alien" proclamation the next month, Muck came under the scrutiny of the Department of Justice. Over and over in the intervening months he was called in for questioning. Why had he refused to play "The Star-Spangled Banner"? What was his current relationship with the Kaiser? Why had he rented a summer vacation cottage on the Maine coast, and did that house really have a wireless radio on the premises that might have signaled German ships?

In March, when Muck's assistant went to the U.S. District Court in Boston seeking passport applications for Muck and his wife, the government placed both of them under arrest. Under the "enemy alien" proclamation, they did not need to be charged and were not even entitled to a hearing. Instead, they were among the few German-born people sent by the United States government to an internment camp at Fort Oglethorpe in Georgia, where they remained in custody through the duration of the war. In 1919, after the armistice, they were deported and never returned to America.

A dazed Muck, on board the ship that would return him to Europe, still seemed bewildered by the whole thing. He had never done anything wrong, had never refused to do anything asked of him, and yet he found himself a reviled figure. "I am not a German, although they said I was," he said upon his final departure. "I considered myself an American."[42]

CHAPTER 11

DON'T NAG

SEPTEMBER 6–16

I n American society at large, another issue was bubbling to the surface: the role of women. The state of Massachusetts had been at the forefront of change for women more than seventy years before the war, when large textile mills located in cities along the state's power-generating rivers recruited young women from around New England to fill factory jobs. This migration from the region's rural farms and small towns resulted in women living on their own, away from their families, and with income they earned themselves. The resulting independence elevated women to a new societal position, and they soon used their leverage to better their lives even further. Living in company-owned housing, the "mill girls," as they came to be called, organized an all-woman union to demand higher pay and shorten the workday from twelve to just ten hours. In one of those factory towns, the Lowell Female Labor Reform Association helped women flex their new political muscles to push for governmental investigation of working conditions and bargain for financial benefits.

During the Great War years, when demands on American industry increased dramatically at the same time that huge portions of the male population were exported to fight in Europe, women suddenly composed an even larger percentage of the workforce. These were not just administrative jobs of the sort traditionally filled by female workers. More and more, these were hands-on technical roles in complex manufacturing settings.

"The women of the United States are willing and capable of anything and everything they may be called upon to do, I believe," said the chairman of the War Industries Board, Bernard Baruch. "The time is fast approaching when they must be mobilized more effectively than at present."[1]

Maud Wood Park could easily have settled into a life typical of so many educated and financially stable women in the early twentieth century; one filled with society gatherings and philanthropy. From early adulthood, however, she showed a propensity to go against the grain.

Born in Boston, she attended the prestigious St. Agnes School in Albany, founded for the stated purpose of teaching upper class young women about a woman's rightful place in the home and the skills she would need to thrive there.

Apparently, it didn't take.

After several years as a schoolteacher, she enrolled in another staunchly anti-suffrage institution, Radcliffe College in Cambridge, the female school associated with the all-male Harvard College. In 1898, after just three years, she graduated *summa cum laude*. Two years later, she was a delegate to the National American Woman Suffrage Association (NAWSA) convention and dismayed with what she found. The meeting was held in the dingy basement of a church, and members seemed to have no seriousness of purpose, with one state committee report actually delivered in rhyme. At age twenty-nine, Park was the youngest woman in attendance. The movement was no longer moving, having largely stalled in its efforts to gain voting rights for women since the days of pioneering suffrage leader Susan B. Anthony. So Park went home and founded the College Equal Suffrage League, first at her alma mater and then at other schools, in an effort to bring youth and energy to the cause.

Shortly afterward, in 1901, she also founded the Boston Equal Suffrage Association for Good Government (BESAGG) with a goal of educating, informing, and empowering women for the purpose of tackling a wide range of societal issues: care for the poor, prison reform, the formation of Boston's first Parent-Teacher Association, and—most importantly—suffrage for women. For the next twelve years, she served as the organization's executive secretary.

A key moment in Park's life, and therefore in the cause of woman suffrage, came when she was elected chairman of the executive board of the Massachusetts Woman Suffrage Association and the group's legislative chairman. It was in this role that she got her first up-close look at the political process. At the Massachusetts State House in Boston, she was exposed to lawmakers and began to study and learn legislative procedures. It was knowledge that would serve her well, first in state capitols across the country and later in the halls of Congress in Washington.

Beginning in 1910, BESAGG focused less on the issues of broad societal good and began to concentrate almost exclusively on the issue of suffrage. Ahead of the 1912 national elections, Park was one of three women named as delegates to the Progressive Party convention in Chicago. In a glimpse of her emerging political pragmatism, however, she declined the invitation. Though the move was unpopular with many suffragists, Park strongly believed that ultimate victory would be reliant on forward-thinking politicians from every party, and she worried that any appearance of partisanship on her part would alienate Democrats and Republicans who were sympathetic to the cause and would be critically important in passing any federal voting rights law.

Park was not inactive in the 1912 campaign by any means. She raised a great deal of money in Boston then traveled across the country to fundraise and campaign against candidates opposed to suffrage. During one stretch, she gave sixty speeches in fifty-four days in the state of Ohio alone. Over the next few years, the movement achieved considerable success in western states, as women gained the right to vote in state and local elections. Despite all of Park's efforts, however, things did not go as well in her home state. In 1913, women campaigned to successfully unseat State Senate President Levi Greenwood, only to see him replaced by a non-committal Republican from western Massachusetts named Calvin Coolidge. A statewide referendum on a suffrage amendment to the Massachusetts state constitution in 1915 failed by a two-to-one margin.

By 1916, leaders of the suffrage movement decided that state campaign efforts had peaked and it was time to turn their sights again on an amendment to the U.S. Constitution to extend voting rights to every woman in the country. At its annual convention, the NAWSA was reorganized from a coalition of state efforts to a national campaign focused on ratifying the Nineteenth Amendment. Rather than state chapters, the group reformed by congressional district and concentrated equally on electing supportive House and Senate candidates. "When we filed out of that room at the close of that meeting [at the convention], I thought I understood how Moses felt on the mountain-top after he was shown the Promised Land," Park often recounted. "For the first time our goal looked possible of attainment in the near future."[2]

At the same time, Park was convinced to move from Boston to Washington, take up residence in the NAWSA headquarters, and concentrate full-time on lobbying Congress. This was a new challenge because, while Park was probably the movement's most gifted organizer, she had no experience in direct one-on-one lobbying of lawmakers. But Park understood a fundamental truth of the suffrage cause at that moment in time: success no longer depended on convincing women. It was now all about persuading men—specifically those in Congress.

That election year also marked the first time Park tangled with her home state senator, Henry Cabot Lodge.

In the lead-up to the presidential campaign and in keeping with Park's bipartisan approach, she felt it critical that each of the three major political parties—Democrats, Republicans, and Progressives—specifically endorse the suffrage amendment in their campaign platforms. The remnants of Roosevelt's Progressive Party were on board. The Democrats, much to her disappointment, would only go so far as to endorse the concept of voting rights for women, not the amendment specifically.

That left the Republicans, where Lodge was the chairman of the convention's Resolutions Committee. With every other plank in the platform already decided, the issue of suffrage was discussed and, by a 26–21 vote, a strongly worded endorsement of the constitutional amendment—written, like those of the other parties, by Park herself—was approved, with Lodge voting against the resolution. It seemed that she had won over two of the three parties.

A half hour later, however, Lodge called the roll of absentees from the first vote in an effort to force reconsideration of the plank. Over the afternoon, votes were counted and arms twisted. The tally varied as committee members entered or left the room, and Lodge kept count of which committee members were or were not present, looking for a moment in which he would have enough votes to defeat the measure. The committee recessed for lunch, and Lodge realized he was not going to find enough votes to win. Instead, he engineered a compromise to avoid complete defeat. He proposed new language which generally supported the cause of suffrage but pointedly called it a matter to be settled by the states rather than the federal government: "The Republican party, reaffirming its faith in government of the people, by the people, for the people, as a measure of justice to one-half the adult people of this country, favors the extension of the suffrage to women," the plank stated, "but recognizes the right of each state to settle this question for itself."[3]

"Our disappointment when we heard Senator Lodge read those last words was indeed bitter, for they had made the plank a practical denial of what the Association had requested," Park wrote later.[4]

Lodge found his votes, and the "compromise" wording was adopted. He hadn't won, but he had kept his opponents from fully winning either.

"Of course, this action is not what we want," one of Park's associates said afterward. "But resolutions and planks count for little. We are asking for action and we expect it from this session of Congress."[5]

Efforts to work within the system did not sit well with every faction of the suffrage movement. Many of the younger women in the cause, inspired and organized in part by Park's own outreach programs, were more impatient for change. Led by a more radical leader named Alice Paul, they took an activist approach and established the National Woman's Party as a vehicle designed to flex women's political muscles ahead of the 1916 elections. The group was organized like any other political party, all the way down to ward captains and precinct leaders. Workers went door-to-door in an effort to reach housewives with literature for them to give to their husbands—the actual voters. Significantly, the "party" reached out to foreign-born women, often including speakers in various languages at their local meetings. In addition, they stepped up public protests. Inspired by the bold, and sometimes violent, actions of British suffragettes, they picketed the White House, demanding more support from President Wilson, and some of them, including Paul, chained themselves to the fence and were arrested. Others began hunger strikes as a form of protest.

Park was determined to take a more moderate and traditional course and gained incremental success. In 1917, she convinced the House of Representatives to appoint a Woman Suffrage Committee and move the issue out of the Judicial Committee. In June 1918, she engineered another major congressional victory. With behind-the-scenes support from President Wilson and public support from former President Theodore Roosevelt, the House approved a Constitutional amendment backing suffrage, reaching the required two-thirds majority with a single vote to spare. It was a dramatic scene, with proponents of suffrage going to dramatic lengths to win approval. Representative Henry Barnhart of Indiana was carried into the House chamber on a stretcher so he could vote. James Mann of Illinois checked himself out of a hospital against doctor's orders to do the same. Most poignantly, Frederick Hicks of New York, at the urging of his wife, left her death-bed to vote in favor of the bill and then returned home to find that she had passed away.

With ultimate victory in sight, Park went to work securing the resolutions of support from the both the Democratic and Republican National Committees, as well as both the Republican and Democratic

Congressional Committees and the American Federation of Labor. She was building the broad bipartisan support she felt was critical.

"When I was sufficiently familiar with the work to have a little sense of humor about it I condensed the rules into a series of 'don'ts,'" Park recounted in her autobiography. It was a declaration of pragmatism in support of her cause.

> Don't nag.
> Don't boast.
> Don't threaten.
> Don't lose your temper.
> Don't stay too long.
> Don't talk about your work where you can be overheard.
> Don't give the member interviewed an opportunity to declare himself against the amendment.
> Don't do anything to close the door to the next advocate of suffrage.
>
> The last "don't" was the one I dwelt on the most in my talks with our workers, partly because it was the most difficult to follow. Knowing that the effect of our work in the case of doubtful members was cumulative, I used to say over and over again, "If we can't do any good, at least we must be sure that we don't do any harm."[6]

For over two years, she had put her moderate, respectful, but persistent approach to work seeking support from senators. When the issue came up in the Senate in the summer of 1918, however, it was tabled under the threat of a filibuster, in a debate memorably marked by Mississippi Senator John Sharp Williams's proposal to confine suffrage just to white women and his frank admission on the Senate floor that he was trying to prevent southern black women from voting.

The clock was ticking. If the suffragists could not get the Senate to join the House in approving the amendment by a two-thirds vote before a new Congress was sworn in, they would have to start over in both houses. Who knew what level of support they would have in either the House or the Senate after the next election?

As summer drew to a close, sensing a momentary advantage, opponents moved to bring the issue up for a vote. "The resolution called upon the Senate to vote on it and get it out of the way, no matter whether it should be carried or defeated, and did not even give it the prestige of a favorable endorsement," reported suffragist Elizabeth Cady Stanton. "Here, one could easily see the fine hand of Senator Henry Cabot Lodge of Massachusetts."[7]

Park was supremely organized, as always. Like a party whip, she was counting votes, trying to determine the best time to bring the amendment to a vote in the Senate. "It looks to me as though we had a better prospect in several ways than at any previous time," she wrote to a colleague on September 6. "On the other hand there are a lot of difficulties. In addition to the three Suffrage Senators who are in Europe, we have the following absences: Senator Gronna, who, according to Senator Curtis, cannot possibly get here for two or three weeks; Senator Page, who is ill; Senator Goff, who can never be counted on; Senator Smith of Michigan, who went away the first of this week to be gone a fortnight; Senator LaFollette, who is up in the mountains with his son and probably will not come back."[8]

This is the way it had gone since the House approved the amendment, a day-to-day accounting of who Park had in her column. It had been a particularly turbulent summer, with a series of deaths and replacements in the Senate, which kept suffrage supporters and opponents coming and going and made Park's vote counting even more difficult.

Yet there was optimism in the suffrage movement that their time had finally come. "During the dark days of 1918, there had come a tremendous advance in the status of woman suffrage," read the official history of the movement. "The magnificent way in which women had met the demands of war, their patriotic service, their loyalty to the Government, had swept away the old-time objections to their enfranchisement and fully established their right to full equality in all the privileges of citizenship."[9]

The war was opening some doors to women, out of necessity if nothing else. In the Massachusetts town of Haverhill, women were being hired for the traditionally male task of reading meters for the gas company. Even this seemingly minor advance, however, was met with opposition. An official of the Boston Consolidated Gas Company was appalled. "Maybe in Haverhill, but not until the last gun's fired in Boston," he huffed when asked if women might find similar opportunities in the city. "Not until it becomes absolutely necessary. And we hope that day will never dawn. For climbing up dizzy step ladders to meters aloft, giddily perched over precipitous coal bins is too much for a woman. Women as meter readers? No, never! The Lord forbid."[10]

Pragmatic leaders like Park and Carrie Chapman Catt, the NAWSA president, were leaving nothing to chance, however. In mid-September, Catt asked Park to arrange a meeting with President Wilson at the White House, which she did. The plan was to appeal to the president for a strong public statement in support of the Nineteenth Amendment. Their lobbying efforts, while effective, needed a final push, and who better to plead the case to reluctant Democratic senators than the Democratic president?

Wilson welcomed the delegation of women to the White House on September 16 and reiterated his support for the suffrage amendment. "I am, as I think you know, heartily in sympathy with you," he told them. "I have endeavored to assist you in every way in my power, and I shall continue to do so."[11]

Members of the NAWSA were happy with Wilson's pledge of support, a transcript of which was made public soon after the meeting. The younger, more radical women in Alice Paul's National Woman's Party were not as easily assuaged. The group held a protest across the street from the White House in Lafayette Park and burned a copy of Wilson's supportive statement. "The torch which I hold symbolizes the burning indignation of women who for a hundred years have been given words without action," one of the protesters said. "For five years women have appealed to this President and his party for political freedom. The President has given words, and words and words. Today, women receive more words. We announce to the President and the whole world today, by this act of ours, our determination that words shall no longer be the only reply given to American women."[12]

   This wasn't going to be easy.

CHAPTER 12

STATE OF DENIAL

SEPTEMBER 16–24

nevitably, because they were exposed to influenza all day, every day, doctors began to die. Dr. Thomas Leen, forty-three; a prominent local physician with a wife and young daughter who lived in Boston's Back Bay; a former member of the Boston School Committee; a lecturer at Harvard Medical School, his alma mater; and the physician-in-chief at Carney Hospital in South Boston, was the first, dying on September 16 as the epidemic picked up speed.[1]

He would not be the last.

Dr. William Kingsbury died in Malden at age forty-five. Dr. Frederick Denning also died from the flu, the first in a hellish but all-too-typical, ten-day stretch at the Denning family home on Third Street in South Boston. Five days after Frederick's death, his mother, Ellen, also passed away from influenza. Four days after that, his older sister, Catherine, succumbed. The very next day, his older brother, William, also a doctor, was dead as well. Four people in the same household. All dead in the span of little more than a week, all carted off to Mount Benedict Cemetery in West Roxbury to rest together.

The wartime paranoia and desire to maintain home front morale remained strong in the face of the viral onslaught, however. That fact had been reinforced just weeks earlier in the journal the *Military Surgeon*. "Ours is now a nation at arms," it said in an editorial aimed precisely at men like Lieutenant Colonel Condon McCornack, the division surgeon at Camp Devens. "Every single activity of this country is directed towards one single object, the winning of the war; nothing else counts now, and nothing will count ever if we don't win it."[2] With that directive in mind, even as thousands of men were streaming into the camp hospital and strong young soldiers began to die, McCornack met with the press. He assured them that there was "absolutely nothing to get fussed up over," that just a small percentage of the troops "are what by any stretch of the imagination could be termed ill,"[3] and that several hundred had already been discharged from the hospital. It was the best possible spin on what was an increasingly dangerous situation, and newspapers across the country dutifully carried McCornack's take under headlines such as "No Danger at Devens."[4] But the career Army doctor also had an uglier rationale as to why most Massachusetts residents should not be overly worried about the contagion, explaining that "many cases were found among Negro soldiers from the South, who were susceptible to any form of ailment and gave in more readily than the white soldier."[5]

In Cambridge, across the Charles River from Boston, the local newspaper poked fun at the spreading sickness, advising the "radio boys" at the Naval Radio School and their girlfriends to "cut out the kissing." At the same time, the paper scoffed at the idea that the influenza striking so many local residents was anything serious. "This so-called 'influenza' is said by the doctors to have the regulation symptoms of a bad cold, headache, running from the nose, bone ache, high temperature and bronchial disturbance," the *Cambridge Chronicle* reported on September 13. "Those afflicted rally from it quickly, the disease taking its ordinary course, except in severe cases where pneumonia follows. It has the exact symptoms of the regular grippe, which has often been prevalent here. Experimentation with volunteers, and with the germ, have indicated that it is not the especially dangerous form once reported from abroad."[6]

And yet, already, someone was dying in Boston from influenza or resulting pneumonia once every hour, and it was killing them quickly. Men and women who felt fine on Saturday afternoon developed a fever on Saturday night and were dead on Monday. Across the city and its nearest suburbs, people were literally dropping in the streets. Over three dozen nurses in Boston had already been infected with the influenza virus. The shortage of nurses, acute before the outbreak, was now even worse.

The government may not have recognized the problem, but one organization clearly did. The Red Cross of New England completely changed its focus from fighting the German army to fighting the Spanish flu. It stopped making surgical dressings and started making gauze masks. Instead of meeting troop trains with snacks and cigarettes, it mobilized to deliver food, clothing, and bed linens to the sick. The Red Cross issued an urgent call for the mobilization of anyone resembling a nurse, such as those enrolled in nurses' training, then put those answering the call to work. "The thirty who responded for immediate service were assigned to an open-air hospital where they worked for nearly a month in all kinds of weather," the division reported up to national headquarters.[7]

North of Boston, the town of Salem, famous for its seventeenth century witch trials, reported over 1,000 cases. Twenty miles further north, Gloucester joined the growing list of communities closing its schools. Officials in Boston, however, stubbornly clung to the notion, publicly at least, that this was nothing but a common wave of old-fashioned flu. Even with the death of young Anna Bloomfield of Dorchester, the first area schoolchild casualty, William Devine, the medical director of Boston's schools, and Dr. William Woodward, the city's health commissioner, opposed closing the schools despite an absentee rate that was topping 40 percent. Devine was most adamant that, "there is nothing alarming, so far as the school children are concerned, and there appears to be no epidemic."[8] Kids, the two health officials insisted, were less likely to be infected "by remaining at their studies," as if they could simply concentrate the virus away by keeping their noses in their textbooks. A seventeen-year-old girl dropped dead on the elevated train platform, and Woodward cheerily welcomed one day's sunny and unusually warm weather, cheerfully maintaining that "a half hour's sun bath means sure death to the germs."[9] On the other hand, the Navy's Captain John Edgar was hoping for a different weather remedy. "If we had a killing frost for a short time, I believe the germ would be knocked out," he predicted.[10]

If government officials downplaying the threat needed any reminder of America's patriotic hysteria, they need have looked no further than the town of Lynn, ten miles outside Boston, where 1,500 people had been stricken. Caroline Dourhauer had come to town in 1898 and had been a teacher in the local schools for nine years. Most of that time she taught German, but when Lynn Classical High School dropped all those language classes after America entered the war, she began teaching French instead. Despite her years of service and her pending application for citizenship, city Councilor John McAuliffe was agitating for her termination on the grounds that she was, solely but undeniably, German. When the School Committee voted to retain her, McAuliffe stoked the flames of xenophobia even further. After Dourhauer's supporters on the School Committee were "energetically attacked" by McAuliffe, he won the city council votes needed to order the city treasurer not to issue her paycheck.[11] He might not have the means to fire her, McAuliffe figured, but he would be damned if he would let taxpayer money go to a German. This was not an isolated incident. Three months earlier, no less a figure than former Boston Mayor John "Honey Fitz" Fitzgerald had suggested a mass burning of German books. "There should be no half-way measure about this situation," he said in a speech. "Every German book in the Boston schools should be gathered together on Boston Common on the Fourth of July and bonfired. By all means, let us tell our school committee that German books and the German language must be banished from the schools."[12]

At Camp Devens, commanding officer Major General McCain flatly rejected a demand from a soldier who had enlisted a lawyer to argue that a fellow soldier, born in Russia in an area that had since been captured by the German army, be dismissed from duty as an enemy alien. "He is no more an enemy alien of the United States than a citizen of France in that part of France temporarily held by the military forces of Germany is an enemy alien," McCain had to explain.[13]

Such were the depths of suspicion and paranoia in Boston at the time. Is it any wonder that something as insidious, as terrifying, as a deadly epidemic would be hidden from the public? The government was determined to keep focus entirely on the shared sacrifices necessary to fight and win the war.

Finally, on September 17, those at the front lines of this deadly battle on the home front realized their fight was as critical as the one taking place in Europe. They decided to break the silence and speak out, civilian morale and government timidity notwithstanding. The *Boston Globe* put their story on page one. "Greater Boston hospital authorities and physicians generally are practically a unit in the declaration that nothing can be gained by denying that the grippe epidemic is making great headway and that the public should be warned of the need for more intelligent cooperation to prevent its spread before conditions become alarming," the story read.[14]

War or no war, the epidemic was too widespread and affecting too many families for medical professionals to pretend any longer. In Boston and the rest of Massachusetts, reality on the ground was swiftly overtaking efforts to minimize the true nature of the spreading influenza outbreak. The death rate in Boston alone was now approaching one victim every half hour. With the civilian death toll from the disease topping 1,000 in the state, Governor Samuel McCall issued a public plea for both doctors and nurses.[15]

The nurses already toiling away to care for the sick witnessed one heartbreaking scene after another. Though death and disease are often great societal levelers, the poor immigrant communities in the commonwealth were particularly hard hit by the epidemic. Advances in hygiene were relatively new, while health codes, building codes, and zoning ordinances were practically non-existent. For the first time, as volunteers mobilized across communities, members of the middle class were getting a look at living conditions of the destitute in their midst, and the view was often mortifying. The secret plight of Boston's impoverished families, many of them recent immigrants, was being exposed as nurses began making home visits.

The young women were appalled by what they found. One nurse, Miss Condell, later recounted the story of entering an infected home to find

> my little patient, eight years old, lying on an old couch with a filthy ragged comforter for cover. The child was slightly delirious; flies literally covered her face and she had played and slept in the same soiled clothes for several days. She had no nursing care. It was a hunt to find the necessary things for a bath and there was not a thing to be found in the house that could be put on the child as a nightgown. In this home, the usual preparation for bed was unknown. One bed that was without pillows and covers served the purpose of three adults.[16]

Horrific scenes of poverty and death were becoming commonplace for social workers. Boston City Hospital staff told the story of a fourteen-year-old pneumonia patient well enough to be discharged. When a hospital employee checked out his home to see if his family was prepared for him to return, what they found shocked and repulsed them. The boy's father and two of his six siblings were sick with influenza. Two other children had died in the previous week, and the youngest, just an infant, had remained on the kitchen table for three days before the Board of Health was notified, as the father was too sick deal with the dead child, let alone work to earn money for funeral arrangements.[17]

At Camp Devens, nurse Margaret Sullivan of Framingham, twenty-nine, who had just arrived in August to care for sick soldiers, also died.

In Boston, government officials were still battling over whether to close schools in an attempt to prevent further spread of the virus. Dr.

Woodward continued to argue for keeping the schools open, reluctant to admit that the situation was as serious as it appeared to be. "I believe the epidemic has reached its maximum," he repeated for yet another day, despite his previous predictions having been proven so wrong.[18] He seemed more preoccupied with preventing widespread panic than preventing the spread of influenza. Rather than offering practical advice, the man in charge of public health for the city of Boston continued to downplay the risks to the civilian population with decidedly non-scientific, almost homespun, public announcements like "the conditions won't improve through worry; on the contrary, they are likely to become worse."[19] Like his argument that kids could avoid infection by concentrating on their studies, he offered a totally unfounded opinion that the disease ravaging his city could somehow be spread further by failure to maintain a positive attitude. In crisis, his shortcomings were being exposed. It was becoming tragically apparent why, after twenty-four years as health commissioner of Washington, D.C., his greatest accomplishments upon leaving the job were "special attention to the milk supply...and the suppression of rabies."[20]

Woodward was under increasing pressure to close schools from more rational voices, however. As Lewis R. Sullivan, a member of Governor McCall's Executive Council argued, "last year the School Committee closed the schools to preserve coal, and it seems to me that they should now be closed in order to protect the health of the little pupils that don't know how to protect their own health."[21]

Still, the cases piled up, and the public health system crumbled under the strain. Somerville's hospital stopped taking new influenza patients. Cambridge's hospital refused all new patients.

On the subject of influenza, the federal government's actions and public pronouncements continued to be in conflict. Internally, the military knew it had an enormously dangerous problem on its hands. Acting Army Surgeon General Charles Richard wrote to the commander of the Army, General Peyton March, with an urgent plea that military units "known to be infected, or exposed to the disease, be not permitted to embark for overseas service until the disease has run its course."[22] Externally, misinformation continued to be delivered to the general public. On the same day that Richard was trying to head off a wider epidemic within the ranks by isolating exposed units as much as possible, Colonel Philip Doane, the officer in charge of health and medicine at the nation's shipyards, was telling the Associated Press that "the so-called Spanish influenza is nothing more or less than old fashioned grippe."[23]

For nothing more than a common flu bug, Doane nonetheless had an ominous warning about its possible source. Influenza, he suggested, could have been brought ashore in America by German spies transported to the U.S. coastline by submarine. "The German agents have started epidemics in Europe," went his fanciful tale, "and there is no reason why they should be particularly gentle to America."[24] Doane had clearly gotten the message: everything—even a burgeoning epidemic—must be used as a weapon to fight the war.

Xenophobia contributed mightily to a sense of fear and isolation among immigrant communities in and around Boston and, later, other American cities. Particularly amongst natives of countries allied with Germany in the war, who were already subject to suspicion, the influenza epidemic would take a severe toll when families dared not emerge into the broader civilian society for medical assistance.

"There was a men's society and a women's citizen group," one Norwood, Massachusetts, survivor of Lithuanian descent recalled years later. "If any member was ill, the society would send people to help. They would take the children to their house. Usually, though, you wouldn't tell anyone outside you were sick or in trouble. I mean, anyone outside the church. People kept to themselves."[25]

Various ethnic groups seemed to favor different home remedies to fight the influenza. Irish families tended to pin bags of camphor balls to their clothing. Germans swore by a shot of whiskey and plenty of fresh air. Italian mothers strung pouches of garlic around the necks of their children. The Finns ate herring. These feeble attempts got so out of hand that U.S. Surgeon General Rupert Blue eventually released a statement. "The Health Service urges the public to remember that there is as yet no specific cure for influenza and that many of the alleged cures and remedies now being recommended by neighbors, nostrum vendors and others do more harm than good," he wrote.[26]

The limited knowledge of an uneducated, isolated, impoverished immigrant population was not aided by government and press efforts to downplay the crisis. Dwindling resources—doctors, nurses, beds, palliative care—were not frequently targeted toward poor neighborhoods overcrowded with recent arrivals, many of whom didn't speak English well anyway, if at all.

"To nurse during an epidemic was like meeting a creeping foe allied with ignorance, poverty, superstition, immorality and hopeless fear," one young nurse said in hindsight.[27] At the time, nursing was one of the most promising areas of opportunity in American society for women seeking careers. The American Red Cross had about eight million workers at the time, and virtually all of them were women.

Jean Stewart Bower was a Girl Scout volunteer at Norwood Hospital, pressed into service by the scarcity of real nurses despite her youth. Many years later, she somewhat bitterly remembered the very first patient she admitted. A man in his twenties was brought in on a stretcher, accompanied by his wife, whose three terrified children clung to her skirt.

"Since she was a foreigner and couldn't speak any English," Bower decided the young mother "must live in The Flats, that section south of the town which the hierarchy pretended did not exist." As she followed her husband into the hospital, the woman suddenly fell to the floor. "To my horror, I saw her lips and ears had turned a dark purple in her ashen face, a sure sign of death."[28] The soon-to-be-orphaned children were left with hospital volunteers.

Afraid of the epidemic as well as vengeful reprisals from a panicked and suspicious population, these ethnic communities were largely on their own and suffering the consequences. "Though I send this sad news, I don't know if I will be around to read them in print," wrote a correspondent for the Lithuanian-language newspaper published in South Boston. "We are, as it were, in a field of battle where no one knows what tomorrow will bring. The streets just resound from undertakers wagons and doctors' automobiles."[29]

Young nurses were not immune from their own prejudices, even as they performed heroically, with some going into two or three dozen homes each day to offer what assistance they could. "The Jews are so afraid of having fresh air in the house that it is a continual fight to have the windows open," recalled one visiting nurse. "Overcrowded! No wonder whole families were stricken. But how can they help overcrowding when there are large families and the man earns small wages and the cost of living is being pushed up every day? Why can there not be some way of regulating the size of a man's family to his wages or vice versa?"[30]

At hospitals across the state, tragic stories were unfolding by the minute. Many involved young mothers, who proved especially susceptible to infection. One study revealed that the death rate among infected women who were expecting a baby could exceed 70 percent.[31] A nurse at Brockton Hospital told a sadly typical tale of a woman, seven months pregnant, who came to the hospital with her lungs already filled by pneumonia brought on by influenza. Failing herself, the woman gave birth prematurely to a child that did not survive.

"She kept begging me to see the baby," the nurse remembered. "I assured her that he was fine and beautiful and she would hold him as soon as she was stronger. She had such a lovely look on her face as she talked about her son, and how happy her husband would be. It was an effort for her to talk as her lungs were filling. She died late that afternoon. I put the baby into her arms and fixed them so that they seemed only to be sleeping. And so the husband saw them when he came."[32]

In towns and cities across Massachusetts, public health officials began to try to cobble together some semblance of a quarantine system. When someone in a home came down with influenza, signs were nailed to the front door identifying the home as infected and silently branding those inside as dangerous.

"I remember Wally Riddell, he was a cop, a big burly guy," recalled a survivor of what he experienced inside one of those houses. "He and Joe Curran's grandfather came up to the house with a great big sign, and the sign it said INFLUENZA in red letters. And they nailed it to the door. I was like quarantined. Kind of scary. I'll never forget it."[33]

The quarantine signs further alienated immigrants from the larger society. They quickly came to be seen as a mark of shame for both the sick and the healthy inside the homes that were singled out for public notice. "I remember them talking about these signs," an impressionable young survivor later remembered. "It was as if, I don't know, they'd done something wrong and they were being punished."[34]

All of this took place despite the admission by the federal government, in the person of Surgeon General Blue, that "there is no such thing as an effective quarantine in the case of pandemic influenza."[35] Nevertheless, in Ayer, health officials were considering one of their own. Rather than locking sick people in their homes, however, they were trying to keep soldiers from nearby Camp Devens out of their town. Newspaper reporters covering the events at the cantonment were buying the official Army line and passing it on verbatim. "While the disease may be spreading in the town, the situation in the camp looks decidedly improved," read a dispatch on September 19.[36] It just wasn't true, not by any conceivable measure. Ten men died that day in the camp, and there were 5,000 cases in all, an increase of 1,500 in just the previous two days. In what possible way could that be considered "decidedly improved?"

In Boston, Health Commissioner Woodward was just as delusional. "Indications are that the epidemic has reached its crest and is receding rapidly," he claimed, with no basis in reality. "The public, by responding to the warnings given for self care, has helped wonderfully." Then came the omnipresent call of the kind Samuel Johnson had once characterized as the last refuge of a scoundrel. "It is a patriotic duty now for everyone to keep well, if possible. Every sick person adds to our country's burdens in this hour of trial."[37]

In Boston on that single Tuesday, forty-two apparent traitors to the glorious American cause died of influenza.

Among those so callous as to put their own needs ahead of those of the country was Philip Buckley of South Boston, who died of influenza-caused pneumonia after being ill for two days. He was the third Boston doctor in a week to catch the disease and die while caring for patients.

Incredibly, the top public health official in the city was pressuring a population under attack from a deadly virus to do everything they could to pretend they were not sick, so as to maintain a veneer of loyalty and patriotism. Further, he was reinforcing his call for those who were foolish enough to fall ill to avoid seeking medical care and crediting his previous potentially fatal advice to practice "self-care" for a totally imaginary peak in the rate of infection. Sadly, it was not the last time Woodward would make outlandish statements of this nature.

Meanwhile, the virus was spreading outside Massachusetts as well, borne by those who left home feeling fine, only to find themselves stricken suddenly while away. That was the case for George Abbott of Charlestown, a chauffer who drove his boss to Yonkers on a business trip and fell seriously ill. Told that his prospects were not good, he sent for his fiancée, Sarah Cone, a nurse from Waltham. She rushed to his side at St. John's Riverside Hospital only to find him slipping quickly. Abbott asked if they could be married immediately, and Cone filled out the requisite forms at his bedside to obtain a marriage license. Before the ceremony began, however, Abbott slipped into unconsciousness and died a single man.

The contagion continued to spread across Massachusetts. Milford closed its schools, as did Somerville. The death toll in Boston jumped 25 percent in a day, with fifty-two people perishing. Even the weather seemed funereal. Day after day after chilled day, torrential rain soaked the state, as it had for much of the month. More than six inches of rain had already fallen in September, over three times the monthly average. In all of 1918, from January through August, the state had experienced just six days in which an inch or more of rain fell. Now, four such storms had taken place in less than two weeks.

Nevertheless, Health Commissioner Woodward could not be dismayed. He told reporters he was not the least troubled by the surface indications of a wider area and a greater virulence of the epidemic. He also said he was convinced that the worst was now over, a refrain he would repeat with pathetic persistence over the next week. Pressure continued to mount on Woodward for more direct action. Louis Sullivan of the governor's Executive Council again urged that Boston public schools be closed. "I am told that in one room where 60 pupils are enrolled only 12 were in attendance this morning, and this shows that absentees are ill, or that their parents have the good sense to keep them out of school."[38] Woodward was having none of it.

The rain may actually have been a blessing, to the extent it kept people isolated and away from others who were infected. Sometimes, however, contact was unavoidable. When Albert Fogwell of Newton died of influenza early in the week, his family gathered for his funeral. Albert's brothers Clarence and W. U. Fogwell, both of whom also lived in Newton, were there with their families. Almost predictably, Clarence came down with the flu himself and died. A few hours later his sister-in-law, Eva Fogwell, was dead as well.[39] One after another, the disease struck and claimed previously healthy people in their thirties and forties.

Illness and death were everywhere. In Quincy, neighbors John Bonafini and Anthony Marini tried to keep working at their jobs in the shipbuilding plant, but both fell unconscious on the factory floor and died on the same day, two of 1,500 reported cases at the Fore River facility. In Milford, sisters Josephine Mazzene, age ten, and Mary, age seven, died within ten minutes of one another. In Cliftondale, Gertrude Collins fell ill just two hours after the burial of her husband and quickly died herself. Two hours later, her two-week-old son died, leaving a two-year-old daughter as the sole survivor in the family.[40]

In addition to doctors and nurses, others who were tending to the sick became victims themselves. Father Simon O'Rourke, a New Bedford native and a graduate of Holy Cross, had been a priest for barely three months. For the past two, he had served as assistant chaplain at the Charlestown Naval Yard in Boston harbor, ministering to the sick and dying. Now he was dead, and his service to the Lord was over before it really even began. Father Patrick Meagher said morning Mass as usual at St. Bridget's in Concord, became ill after lunch, and was dead by sundown.

The hastily erected tent hospital built by the Navy in nearby Framingham to house the massive overflow of sailors stricken by the disease was opened on September 20, barely ten days since Navy Captain John Edgar had cavalierly proclaimed that the uptick in cases at Chelsea Naval Hospital were "just plain grippe, without any fancy Spanish influenza trimmings."

His Army counterpart stuck with the company line as well. At Camp Devens, where fifteen soldiers died during the day, division surgeon McCornack announced, without any foundation, "the epidemic is really on the wane."[41] Officials in Ayer, right outside the Camp Devens gates, continued efforts to keep soldiers from coming to town. They closed the theater. They asked pastors to postpone services. It had no effect. Uniformed personnel continued to move freely between the camp and the town, and Army officials even issued a terse statement that denied there was a quarantine, emphasizing that this was "official and final, regardless of all unauthorized reports to the contrary."[42] A federal judge held a massive naturalization ceremony, where 2,300 soldiers became American citizens in three separate shifts of hundreds of immigrants each. Despite every effort, more than 500 additional soldiers were too sick to show up and take the oath.

In the face of all the sickness, however, was the constant reminder of the harsh reality of death being experienced by the fathers, sons, relatives, and friends from New England who were on the front lines "over there." The back page of the newspaper brought the latest statistical update. The Twenty-Sixth Division had thus far taken 3,266 casualties in the Great War, including 572 dead. All by themselves, the men of the Yankee Division had accounted for nearly 10 percent of total American casualties since the fighting began.[43]

On September 21, for the second consecutive Saturday and in direct conflict with every known scientific fact about the nature of contagion and the virulence of the influenza strain burning through the populace, another mass gathering was planned to promote the war effort. Like Major General McCain's massive review at Camp Devens the week before, the purpose was to boost civilian and military morale. Just when crowds of tightly packed people meant the transmission of a deadly disease even faster and wider, the demand for a celebration of war trumped medical common sense. So, at 6:00 p.m., some 7,000 laborers involved in building an Army supply base in South Boston assembled for a parade to Boston Common. The event was arranged by the Patriotic Promotion Section of the Army's Construction Division, which clearly was not going to let infectious disease and widespread death get in the way of its duty to promote patriotism. So the workers jammed together in something resembling formations, and a dozen bands marched along as well, all to entertain and inspire the crowds that lined the streets. All this offered the virus ready access to new and vulnerable hosts.

In another move that defied understanding, Camp Devens was opened to visitors. Soldiers had been restricted to base, with no passes being issued to those wishing to leave, but families were welcomed in instead, with only the barracks being declared off limits. Camp officials made an announcement stunning in its contradictions on multiple levels. "In reality," the press dutifully reported, "the epidemic is well in hand; although there are 6,000 hospital cases, many of them are scarcely ill at all."[44] Less widely noted, another twenty soldiers were no longer "scarcely" living at all.

Alarmed local officials in the town of Ayer, just outside the Camp Devens gates, finally decided it had to do something to try to protect its citizens. The Board of Health—which consisted of the town druggist and the owner of a tannery—went ahead with its ban on soldiers from the camp entering the town. Ayer had 2,500 citizens but another 2,500 transients staying within city limits, mostly wives of officers and soldiers based at the cantonment. This time, Major General McCain, the commanding officer at Devens, agreed to cooperate. He signed an order confining soldiers to the camp. The attempted quarantine had little effect, however, given that the camp remained open to visitors coming in. As a result, rather than soldiers bringing infection back into town, those who visited and returned brought it instead.

Despite Commissioner Woodward's claim the day before that the worst was over, civilian deaths in Boston spiked. In the twenty-four hours

between Friday and Saturday nights, eighty-five more people had succumbed. Now, for the people of Massachusetts, the influenza epidemic
finally had a face.

William F. Murray had been elected to Congress before he turned
thirty, and he achieved nearly as much popularity in Washington as he
had at home. The engaging young man got tagged with the nickname
"the Baby of the 63rd," which stuck and was subsequently updated when
he was re-elected to serve in the 64th and 65th Congress as well. President
Wilson then appointed Murray to be Boston's youngest-ever postmaster,
at the time a prestigious and powerful position, even more so than serving in the House of Representatives in Washington.

On Saturday, September 21, two weeks after his thirty-seventh
birthday, Murray was dead of influenza.

This was not another anonymous, if tragic, case from the neighborhood or the next town over. Billy Murray was famous. This was not a
poor immigrant living in cramped, unsanitary conditions without access
to medical care. This was a well-loved public figure from the city's version of Irish aristocracy, a gifted public speaker known as the "kid
spellbinder." If influenza could kill him, it could kill anyone.

The Army, the Navy, and the local government were losing control
of the narrative. Home remedy recommendations and sloganeering were
not going to appease the masses any longer. It would now be almost
impossible to deny the serious crisis that had befallen the city and state,
though some would continue to try. The Navy's spokesman, Captain
John Edgar, made what was described as a cheerful announcement on
September 21 that only seven sailors had died that day. On September
22 he boldly declared "we have defeated the germ here."[45]

And yet, death was relentless. Carmine Varrasco died in Quincy just
hours after his brother Barrazio. The two would be buried together at
Mt. Wollaston Cemetery after a joint funeral, but not right away. Graves
could not be dug fast enough to keep up with demand, so caskets were
being stacked in the cemetery's winter storage tomb, which was running
out of space itself. The Fore River shipyard in Quincy, where Red Sox
pitcher Dutch Leonard had taken a job in midseason, set up a second

onsite hospital, with fifty additional beds, to treat its employees too ill to make it home from work. Some three thousand workers were now sick at this single facility. A tragedy that would normally have shaken a city went almost unnoticed in the carnage, as a triple funeral was held for sisters Madeline, Ina, and Esther Smith, ages eight, seven, and five.

Adding to the fear was the fact the contagion seemed to kill so randomly. No one could be sure they would escape. One nurse described seeing two families in a single day on opposite rungs of the social ladder. In one home, which she described as "very comfortable and clean,"[46] she found a mother, father, two children, and an aunt with temperatures ranging up to 106 degrees, and an eight-year-old boy trying to care for them all. Another aunt came to care for them but was dead within a day, and the mother plus one of the children soon followed. In the other home a mother and six children were living in filth amid dirt, garbage, and flies. All seven of them had temperatures between 103 and 105 degrees when she found them, and there were no relatives or friends to help them through the crisis. All of them survived.

While bodies piled up at military installations, hospitals, and homes, government officials continued to act nearly incoherently in the face of the mounting crisis. The same surgeon general who had warned about home remedies and cures issued tips to the general public on how to avoid influenza, including the pathetically comical advice to "avoid tight shoes."[47] The *Boston Post* reported that total influenza deaths in the city had increased from nineteen to 342 in just the previous seven days.[48] The report seemed to directly contradict another claim by Woodward that he was "optimistic" the worst had passed and that the day's sharp increase in the number of cases was not alarming. "I believe the plateau, if not the peak, of the contagion has been reached," he once again told the city's residents. What was the basis for Woodward's optimism this time? Just three days after claiming that warm weather was helping matters, he touted cold weather as good news. "The air had lots of snap today," he said. "It is good advice to the public to get outdoors as much as possible. Fresh air is an aid to health at all times. Walk briskly in the open air and one will feel better."[49] So long as they wore loose-fitting shoes, presumably. Every forecast was purported to be welcome—warm weather and cold, sunshine and frost—it was all supposedly good news.

Outside the city, civilian authorities began to act more urgently. The town of Quincy realized it was overwhelmed and turned control of all medical and health issues over to the Navy. Lieutenant I. E. Stowe was placed in charge, mapped the city into districts, and placed a doctor in charge of each, with a small staff to support each one. "From what I have seen of the situation here in Quincy today, I feel the epidemic can be systematically fought and, I hope, controlled," Dr. Stowe said. "We are carrying on."[50] Still, two people collapsed in the streets, and Stowe banned all public funerals, ordering undertakers to seal caskets immediately after embalming, not to be reopened before burial. The mayor asked all local clubs and societies to cancel their meetings. The annual Harvest Festival was canceled.

The Massachusetts state health commissioner, Dr. Eugene Kelley, had been resisting calls to close schools statewide. "Schools should not be closed except in exceptional instances," he said in a letter to local Boards of Health, as if current circumstances were somewhat normal. "Children coming from homes in which there has been an active case should be excluded until the danger of carrying the infection is past, also those who show symptoms of beginning infection are to be immediately sent home."[51]

On September 22, Woodward boldly predicted that by the end of the week, deaths among the civilian population would be "reduced to a minimum."[52]

In fact, they would nearly double.

CHAPTER 13

COOLIDGE

SEPTEMBER 22–24

I t was increasingly apparent that the influenza crisis was out of control. A vacationing Governor Samuel McCall held a call with Kelley, Woodward, and representatives of the state's Public Safety Commission and the New England Division of the American Red Cross. Finally, the nature of the crisis was addressed directly. Convinced that the public health system was overwhelmed and hampered by a lack of doctors and nurses due to military service, the governor decided on a proclamation asking municipal officials across the state to take steps to prevent people from congregating and spreading the influenza virus. "I earnestly urge the authorities to consider the advisability of closing the schools, places of amusement, churches and all places where people gather in considerable numbers," it read.[1]

Being absent from the state, McCall asked Lieutenant Governor Calvin Coolidge to sign it.

A native of tiny Plymouth Notch, Vermont, Calvin Coolidge had entered Amherst College—on his second try, having failed his first entrance exam—in Northampton, Massachusetts. After graduation, he remained in Northampton, where he attached himself to a local attorney and "read the law" rather than attend law school in preparation for taking the bar exam.

The son of a full-time farmer and some-time politician, Coolidge carefully cultivated a local political following while practicing small-town law. The taciturn redhead somehow connected with voters, despite his economy of words. In personal conversation he was reserved and somewhat awkward, but he made his reputation, first in college and then in politics, as an effective and persuasive public orator. His speeches were often methodical, logic-based efforts to stake out a middle ground. On the campaign trail, he maintained a steadfast refusal to offend anyone. He even declined to criticize his opponents in his political races. "It is much better not to press a candidacy too much," he believed, "but to let it develop on its own merits without artificial stimulation. If the people want a man they will nominate him, if they do not want him he had best let the nomination go to another."[2]

As a state representative, Northampton mayor, and state senator, Coolidge's political positions matched his personality: prudent, frugal, conservative, but practical. Early in his career, he supported many of the progressive causes championed by the Republican Party and President Theodore Roosevelt, but he later distanced himself from the movement when he felt the party was moving too quickly on many matters, particularly government spending programs.

Above all, Coolidge believed in governmental restraint, legislatively and especially fiscally. Among his chief motivations for seeking the position of president of the Massachusetts Senate in 1914 was the power he could wield to kill bills. "Don't hurry to legislate," he advised his colleagues in his first speech upon taking the gavel as Senate president.

In 1915, Coolidge was chosen as the running mate for McCall's campaign for governor, mainly to provide ideological and geographic balance to the ticket. He differed from McCall on many progressive issues, though he took pains not to publicly contradict the top man on the ticket. He was from western Massachusetts, while McCall had been a congressman representing the Boston suburbs across the Charles River from the city. While he would have to relinquish nearly all the legislative power he had gained and freely exercised in the state senate, Coolidge had bigger plans.

"It was no secret that I desired to be Governor," he wrote in his autobiography. "Under the custom of promotion in Massachusetts a man who did not expect to be advanced would scarcely be willing to be Lieutenant-Governor."[3]

While serving in the state legislature, even as president of the Senate, the thrifty Coolidge rented a single room at the Adams Hotel in Boston, paying $1 per day in rent. When he became lieutenant governor, he splurged a little, renting another room across the hall so his family could visit. From those little rooms, for three one-year terms, Coolidge bided his time, something akin to a crown prince awaiting his ascension to the throne. Massachusetts had been solidly Republican for half a century, and securing the GOP nomination had always been tantamount to winning the general election itself. But demographics were changing across the country, particularly in Massachusetts. Nearly one million immigrants were coming ashore in America every year. The upcoming postwar 1920 census would be the first in the country's history in which there were more urban than rural residents. In the Bay State, long-standing control of the gears of political power by Yankee Republicans was about to be loosened as immigrants, mainly Irish, flooded into Boston harbor and onto the rolls of the Democratic Party.

By 1918, McCall had served the traditional four terms as governor. Though he was not prohibited from running again, he told Coolidge very early in the term that he would not do so. McCall thought there was a chance he could replace fellow Republican John W. Weeks in the Senate. Direct election of senators was still a relatively new phenomenon. Weeks was the last senator chosen by the state legislature before the Seventeenth Amendment to the U.S. Constitution was ratified in 1913. He was selected after thirty-one ballots in the Massachusetts legislature, defeating McCall. But Weeks was a dull bureaucrat, not particularly well-liked back home, and McCall thought the party might turn to an experienced vote-getter for the 1918 campaign, when the seat would be filled for the first time by voters. But the Republicans stuck by Weeks, and McCall did not get his chance to avenge his earlier loss. The way was cleared, however, for Coolidge to ascend to the governorship.

"You will see by the Monday paper that I am to run for governor," Coolidge wrote to his father after announcing his bid in June. "Mr. McCall will not run. I do not think I shall have opposition. I feel certain of election, but in politics anything may happen, so you better wait until November before you prepare for the inauguration."[4]

Reserved, shy, and cerebral, Coolidge was anything but a natural politician. One local government official told the story of being asked during the campaign what he thought of Coolidge and responding, "I like him all right, but he makes me think of a human icicle." Two weeks later he received a surprise invitation to lunch with the lieutenant governor at Boston's Parker House hotel. Coolidge managed some small talk, including on the topic of the weather, and little else. The man found the encounter "painfully embarrassing because of the long intervals of silence," until, unexpectedly, Coolidge looked at his watch and got up to leave. "The House comes in at two o'clock. Glad you could take lunch with me." He shook hands "very limply" and left, leaving the man he was trying to win over bewildered but nevertheless favorably inclined to Coolidge on a personal basis. The human icicle hadn't exactly thawed, however.[5]

Despite his lack of interpersonal skills, Coolidge found a way to win race after race as he climbed the political ladder. "I think Coolidge can beat any Democratic candidate," Senator Henry Cabot Lodge told the state GOP chairman a week before the party primary. "Coolidge seems to be the best vote-getter I have known in Massachusetts politics."[6]

The Massachusetts state constitution was subject to revision by a constitutional convention being held in Boston through that fall, but until and unless changes were made, it held that the lieutenant governor assumed the role of acting governor any time the governor himself was away from the State House. With McCall first maneuvering for a Senate bid then traveling through Canada on vacation, and Coolidge preferring a laconic non-campaign style in his own race, the cautious conservative was effectively running Massachusetts on a day-to-day basis.

"The duties of governor of the commonwealth are not intricate or burdensome," Coolidge claimed in one rare campaign speech, "if a man looks upon their discharge as a public function and not as a personal prerogative. If chosen to be your governor, I shall try to conduct the duties of the office so as to merit the sincere endorsement of men of fair mind and in all parties. I would not deem myself worthy of your support if I promised anything less."[7]

Tuesday, September 24 was primary day, but Coolidge was not focused on politics. He was unopposed in his race, though the Democrats would be choosing his general election opponent. His focus was on the job at hand, including managing the state's reaction to the influenza crisis. In a letter to his stepmother earlier in the week, he had summed up his attitude toward the campaign. "There is no occasion for you or father to worry about the election," he wrote. "It looks very favorable; but of course it is impossible to forecast it, as elections are always very uncertain. I have been handsomely treated in Massachusetts, whether I happen to secure this election or not."[8]

The Democrats selected Framingham shoe factory owner Richard Long as the party's candidate for governor in their primary. Long would play to the immigrant and working-class voters in and around Boston during the race, hoping to overcome the advantage any Republican, especially Coolidge, had in the more rural areas in western Massachusetts. He would also run a more vigorous style of campaign, spending his own money freely and attacking Coolidge and the Republican establishment directly. This was not at all Coolidge's style. Shown a proposed newspaper ad prepared to respond to a particularly sharp ad on Long's behalf, Coolidge killed it immediately. "It is a good advertisement," he admitted, "but I will not get into a controversy of that kind. I will not attack an individual. If the people of Massachusetts do not know me well enough to understand the animus of such an advertisement and are not willing to elect me without my answering every indiscriminate attack, then I would rather be defeated."[9]

Instead, Coolidge's infrequent campaign speeches emphasized patriotic themes and, inevitably, the need for all citizens to share in the sacrifices necessary to support the government and the troops. "The war is won," he said at one September appearance. "It is being overwhelmingly won. A righteous purpose has not only strengthened our aims abroad but exalted the nation at home. The great work before us is to keep this new spirit in the right path. The sacrifice necessary for national defense must hereafter never be neglected."[10]

One candidate on the ballot would not be taking office, regardless of the vote tally. Alexander Stoneman, age thirty-one, a Republican candidate for the state legislature, died thirty-six hours before the polls opened, another influenza victim.

Coolidge and other state officials conferred with the vacationing governor by phone. McCall instructed his lieutenant to issue a statewide appeal for help. "It is earnestly requested that everyone who has had medical or nursing experience or who can assist in any way communicate with the Commissioner of Health at the State House," it read. The need was clearly real, but the request had serious ramifications. Anyone heeding the call was going to put himself or herself directly in harm's way, as evidenced by the death the day before of twenty-three-year-old Irene Foucher, a nurse at Carney Hospital.

As Coolidge remained focused on policy rather than politics, heartrending tragedy lurked in virtually every neighborhood around Boston. Across the harbor in Charlestown, on the north side of Bunker Hill, site of the famous Revolutionary War battle, James Harvey passed away at his house on Green Street. On the same day, barely a block away and in the shadow of the granite obelisk honoring the brave colonists, his brother John Harvey also died, along with John's wife. The couple left behind four children aged nine months to seven years.[11] It was a story being replayed, in one fashion or another, across Massachusetts.

Nearly 600 Boston residents had lost their lives in just over ten days, including 109—the highest daily total yet—on September 24 alone. There were over 6,000 cases in the town of Salem, and the hospital there had been closed to all new patients, with no space to hold anyone else.

There were 10,000 cases reported in Lynn, and the city got a court order to seize the Martin family mansion in town and convert it into a temporary emergency hospital with room for seventy-five patients.

In the midst of the devastation, however, the indoctrinated need to support the war effort and display an overly enthusiastic level of patriotism remained strong. Just now, when contact with masses of other people might mean death, the city held *another* parade; the third since the epidemic began. This one was to build awareness for the nation's fourth Liberty Loan campaign, a concept that seems foreign today under which the government raised money to fund the war by borrowing it from the American people rather than allocate it from off-the-books federal budgets. The loan campaign was to kick off on Saturday across the country, with a goal of raising billions of dollars through small individual bond purchases. Here again was an instance of the rationale behind President Wilson and Committee on Public Information director George Creel's omnipresent campaign to paint every aspect of American life in patriotic colors. Knowing that the funds needed to build a massive war effort would have to come from the people increased the urgency to sway the entire population to accept sacrifice for the cause. Mixed with the appeals to patriotism, however, was something darker, a smothering peer pressure best exemplified by the CPI Liberty Loan poster that ominously read, "I am Public Opinion. All men fear me! If you have the money to buy and do not buy, I will make this No Man's Land for you!"

Here, too, was an explanation for some of the governmental calls for people to get outdoors to avoid being infected with influenza. Isolation was undoubtedly a far more effective means of avoiding contagion. Certainly some of the governmental advice to take in the fresh air was a misguided, naïve reflection of nineteenth-century medicine, but some officials were undoubtedly looking ahead to the important mass events like parades and military sports exhibitions as critical in the ongoing efforts to build morale, maintain support for the war, and fund its execution.

So, captured German guns were hauled through the streets of Boston. Military bands, soldiers, and sailors, directly out of the viral hot zones at Commonwealth Pier and Camp Devens, marched along the parade route in front of throngs of people. Together they produced, and therefore shared, an atmospheric soup rich with influenza germs. America needed to raise another six billion dollars, and, epidemic or not, New England was expected to come up with $500 million. So the people needed to be persuaded.

With Lieutenant Governor Coolidge's proclamation as political cover, local authorities suddenly felt free to acknowledge the true nature of the health crisis as well. On Monday night, Health Commissioner Woodward steadfastly insisted on keeping Boston's schools open. He also argued against closing churches, reasoning that, unlike theaters, they were only filled one day per week. After McCall and Coolidge announced their request that public gatherings in the state be curtailed, he was finally persuaded to reverse his stand on Tuesday and order the indefinite closing of the city's public schools. Still, he did not blame the threat of contagion for the move but rather citied a shortage of healthy teachers and high absenteeism. Boston Mayor Andrew Peters then acted to appoint an Emergency Committee, which moved to turn the city's 265 suddenly vacant school buildings into temporary hospitals and suggested that teachers be utilized as emergency nurses. That committee—some undoubtedly just in from watching the parade and oblivious to the irony—complied with the governor's request and ordered theaters, movie houses, and concert halls closed as well, in an effort to prevent large crowds from gathering.

Even the press seemed liberated by Coolidge's pronouncement. The *Boston Herald* became the first newspaper to use the word "plague" in its page-one headline on the day's epidemic news, a far cry from the steady stream of "all is well" boosterism that had marked local coverage to date.

In spite of the new restrictions, 2,500 people showed up at St. Mary's Church in Charlestown for the funeral of Postmaster William Murray and a Mass concelebrated by his brother, Reverend Stephen Murray, and six other area priests. Hundreds, if not thousands, more gathered outside in the rain, unable to get a seat. Additional hundreds more lined the streets as the funeral procession made its way to Holyhood Cemetery in Brookline. On the same day the government was finally urging the public to avoid large gatherings, virtually every democratic office holder joined the long list of dignitaries in attendance, including Mayor Peters and former mayors, as well as current and former congressmen and city officials.

In contrast, no service at all was held for Francisco Catolina, a twenty-year-old shoe worker from Brockton. When he died, doctors checking his belongings found $2,000 in his pockets, along with a bank book with $578 on deposit and another with a $1,200 balance. But no relatives or friends could be found to claim the money or the body.[12]

CHAPTER 14

THE HORROR AT DEVENS

SEPTEMBER 22–23

Not every government official had his head buried in the sand. Some of the country's foremost medical experts—William Welch, Vincent Vaughan, Rufus Cole, and Frederick Russell, all now officially enlisted in the armed forces and each holding the rank of colonel—had completed their inspection of southern military bases and the efforts underway in those camps to head off the kind of widespread epidemic they feared might break out among tightly billeted soldiers. Beginning in 1916, Welch had recruited the others to help prepare for, and try to prevent, a major infectious disease epidemic such as meningitis, measles, or pneumonia among American troops.

"Our organization had no official standing, no government support," Vaughan said of the National Research Council's preparedness efforts. "The National Academy of Sciences had volunteered its services to the President and he had accepted, but we were not under his direction nor that of Congress. Even among ourselves we did not speak of our work as a preparation for war, but as preparation for an 'emergency.'"[1]

Still, the medical experts had worked feverishly for more than two years to bring military medicine up to modern standards. Among the issues they tackled were the sterilization of drinking water, smallpox and typhoid vaccination programs, treatment of gas poisoning, and the prevention of infection from wounds. Foremost on all of their minds, however, was the fear of an epidemic of infectious diseases.

"Digitalis was considered an essential agent in the treatment of pneumonia," Vaughan explained, by way of example.

> The "emergency," if it came, would be accompanied by a high morbidity from this disease. All the digitalis used medicinally in this country had come from Germany. There was not enough in stock here to serve a small hospital six months. A species of the plant from which medicinal preparations are made grows wild in this country, especially in the states of Oregon and Washington, but this is not the species from which the preparation had been made. Would this species serve our purpose? Boy Scouts in Oregon and Washington gathered the wild leaves; these were assayed at the University of Minnesota and when the "emergency" did come we had enough of this drug to supply the world.[2]

Such was the depth of forethought these scientists had given to their service toward the war effort. They all had firsthand experience fighting yellow fever and typhoid among military troops in the Spanish-American War twenty years earlier, they were among the most accomplished infectious disease specialists in the country, and they were each Welch's hand-picked protégés.

Vaughan, for example, was a former president of the American Medical Association. Cole had developed a pneumonia serum. Russell had developed a vaccine for typhoid a decade earlier and, having vaccinated every member of the U.S. Army, had virtually wiped out the disease among military personnel. These were the country's foremost experts, and they had been intent on preparing for precisely the events that were unfolding, of which they were as yet unaware.

Their tour of southern military bases complete, the group was fresh off a few days of rest and recovery at an Asheville, North Carolina, resort. "The medical service of the army is now well organized and conditions are very much improved in our camps," Welch noted in his report.[3] On Sunday, September 22, they returned to Washington, D.C., and, despite the weekend, were summoned directly to the Army surgeon general's office. There, without taking the time to even look up from his paperwork, General Charles Richard gave the doctors urgent new orders.

"You will proceed immediately to Devens."[4]

They boarded a train and headed north to Massachusetts. What the eminent medical men found at the cantonment when they arrived was the full embodiment of their worst fears. A virulent epidemic was roaring through the camp; the deadly virus was feasting on the young men packed together like a bacteriological buffet.

"One day fifty were admitted; the next day 300, then the daily average became 500; into a 2,000 bed hospital 6,000 patients crowded," lamented Jane Malloy, the camp hospital's chief nurse. "Every inch of available space was used. Three miles of hospital corridors were lined on both sides with cots."[5]

Sickness and death were overwhelming the Camp Devens infrastructure. Over 10,000 soldiers had already been diagnosed with influenza. More than sixty died just in the eight hours it took Welch and his doctor colleagues to make their way to the camp from Washington.[6] Many of the healthy soldiers were put to work caring for their ill brothers-in-arms.

"We had to take men from the Sanitary Train and send them to the Base Hospital for duty," the division surgeon, Lieutenant Colonel Condon C. McCornack reported.

> Most of these men were new to the service and they didn't know anything about hospital work. They were told what they were up against. They knew that many of them were going to contract the disease and that some of them would

die. But when they knew that men were dying at the hospital because their help was needed, and when the order came to go up there for duty, not a man of them so much as looked back. And some did contract the disease and some of them did die. But they knew that it was part of the army game and they did it willingly and gladly, like true soldiers. They are just as truly heroes as though their lives had been given on the battlefields of France.[7]

When Welch and his party arrived, almost one in five soldiers at Camp Devens was suffering from influenza, and three-quarters of those required hospitalization. Of the 200 nurses in camp, seventy of them were sick themselves. Corpses were stacked like firewood set aside for a New England winter. The infected were immediately identifiable by the blue-black cast of their faces.

"We were at once struck by the cyanosis which most of the patients exhibited," Cole recalled. "One could pick out the infected men among those standing about, by the color of their faces."[8]

Blood is only red when it has been enriched by oxygen in the lungs and is being pumped out to the circulatory system by the heart. On its return route, when the oxygen has been depleted, the blood is bluer in color. Because the lungs of those infected with this strain of influenza were so compromised, they were not infusing that blood with enough oxygen to turn it back to red, and, over time, the patients took on a blue tone, especially away from the body's core.

Vaughan likened the scene to a battlefield in the aftermath of conflict. He called it a "picture painted on my memory walls."[9] He described seeing "hundreds of young stalwart men in the uniform of their country coming into the wards of the hospital in groups of ten or more. They are placed on the cots until every bed is full and yet others crowd in. The faces wear a bluish cast; a distressing cough brings up blood-stained sputum."[10]

Cole remembered it vividly as well. "It was cold and drizzling rain, and there was a continuous line of men coming from the various barracks, carrying their blankets, many of the men looking extremely ill," he recounted. "There were not enough nurses, and the poor boys were putting themselves to bed on cots, which overflowed out of the wards on the porches."[11]

The dead were everywhere, too many to be handled with the care and respect anyone, let alone American soldiers in a stateside base during a time of war, deserved. Nearly seventy more men died on the day the visiting doctors arrived.[12]

"Owing to the rush and the great numbers of bodies coming into the morgue, they were placed on the floor without any order or system," Cole later wrote to a colleague, "and we had to step amongst them to get into the room where an autopsy was going on."[13]

When the doctors conducted those autopsies, they were shocked by what they found. "We went to the morgue, and saw a large number of bodies piled up waiting to be examined," said Cole. "In one after another of them, when the chests were opened we saw large amounts of bloody fluid in the pleural cavities, and on cutting open the lungs there were large areas of wet, hemorrhagic consolidation."[14]

This was not the "old fashioned grippe," as some in the military were still insisting publicly. Typical influenza killed the weak: infants, the aged, and the infirm. This was not even familiar pneumonia, filling its victims' lungs with fluid. The yet-unidentified virus was preying on strong young adults, men and women in the prime of their lives. It was literally turning their pulmonary systems to jelly. Welch—a giant of American medicine who had transformed the nation's medical system from an often-barbaric tradition of superstition and guesswork into a modern scientific profession—was stunned and shaken.

"This must be some new kind of infection," he said darkly. "Or plague."[15]

The doctors were confused and afraid. Welch's reaction was anything but reassuring.

"It was not surprising that the rest of us were disturbed but it shocked me to find that the situation, momentarily at least, was too much for Dr. Welch,"[16] Cole remembered. "It was the first and only time I ever saw him lose his customary calmness and self possession."[17]

While Welch was shaken by the science of the infection, Vaughan was petrified by the math. "If the epidemic continues its mathematical rate of acceleration," he calculated, "civilization could easily have disappeared from the face of the earth within a matter of a few weeks."[18]

Welch did not hesitate for long. He immediately called the surgeon general and urged "immediate provision be made in every camp for the rapid expansion of hospital space."[19] He had done some math in his own head, and he knew that troops previously departed from Camp Devens had likely already infected men in cantonments and military installations across the country and that those infected men had, in turn, fanned out to still more facilities. He knew that what he and his colleagues were seeing in Massachusetts had already been unleashed across America.

"The realization of the utter helplessness of man in attempts to control the spread of this disease depressed me beyond words," said Vaughan, who was all too familiar with disease in a time of war, having contracted yellow fever himself in the Spanish-American War in 1898.[20]

Acting Surgeon General Charles Richard immediately understood the gravity of what Welch was calling to report, and he wasted no time sending the ominous news up the chain of command. "Epidemic influenza has become a very serious menace, and threatens not only to retard the military program, but to exact a heavy toll in human life, before the disease has run its course throughout the country," Richard relayed to Army Chief of Staff Peyton March.[21]

Richard made a series of recommendations: cancel the call-up of all troops headed to infected facilities, stop sending troops to Europe until the epidemic had run its course in their camps, quarantine all soldiers for one week before moving them overseas, and then reduce troop ship capacity for those heading across the Atlantic by 50 percent. March rejected almost all of the suggestions, choosing instead to order camp commanders to increase medical staff and cut troop ship capacity by just 10 percent. That was it. No quarantines, even for soldiers from camps where influenza was rampant. As with so many of the mistakes made during the epidemic, the rationale was once again about keeping up appearances in wartime. March was concerned, he said, about "the psychological effect it would have on a weakening enemy to learn that the American divisions and replacements were no longer arriving."[22]

Welch made another call as well, reaching out to a colleague at the Rockefeller Institute, Dr. Oswald Avery, an expert diagnostician. Welch asked him to catch the next train from New York and get to Devens as quickly as possible.

Avery was a Canadian native who had joined the Army in 1917 as a private and upon becoming a U.S. citizen was promoted to captain and placed in charge of teaching Army doctors how to diagnose acute respiratory diseases—part of the preparedness Welch had put in place out of fear of an epidemic just like the one currently raging. Avery, a brilliant doctor who would be repeatedly nominated for a Nobel Prize in medicine later in life, was at Devens by the afternoon and immediately began conducting autopsies and running tests on lung tissue from the victims. He was searching for the particular bacteria causing the disease. If he could isolate it, he might be able to produce a serum. It was the same search Milton Rosenau and John Keegan had been conducting for the past three weeks at the Chelsea Naval Hospital, to no avail. Nearly 100 new cases a day had been diagnosed there over the weekend and now, alarmingly, another 116 cases had sprung up among workers in a single office, the Naval district headquarters at the Little Building on the corner of Boylston and Tremont in the heart of downtown Boston.

Even as Welch was alerting Washington to the grave crisis he and his colleagues had found, the commanding officer at Camp Devens, Major General Henry McCain, was telling the public that "the new cases of influenza have materially decreased,"[23] perpetuating the lie that there was nothing to see here, no need to worry, everything was under control. Behind the scenes, however, Welch convinced McCain to take action. After touring the camp hospitals, the general ordered preventative measures that, by today's standards, seem so elementary: ventilate the barracks and mop the floors, order the men not to spit on the floor, isolate soldiers with coughs and those just discharged from sick bay, supply blankets to keep men warm in the autumn night (but do not turn on the heat in the barracks).[24] How could these simple measures have not already been in place, especially as thousands took sick?

The *Globe* reporter embedded at the camp walked a line between his patriotic duty to put the best possible spin on America's military effort and the clearly growing skepticism regarding the absurdly upbeat pronouncements from some of the Army brass and the civilian authorities. "That the situation is grave, no one denies," William Robinson wrote. "That there is any occasion for panic on the part of the public is most emphatically denied. The military authorities declare they are making no effort to conceal or minimize the situation." Then he passed on perhaps the most incredible statement of the crisis. "All in all, the situation is regarded as satisfactory."[25]

Satisfactory. The scene that had visibly stunned the country's preeminent physician and most respected infectious disease specialist that same day—as he walked among thousands of sick American soldiers, stepped over the corpses of so many cut down before they could even make their way to the actual warfront, and peered into dead men's chests to see lungs turned gelatinous in a matter of hours—was apparently satisfactory to the U.S. Army.

CHAPTER 15

THE YANKEE DIVISION

SEPTEMBER 19-27

In the early morning hours of September 19, after midnight, the phone rang at the home of Mrs. Janet Putnam on Englewood Avenue in Brookline. In wartime, with a son serving at the front, it was a sound that undoubtedly brought instant dread. So perhaps, for a moment, she was relieved, if confused, when the person on the line identified himself not as an official of the U.S. Army but a reporter for the local newspaper. His question, though, was devastating. Could she confirm the report just received at the paper from Europe that her son, David Putnam, the celebrated flying ace, had been killed a week before? No, she managed, no one had told her that. Her son was getting ready to head back to the United States for a furlough, she insisted. The family had set aside a room in their new Brookline home. She reread the letter from her son that had filled her with both fear and hope. "This I will say," he wrote, "that, if I go, I will die fighting. But I do not think I will go. I will come back to you."[1]

Mrs. Putnam telephoned the adjutant general's office in Washington and was told that there had been a cable from the front reporting her son's death, but it was not yet fully confirmed.

There it was, though, emblazoned across the front page of the *Boston Globe* in the morning, complete with Putnam's portrait. Now, everyone knew what his family had not known even as they gathered to celebrate his sister's wedding just five days earlier; the young man who had been America's Ace of Aces was dead.

A reporter from the *Boston Herald* sat with Mrs. Putnam later in the day. "The mothers of the United States and in all the countries of the allies are doing what God did," she managed to say through her grief. "He gave His only begotten son that liberty might have life. What could be more glorious than to die fighting the enemy? It was a glorious death my son had, to glide down to earth on territory held by American troops after he had done his best and given his all."[2]

The *Herald*'s sports columnist, Burt Whitman, recalled Putnam's days as a local athlete and suggested a statue of the young hero be erected in front of Newton High School. "On two continents," Whitman eulogized, "he had made his name a byword, a synonym, for all that is epic and brave. He did more than the work of many an entire regiment before he finished the last period of the Great Game. He belongs on America's all-immortal eleven."[3]

As the Yankee Division pulled out of the St. Mihiel region of France, the liberated residents of area towns and villages came to grips with what had happened. Father A. Leclerc, a Catholic priest in the village of Rupt-en-Woevre, wrote a letter to General Clarence Edwards expressing the feelings of his fellow countrymen.

"Sir, your gallant 26th American division has just set us free," it said. "Several of your comrades lie at rest in our truly Christian and French soil. Their ashes shall be cared for as if they were our own. We shall cover their graves with flowers and shall kneel by them as their own families would, with a prayer to God to reward with eternal glory these heroes fallen on the field of honor and to bless the 26th Division and generous Americans."[4]

Among the men laid to rest was Captain Joseph McConnell, the Boston lawyer, whose death deeply affected the Yankee Division in the aftermath of the St. Mihiel offensive.

"Captain McConnell was buried in the little cemetery at Troyon," *Boston Globe* reporter Frank Sibley wrote.

> There was no officer in the whole Division whose death was more deeply felt. Captain McConnell had a quality that endeared him to everybody who knew him, and a personality that was rare indeed. His earnestness, his common-sense facing of problems, his devotion to his men and his resolute reticence about himself were characteristics for which he was well known. His work as a commander and his sturdy mentality made him respected, but beyond all these things was the quality, indefinable but appealing, that made him one of the best-loved men I have ever known.[5]

The loss was felt all the way to the top of the divisional command.

"General Edwards told me one day that the death of Captain McConnell had a peculiar effect on him," said Father Michael O'Connor, the chaplain with the Twenty-Sixth who had discovered McConnell's body by the side of a French road. "He said it impressed him in an unusual manner and that he could not get it off his mind. Our division commander and all the men of the 101st Regiment and everybody who knew him thought a lot of Joe."[6]

The war was only over for those who had fallen. The rest of the Yankee Division faced still more combat.

The men of the Twenty-Sixth had been away from the front line of the conflict for a few days following their rousing victory at St. Mihiel. That did not mean that they were resting, or even out of danger. Battery C had rarely fired its guns in the intervening days but was under near constant bombardment at night, and conditions were difficult. "The food all this time was very poor indeed," artilleryman Ed Sirois of Lawrence complained. "The inevitable rain set in once again and made things very miserable. We were living in pup-tents and the result was that we had a wet bunk every night."[7]

In shifts, men were sent to the nearby town of Dommartin, where there was a delousing machine the troops called the "cootie incubator." After their bath and disinfection, they were sent back to their positions with food and supplies from the Red Cross.

Finally, after six separate orders to move were rescinded or delayed, the division was leaving the area the French called the Troyon Sector, but the Americans had come to refer to it as the New England Sector. It was a short trip, just two kilometers, and Battery C took up its new position at the top of a steep hill, among a small grove of trees, overlooking the French countryside. Its most memorable characteristic, however, was mud.

"This new position was the best of any that we had occupied on this sector as far as dugouts and personal comforts went," Sirois said.

> The dugouts were in the side of a hill and fairly shell proof. There was also a running spring nearby where we could get good drinking and washing water. The approaches to the position were terrible, however. There were no roads, simply a path, with the mud two feet deep for a stretch of 500 meters. The horses were unable to pull the guns in here, so each carriage had to be taken in by hand. We commenced at 9:00 o'clock at night to bring the guns in here and at daylight next morning we were hardly ready to open fire.[8]

The logistical difficulties were manageable, however, since the men of the Twenty-Sixth would not be "going over" for another couple of days. Allied and German forces continued to attack each other from a distance near the town of Fresnes-en-Woëvre, even as General Pershing and Marshal Foch were making plans for what they hoped would be the decisive battle of the war, the Meuse-Argonne offensive.

Given some down time, Lieutenant Paul Hines decided a party was in order. A soldier, particularly one of those in the Yankee Division who had stared death in the face for seven months, needed a chance to have some fun, he felt—even, perhaps especially, in the midst of war.

"Hines had been a Boston newspaper man," recalled fellow reporter Frank Sibley, "a quiet, smiling chap who had become a lieutenant and gone over to the 102nd Infantry to become assistant to the adjutant. But as no reporter likes a desk job, he grabbed eagerly a chance to have a party of his own."[9]

The 102nd had captured a big six-inch artillery gun in the Battle of St. Mihiel, and Hines decided that, despite knowing nothing about firing artillery, they should scrounge up some ammunition, haul the gun into No Man's Land at the edge of the town of Saint-Hilaire, fire it from point-blank range into the German lines, and then run for cover before the enemy could return fire.

In a nearby dump they found some round bags they assumed to be ammunition, filled with what they took for gunpowder. Hines and some cohorts commandeered a couple of horses and a wagon and tried to drag the gun into position. Predictably, the whole parade ended up in a ditch, but that didn't stop the doughboys from turning the gun toward the Germans, packing bags of "ammo" down the barrel, and rigging a long string of telegraph wire to the trigger. Time and again they primed the massive gun and yanked the wire, only to have it fizzle and fail to fire. Eventually, they gave up and returned to camp with some of the bags of powder.

"They went down into a dugout, a place perhaps twenty feet square, and tested the ammunition by putting most of it on a table and a double handful in a piece of newspaper on the floor, and then lighting the newspaper," Sibley reported. "If it had been powder none of the young officers would have gone in to report that fact. As it happened, the stuff was flash reducer, which the Germans put on top of charges to smother the flame when the gun was fired. It wouldn't burn on a bet."[10]

All Hines and his fellow partygoers had blown off was steam.

The real artillerymen in Battery C of the Twenty-Sixth Division, made up almost entirely of men from Lawrence, had front row seats in the hours leading up to the first action of the offensive. "When the weather was clear, excellent observations of the Hun lines were afforded," Sirois later wrote. "We could look out over the Woëvre plain. The big manufacturing cities of Étain and Conflans, twenty kilometers away, could easily be seen and the smoke rising from the chimneys told us that the Germans were working the factories for all they were worth. Almost every movement of the Germans, on the plain, could be seen and they were carefully watched."[11]

More importantly, as it turned out, the Germans could also see what the Yanks were up to.

The Allies had plans for what became known as the Grand Offensive, a coordinated attack up and down the entire length of the Western Front. In the Meuse-Argonne, Americans were at the left flank and due to make a major push at the western end of the front. On September 26, in an effort to confuse the Germans, the Yankee Division was ordered to conduct two raids on the villages of Marchéville and Riaville and to hold those towns for twenty-four hours.

This was not the main Allied point of attack. The Twenty-Sixth was to be the bait in a diversion designed to take attention away from the real location of the Allied offensive in this region, at Verdun. The men of the Yankee Division were supposed to tie down German units and create doubt in the Germans' minds about whether this was, instead, the start of a major offensive aimed at the key city of Metz. Two meals were cooked for the men that night, dinner and some food set aside for breakfast, and orders were reviewed for the attacks that would begin at dawn.

Stanhope Bayne-Jones was a native of New Orleans who graduated from Yale and then studied medicine at Johns Hopkins, where he lived one floor above Dr. William Welch. The two became friendly during Bayne-Jones's study of bacteriology and immunology, subjects dear to Welch's heart. The great doctor arranged for Bayne-Jones to study at Columbia then return to Johns Hopkins as an instructor in pathology.

As the war in Europe raged, but before the United States entered the conflict, Bayne-Jones was in the Army's Medical Reserve Corps. In 1916, Welch sent him to Washington for a meeting with Army Surgeon General William Gorgas. It was Welch's plan to have Bayne-Jones assigned to

Johns Hopkins while on active duty, but the visit turned into a rare instance where things didn't go as Welch wanted. Gorgas was actually Bayne-Jones's cousin, whom the young doctor affectionately referred to as "Uncle Willie." When he arrived in the surgeon general's Washington office, Gorgas had plans of his own. "I'm glad you came," he told Bayne-Jones. "I need you."[12] Less than a week later, Bayne-Jones was headed to England to fill an urgent need in the British army for doctors at the European front.

When America entered the war, Bayne-Jones became regimental surgeon for the Twenty-Sixth Division and, on the night before the raids on Marchéville and Riaville, he was dirty and uncomfortable.

"If the cooties and a species of red German fleas that I never saw before will allow me to stop scratching for a few moments, I will take pen in hand," he wrote that night. "We've been knocking about the woods and lousy shacks and Boche dugouts for so long that I have completely forgotten when I had a bath last. I am in a disgraceful state of decomposition. My only uniform is snagged on barbed wire, frayed at the cuffs, and one elbow is worn through in ravels and when I sit down on a wet plank something tells me coolly that there is a bald spot in the seat of my trousers."

More than likely, as the Yankee Division's doctor, Bayne-Jones was in comparatively better shape than the infantrymen he cared for. "It's not so bad, only wet and muddy," he continued. "This division is a good fighting division and so has *beaucoup* work to do these days. Perhaps they will get the bloody job done quicker, *toute suite*, and the 'tooter the sweeter.'"[13]

General Edwards was not happy that his men were being used as a sacrificial ploy. He thought the raids would result in "unwarranted bloodshed," especially after he got a new intelligence report the night before the battle was to commence.[14] He had his orders, however, and the Yankee Division was about to become a loud, obvious target for their German foes.

As had been the case at St. Mihiel, the battle plan was an overnight artillery barrage, followed by an infantry advance around dawn. "Riaville and Marchéville are each in a little group of perhaps 30 or 40 houses along a country road, with a few big farm granaries and a few buckstreet houses," the *Boston Globe* reporter's dispatch recounted afterward.

> Only two or three houses in each town had a roof yesterday morning. Hardly one roof is left this morning.
>
> At 5:30 it was still dark. The faint moonlight, a great fat morning star towing one of the fixed stars along for company, and a cold windless air, pulsating under the thump of the guns—and everywhere these mad French birds, who don't know enough to move out of the fighting country, trilling away in the midst of the racket. From the prow of one of the hills all that could be seen was a great white blanket of smoke, the accumulation of all-night fire without a breath to drift it away. Round the two towns pink flashes twinkled constantly. But what the boys were doing down underneath that blanket, no man could tell.[15]

Battery C and other Allied artillery units continued their bombardment all night, pounding the elite Prussian Divisions that the Allies so desperately wanted to keep away from the real offensive, which was starting this same day about six miles away.

"The Infantry, a few hours later, just at daybreak, under cover of dense fog, sallied forth onto the plain and entered the village of Marchéville and then proceeded to Riaville," Sirois recalled. "Their orders were to take the towns, hold them all day and capture prisoners." This limited objective proved much more difficult than it sounded. German resistance was much stiffer than the Allies had planned. General Edwards's fears about "unwarranted bloodshed" were sadly being realized.

"Our Infantry had no sooner started than the Boche laid down terrific defensive fire," according to an artilleryman supporting the 102nd Infantry. "At about 10:30 A.M. the report came in that the Infantry had gained their 5 kilometer objective with heavy losses."[16]

Throughout the day, two regiments of New Englanders each attacked a town: one at Marchéville and one at Riaville. In both places, they met stiff resistance and withering machine gun fire. Twice the Americans were repulsed just short of Riaville by Germans ensconced in concrete pillboxes, immune from artillery attack. The troops who made it to the center of Marchéville soon found themselves under a relentless artillery bombardment, causing them to retreat. While the fighting was fierce and the casualties high, the Twenty-Sixth was achieving its objective of holding the Germans' attention and keeping firepower from the real offensive.

At one point, in Marchéville, American offices found their small headquarters, no more than a sheltered space in the town's main square, surrounded on three sides. Two colonels and a major were low on ammunition and men. They sent one of their few remaining soldiers, Lieutenant Frederick Linton of Roslindale, a Boston suburb, into the field of fire with a message to the rear reporting on the dangerous conditions shaping up in the makeshift command center. Linton was the man who had made a frantic run to the front in St. Mihiel, delivering direct orders passed from Pershing to General Edwards for a more aggressive nighttime offensive. Now, once again, he headed into danger alone.

"It was a murderous kind of day," wrote Emerson Taylor in his history of the Twenty-Sixth Division. "The enemy artillery played havoc with the lines of communication, whether wire or runner relays, the former being destroyed beyond repair and the runners undergoing so many casualties that the delivery of orders or information was delayed for hours."[17]

As the Germans closed in and things seemed bleakest for the Yankee Division officers, Linton somehow miraculously returned, in the nick of time. He had corralled a couple dozen men and once again raced across open ground, drawing torrents of enemy fire, to get to them. The added manpower was enough to turn the small tide and allowed the officers to retreat to safety.

Linton wasn't done. He volunteered to take a platoon back into Marchéville in a counterattack. Under his command, the Americans retook the town square, though Linton was wounded in the process.

Mindful of the orders to occupy the town for twenty-four hours, Linton retained his command, and his men held their ground in the face of heavy enemy fire. The second wound Linton received in the little town—a town which had no strategic value other than as a diversion—was the one that killed him.

Lieutenant Linton was far from the only hero.

Paul Hines was barely thirty-six hours past his ill-fated party with the captured German howitzer, and in that small group of officers nearly surrounded by enemy German troops with machine guns, when Linton arrived to rescue them. When Linton led his men back into the town, one of them fell wounded, and it was Hines's turn to be the rescuer.

"He was all through the fighting," Sibley said, "everywhere grinning as if he enjoyed the mess. He distinguished himself by rushing out over the open ground from the trench to rescue a wounded officer. He took two men with him to what looked like certain death; but the party in the trench spread out and opened up such active fire on the Germans at the southern end of Marchéville that Hines was able to get to safety."[18]

Both men, Linton of Roslindale and Hines of South Boston, along with a number of other Massachusetts natives in the Twenty-Sixth Division, were awarded the Distinguished Service Cross for their actions on the field that long and bloody day.

By nightfall, the order was given for the men of the Twenty-Sixth to pull back to that morning's original lines. They had occupied German forces all day with their feint at Marchéville and Riaville, even as the main offensive took place ten kilometers to the north. "The wounded doughboys straggled back singly and in small groups, discouraged at the evident uselessness of their attack, for they had received order to relinquish their hard-won 5 kilometers to the Boche," an artilleryman from Battery A remembered. "All day long and all that night we heard the heavy, continuous boom of artillery away to our left, and we knew that the big attack on Verdun was on in earnest."[19]

That offensive, at the Meuse-Argonne, would last until Germany surrendered and the war came to an end six weeks later.

While the Twenty-Sixth was not yet involved in the thick of the main battle, it was far from idle. Skirmishes continued, and the division suffered through perhaps the most dreaded aspect of the Great War: gas attacks.

On September 27, the 103rd Infantry, along with men from the 102nd and 103rd Machine Gun battalions, who had become separated from their units during the action around Marchéville and Riaville the day before, were shelled by German artillery. Over the course of six hours, shells dropped all around them, including some loaded with mustard gas. The cloud of gas was thick enough that even some of the horses were affected and had to be moved further away from the front lines. Within fifteen minutes of the artillery barrage's end, however, troops were told they could remove their gas masks. Thinking the concentration of gas was light, one company served breakfast to its men, as well as some soldiers from another company, even as the gas lingered in the air around them. Every cook and all the men who ate that breakfast were soon evacuated out for medical treatment resulting from the gas. It was, the Twenty-Sixth's Division gas officer reported, an almost perfect example of "how an organization should not act during a gas attack."[20]

One would think that the Yankee Division, of all American units in the war, would understand the critical nature of gas attack preparedness and proper procedure. After all, it was the men of the Twenty-Sixth who, as one historian put it, "had the unhappy distinction of suffering the greatest number of gas casualties, most of them on quiet fronts, in the American Expeditionary Force."[21]

Gas drills had been part of the training regimen for the New England troops in the Yankee Division since before they left American soil in 1917. They were taught about the various types of gases employed by Germans against the British and the French: paralyzing gases like prussic acid, lachrymating gases, which we know now as tear gas, and more deadly weapons such as cloud gases, like chlorine and mustard gas, which could cause pneumonia and death with as little as three or four breaths in certain concentrations. "The enemy brings this gas to the front in liquid form, confined in drums through which pipes are led toward the foe," read an official report on the Twenty-Sixth Division's experiences with chemical warfare. "When the wind is in the right direction the air is let into these drums, which vaporizes the contents, and the gas, being heavier than air, rolls over the surface of the earth and into the trenches and dugouts, in the form of a cloud, visible by day, but invisible by night."[22]

The men of the Twenty-Sixth had been issued two kinds of gas masks, for which they had repeatedly trained and were often forced to use. "We were issued a French gas mask and an English gas mask, the latter called a respirator," recalled Private Connell Albertine.

> The French gas mask was a small pouch with two pieces of glass set in the upper part so one could see, and the bottom part that went snugly under the chin was padded with cotton impregnated with some kind of chemical. The English mask seemed far superior, for it had a good facepiece with good glasses and a mouthpiece connected to a rubber-covered flexible tube, which was connected to a canister containing granules of charcoal and other chemicals. It also had a nose clip fastened to the inside of the mask, so that when the gas mask was put on the nose clip kept one from breathing through the mouthpiece. At the bottom of the mask was a flap where the exhaled air went out, but because of the suction the air could not get in. The mask with the canister was carried in a square pouch, but the gas mask could be taken out very quickly. Considerable time was spent every day with gas mask drills, and after a while we got so that we could put on our masks in a couple of seconds. We had to carry these masks at all times, no matter where we went.[23]

The easy availability of the masks was critical, as the soldiers were told time and again during their training drills. "These masks have to be put on within six seconds from the moment the signal is sounded, else the damage is done and the soldier's death is only a matter of time, or if he has not breathed enough gas eventually to cause his death, he is rendered useless for further service," read a particularly blunt assessment of chemical warfare readiness. "In other words, a man once gassed is considered useful for only for civilian life and is often not much good for that."[24]

For whatever reason, the men of the Yankee Division could not seem to grasp the subtleties of gas masks or chemical attack procedures. During combat in March, there had been an incident in which the men of the 104th Infantry had been caught unaware and without their gas masks hung at the ready around their necks. When the men smelled a faint whiff of gas, the aid station was soon overrun with doughboys certain that they were suffering the effects of gas. The regiment's medical officer, however, attributed most of the symptoms to a mass mild hysteria, finding they "were suffering from suggestion rather than from the effects of enemy gas shells. In spite of large numbers who reported, not one man showed any signs of gas intoxication after his mental anxiety had been allayed."[25] All the men returned to action with the 104th by the next day.

Later that month the problem arose again, with more serious consequences. The 102nd Infantry found itself under attack along with French troops, and German artillery lobbed some 15,000 shells containing chlorine, mustard gas, and tear gas at their positions. Not recognizing the attack as including gas, the men were slow to don their masks, and, as a result, over 150 soldiers in the regiment suffered burns or respiratory problems.

The most serious gas attack experienced by the men of the Twenty-Sixth came in May. It was a blunder so severe as to be initially covered up by divisional command and eventually result in significant changes in procedure because the attack on the 101st Infantry came from their own artillery units, and it was severe enough to cause Allied battlefield commanders real trepidation in using chemical weapons themselves.

In an attack at Camp du Moulin, the Fifty-First Artillery brigade used phosgene shells in what was known as a box barrage around the target. This is a procedure in which the enemy is shelled to the right and left and behind, leaving only one open side to the "box," from which the attack would originate. No one told the infantrymen of the 101ˢᵗ about the plan. At 2:30 a.m., after more than three hours of conventional bombardment by the artillery, the infantrymen advanced on German positions. As they arrived at the outer line of German trenches, the artillery began to fire the phosgene shells into the village of Lahayville, about 600 yards to the east. A westerly wind then blew the gas clouds, smelling distinctly of new mown hay and ammonia, directly into the path of the advancing New England men. "The men were bothered considerably by the fumes from our shells," read the understated post-engagement report, "many men being rendered very sick, vomiting and gasping."[26]

Smoke from artillery fire concealed the gas cloud, and the Yankee Division men ran right into it, never pausing to put on their gas masks. They were completely exposed to the gas for thirty- to forty-five minutes. When they reached the German positions, they found them abandoned, as the enemy had retreated over the course of the lengthy overnight artillery attack. So the regiment hiked four miles back to camp. By noon, however, every man involved in the raid began to show the ill effects of being gassed. By nightfall, they were all receiving medical treatment. Within five days, 231 were evacuated to base hospitals. Five men eventually died.

Colonel Logan, commander of the 101ˢᵗ regiment and a judge in the South Boston police court prior to the war, demanded an investigation and punishment for those responsible for gassing his men, but none was ever handed down. The Army did institute new rules of engagement, however, that increased the "safe" distance for gas attacks from half a mile to roughly two miles away from friendly troops.

By the end of the war, an estimated 1.2 million troops from both sides of the conflict were casualties of chemical weapons, and 90,000 soldiers died from increasingly deadly forms of gas attacks. The victims suffered from a variety of symptoms, depending on the chemicals used: respiratory problems, loss of eyesight, blistering skin.

As September neared to a close in France, Boston artist John Singer Sargent finally settled on the subject of his "epic" painting: gas attack casualties lined up for medical treatment at an aid station. "A harrowing sight, a field full of gassed and blindfolded men," he called it.[27] In the painting, a massive canvas with nearly life-sized figures, men walk toward a relief station, their hands on the shoulder of the soldier in front of them, while the bodies of the dead and wounded lie all around. The painting, entitled simply "Gassed," went on to win Picture of the Year honors from the Royal Academy Exhibition in London in 1919 and hangs today in the Imperial War Museum.

Even as he made the decision, Sargent was himself bedridden. More than 3,000 miles from the epidemic that was sweeping through Boston, he had contracted influenza. "In a hospital tent, with the accompaniment of groans of wounded and the chokings and coughing of gassed men, which was a nightmare," he reported in a letter to a friend. "It always seemed strange on opening one's eyes to see the level cots and the dimly lit long tent looking so calm, when one was dozing in pandemonium."[28] Though his condition improved slowly, Sargent was still feeling the effects of his flu symptoms when he went back to London in late October.

CHAPTER 16

THE PATH OF PROGRESS

SEPTEMBER 26–30

President Wilson had to confront a monster of his own making. The administration's unrelenting campaign to whip Americans into a frenzy of war support necessitated the constant denigration of Germany and the German people. In order to swing public opinion from the anti-war platform on which he had been re-elected to the total societal commitment required to bring the nation to a war footing, the enemy had to be built into an evil and looming threat to everything Americans held dear.

As the still-nascent prospects of peace dawned, however, the president faced the daunting task of turning public opinion yet again if he was to return to his original case for a negotiated peace. Surprisingly, at least one member of Wilson's own cabinet seemed caught off guard by the hatred that had emerged regarding "the Boche" and the insistence by Wilson's political opponents on nothing less than complete and unequivocal victory for the Allies.

"The psychological effect upon the American people has been peculiar," Secretary of State Robert Lansing—a graduate of Amherst College like Calvin Coolidge—wrote in his diary.

> The natural enthusiasm and joy over daily victories have been accompanied by an increasing bitterness toward the German people and by louder demands for retaliation which are almost savage in their vindictiveness. On the crest of this wave of passion which is sweeping over this country rides the malignant Roosevelt, the partisan Lodge, the narrow minded politician Gillette and all the lesser enemies of the Administration who have [been] seeking for a chance to bite.[1]

Wilson, thanks in large measure to Creel and his relentless propaganda campaign, faced a real challenge. How to convince the American public, fed a steady diet of hate for Germany by his own administration for almost a year and a half, to embrace peace rather than punishment? In this atmosphere, the president traveled to New York on September 27 to deliver a speech, ostensibly to kick off the Fourth Liberty Loan campaign, though the president had a higher goal in mind.

"I'm not here to promote the loan," he surprised everyone by beginning, before drawing a line that must have pleased Lodge and the Republicans.

> We are all agreed that there can be no peace obtained by any kind of bargain or compromise with the governments of the Central Empires, because we have dealt with them already and have seen them deal with other governments that were parties to this struggle. They observe no covenants, accept no law but force and their own interest. We cannot "come to terms" with them. They have made it impossible. The German people must, by this time, be fully aware that we cannot accept the word of those who forced this war upon us. We do not think the same thoughts or speak the same language of

agreement. It is of capital importance that we should also be explicitly agreed that no peace shall be obtained by any kind of compromise or abatement of the principles we have avowed as the principles for which we are fighting. There should be no doubt about it.

Then Wilson made a rhetorical turn, right into Lodge's crosshairs.

"If it be in deed and in truth the common object of the governments associated against Germany, and of the nations whom they govern, as I believe it to be, to achieve by the coming settlements a secure and lasting peace, it will be necessary that all who sit down at the peace table shall come ready and willing to pay the price, the only price, that will procure it," he said. "The price is impartial justice, in every item of the settlement, no matter whose interest is crossed; and not only impartial justice, but also the satisfaction of the several peoples whose fortunes are dealt with. That indispensable instrumentality is a league of nations."[2]

The concept was not new. Wilson had broached the idea of a league of nations in his famous "Fourteen Points" speech earlier in the year. Now, however, the president was using the distrust of Germany he had helped build as a new rationale for his plan. He was co-opting the arguments of Lodge and Roosevelt that the Germans could not be taken at their word on any matter and making it the rationale for an international organization that would hold them responsible going forward.

It was a clever tactic. Lodge's response lacked all subtlety.

"I believe that the great mass of the American people are with me and mean to have an unconditional surrender," he wrote. "The thing to do is to lick Germany and tell her what arrangements were going to be made."[3]

Wilson's push for a formal League of Nations, and Lodge's bitter opposition, would be the central political fight in America in the post-war years and, in the end, the Massachusetts men leading both houses of Congress, Lodge and Gillett, would prevail.

One issue that Wilson seemed to be too preoccupied to address, as he had yet to make a single public statement on it, was the influenza epidemic. Others in Washington, however, were speaking up. On September 28, in a Saturday session of Congress, Gillett introduced a bill in the House of Representatives to appropriate $1 million to fight influenza and other communicable diseases and to distribute a serum thought to be promising in the battle with influenza. "Tens of thousands of people in New England are affected, with hospitals full to overrunning, no nurses available and doctors worked near 24 hours a day as humanly possible," Massachusetts Senator John Weeks, the bill's co-sponsor, said on the floor of his chamber. "The Public Health Service informs me that it is spreading to other portions of the country, and they must have the funds to cope with it."[4] With that ominous prediction, the bill passed unanimously in both the House and the Senate.

Even in light of the devastating toll influenza was taking on the citizens of his home state, Senator Lodge rationalized his vote on familiar terms. "The epidemic is stopping the war work in the states," he said in explaining his support for the appropriation.[5] "If the disease is not arrested, it may spread to every part of the country. Already it has affected our war munitions plants. Its ravages may be more severe unless we grapple with it now, and we cannot do it without money."[6]

The money would be sorely needed. Despite the lessons coming to light in Boston regarding the infectious nature of influenza and the need for isolation to prevent its spread, thousands of people crowded together in Philadelphia for a Liberty Loan parade. Almost immediately afterward, the epidemic exploded in that city. By the end of autumn, Philadelphia would suffer far more than even Boston had. Over 12,000 people would die, in a city whose morgue was built to hold thirty-six bodies.

While Lodge was fighting for funding to battle influenza, he was also fighting a familiar foe in his efforts to defeat a constitutional amendment giving women the right to vote. As the Senate entered the last week of September, the suffrage issue was coming to the forefront, and Boston's Maud Wood Park faced parliamentary obstacles thrown in her path by her old nemesis. With the session winding down ahead of the recess that would allow members to return home to campaign for the November election, Lodge was stalling. He wasn't sure he had the votes. "This question must not be decided by a thinned Senate," he said. "There will be no vote until all are here."[7]

As in the 1916 GOP convention platform fight, Lodge wasn't sure he had the votes to kill the amendment outright—like Park, he was counting allies among the ever-changing Senate roster—so he was looking for a tactical victory instead.

"I am getting more than one hint of a systematic attempt to keep us from coming to vote before election if we are likely to go through," Park said of Lodge's maneuvers.

> It is also said that there is a subtle and intricate plan to bring forward several other issues to stave off that vote, as well as our own, until the Revenue Bill is reported into the Senate thus to avoid action until after the election. I have no doubt that we shall have to make a hard fight for a chance to get the vote provided we have the votes to win. However, we all knew that we were not going to have an easy time. This is simply another way of saying that we must fight with every ounce of force that is in us.[8]

President Wilson kept the promise to Park and the other NAWSA members he made at the White House meeting earlier in the month. He politely twisted the arms of Democratic senators, urging their support. "I know that you will forgive and justify me as leader of our party in making another direct and very earnest appeal to you to vote for the suffrage amendment," he wrote to Senator Christie Benet of South Carolina. "I know that I am asking a great deal, but I also know how generous you are in your purpose to accept leadership and serve the present unusual interests in an unusual way."[9] Like Park and Lodge, the president was counting votes and attuned to the pending tally as it fluctuated. "I am so deeply interested in the passage of the suffrage amendment that, learning you are about to leave town, I am taking the great liberty of asking if you will postpone your absence," he wrote to Senator

Robert Owen of Oklahoma. "I know that you will pardon your party's leader for this liberty."[10]

The fight over suffrage was not confined to Washington. It raged in Boston as well, where Lodge and Weeks had sympathetic allies. The suffragists were not deterred. "Formerly, there were many men who said they did not believe in suffrage because they did not think women wanted to vote," noted Mrs. Theodore Tillinghast of the Massachusetts Woman Suffrage Association. "If they have not found out differently, they will."[11]

In opposition to the amendment, a group called the Women's Anti-Suffrage Association of Massachusetts sent out an appeal for donations, playing to the patriotism of potential contributors through innuendo. "There is a growing conviction among thoughtful people that Germany, while repudiating Woman Suffrage at home, is, and has been during the war, working to further the measure in this country," the letter said, stopping short of an accusation but clearly implying no less than treason on the part of women seeking the franchise. "Will you not give us One Dollar to help keep our Government at its maximum strength while our boys are fighting for its safety at the front?"

In a front-page ad in the *Boston Post*, the suffragists fought back, reprinting the text of the fundraising letter and saying, "we call upon the Women's Anti-Suffrage Association of Massachusetts to repudiate this untruthful and insulting 'appeal' or failing to do that to stand convicted before the citizens of Massachusetts of a discredited and dishonorable act."[12]

Another group, calling itself the Massachusetts Public Interests League of Anti-Suffragists, was even more blatant. They issued a leaflet that was entitled "Is Woman Suffrage Pro-German?" In September 1918, this was the worst accusation that could possibly be leveled against any person or organization. The pamphlet was not subtle. "To weaken the countries of her enemies through Socialism and Woman Suffrage is Germany's cleverest device," it read. It made the case that the suffrage movement was no more than a front of America's enemies, with claims like "George Sylvester Vierick, the Kaiser's alleged cousin, was the first to agitate for Woman Suffrage among the Germans in New York!" and

"It was owing to a 'deal' between suffragists and Germans in the Nebraska legislature that the Presidential Suffrage bill was passed in that state, and that German teaching in the public schools of Nebraska was endorsed by law."[13]

Political disagreement over the issue of a woman's right to vote had devolved into a bare-knuckles brawl across Massachusetts.

Undeterred, the Massachusetts WSA gave notice to the state's elected officials in the week before the anticipated vote. "We intend that through the hundreds and thousands of letters and telegrams which Senators will get between now and the time that the bill comes up for final vote, our own Senators shall have no doubt left in their minds of the real sentiment of the people at home, and shall be made to understand that if they vote against the measure, they do so according to their own preference in the matter and in doing so act contrary to the wishes of the constituency which they represent and according to whose desires they are supposed to act."[14] Senator Weeks had a succinct response. "I would not vote for the suffrage amendment if the whole state of Massachusetts urged me to do so."[15]

Finally, on Friday, September 27, the amendment was brought up for debate and a vote. By Park's count, there were sixty-two senators in favor of the amendment, thirty-two opposed, and two on the fence. She needed the votes of both undecided members to get the two-thirds majority required to send the amendment on to the states for ratification. "As soon as the date for taking up the amendment was settled, our women flocked to Washington," she recalled in her memoir of the effort. "Although I did my best to make them realize that we were still two votes short, they would not believe that we could fail to win that small number."[16]

Friendly senators had given all one hundred tickets in the Senate's northeast gallery to the National American Woman Suffrage Association for its members to be present when the historic vote was taken. The suffragists came to Capitol Hill prepared to sit through every minute of the debate, determined to be present for the vote that could end the movement's nearly seventy-five-year campaign for voting rights. "Packages of sandwiches, nuts and apples were again ready for all of us," Park remembered, "for by that time our house manager had become expert in choosing the kind of food that could be eaten quietly and in putting it up in paper that would not rattle in the gallery."[17] The women were trying to be quiet, but the senators on the floor were anything but.

"Debate [began] with a long speech in support of the amendment by Senator Vardaman of Mississippi," according to Park. "Why he was in favor was almost as much a mystery when he concluded as when he began, for his address was about equally divided between extravagant praise for women and violent attacks upon the Negro. He went on for the better part of an hour, balancing, as it were, the emotions of admiration and hatred."[18]

This was not a typical dispute between two parties. There was a clear bipartisan majority in favor of passage. In fact, Lodge's Republicans supported the measure by a wider margin than the Democrats, despite his unrelenting efforts to scuttle it. In the absence of party wrangling, the arguments turned personal, with senators hurling insults and accusations at their foes—real or imagined—and at each other.

One Senator, Democrat James Reed of Missouri, made Maud Wood Park herself the object of his scorn. "It is a strange charge to hear on the floor of this house that faith has been broken because a pledge made to a female lobbyist has not been carried out," he said before launching into a sexist tirade that revealed much of the paternalistic mindset of suffrage opponents.

> Is it not a fine state of affairs that the general of this battle is outside of the Chamber, and that the generalissimo is summoning the leader of her cohorts from the Republican side and saying "How many men have you recruited?" Here we have a situation where a petticoat brigade waits outside, and the Senate sends out its leaders, like little boys, like pages, to these women to receive their orders. Put on a cap and bells if you are to do that, and get a stick carried by the court fool of the Middle Ages, and go and do your truckling in a proper garb.[19]

Park was alarmed at the broadside but not because she was the target. "I rushed down to see some of our friends because I was afraid that Senator Reed's attack might have done harm to the cause," she recounted. "But they laughed my fears aside. 'Everyone knows that Reed loves to shoot off his mouth,' one of them assured me, 'and nobody pays any attention to him.'"[20]

Over the course of the day, it became clear that the suffragists still did not have the two-thirds majority they needed, so supporters began a filibuster that succeeded in delaying a final vote into the next week. Park and NAWSA President Carrie Chapman Catt decided they needed to persuade their most powerful ally to take a more active role if they were to have any chance of victory.

"We hope that you who have proved yourself a miracle worker on many occasions may be able to produce another wonder on Monday," Catt said in a note to President Wilson. "The wonder of putting vision where there was none before."[21]

Most immediately, the president was focused on matters of war. On Saturday, September 28, Bulgaria signed an armistice with the Allies. On Sunday morning, however, Secretary of Treasury William McAdoo—who was also Wilson's son-in-law—met with the president to urge him to agree to the suffragists' request and go to Capitol Hill to address the Senate before the vote. "I knew that the President did not like to discuss, or consider, any public question on Sunday," McAdoo recalled.

This was an immutable rule with him which he never violated except in case of emergency. Nevertheless, I felt this matter was of sufficient importance to justify me. The President listened patiently, as he always did, until the case had been presented to him. He said, at once, that there was no precedent for such a course on his part and that he thought the Senate might resent it. It was a question of bringing just two senators to our side. He thought it would be hardly possible to get them to change their minds—nothing whatever could change them, he thought—but he promised to consider my suggestion.[22]

Wilson and the First Lady went to church, and later on Sunday afternoon he agreed to take the unusual step of personally addressing the Senate in favor of the amendment, in an effort to sway the last two votes needed for passage.

"When I came to think over the situation in bed that night, I was by no means certain of victory," said Park of the eve of Wilson's speech. "The next morning, as we were driving up to the Capitol, Mrs. Catt took me to task for not looking jubilant. When I told her that I was not so confident as she was, I did not shake her faith at all, nor did [fellow suffrage leader] Miss Hay, who said, 'I think Maud's right. He may not be able to change any votes.'"[23]

At 1:00 p.m., the president and his cabinet entered the Senate chamber. "The excitement that we, in the gallery, felt keenly was plainly evident below, where all the senators except Mr. Reed of Missouri were standing to show their respect for the nation's chief, if not for Woodrow Wilson himself," wrote Park. "I should have given more thought to Reed's surprising lack of courtesy if my mind had not been so intent on the President and what he was about to say."[24]

Today, we are accustomed to presidents addressing Congress. The annual State of the Union speech is a familiar television event. But a sitting president addressing a single chamber in support of a specific piece of legislation—even one as momentous as a constitutional amendment—was highly unusual. "It was clear," McAdoo could see,

> that his appearance was bitterly resented by all those opposed to the amendment and that even those who favored it were influenced by senatorial tradition and the feeling that the Chief Executive should not plead for any particular measure which the Senate had under consideration. An air of hostility, a frigid atmosphere, always heightened President Wilson's powers. It did on this occasion. He spoke only fifteen minutes.

His speech was powerful and impressive and carried a fighting edge.[25]

Predictably, Wilson framed his appeal in the context of the war. "I regard the concurrence of the Senate in the constitutional amendment proposing the extension of the suffrage to women as vitally essential to the successful prosecution of the great war of humanity in which we are engaged," he began. "It is my duty to win the war and to ask you to remove every obstacle that stands in the way of winning it."

He reinforced that both parties were on record in support of extending the right to vote to women, and he noted that the only thing standing in the way was a dispute over the method of doing so. He came down squarely on the side of federal action rather than state-by-state decisions and again reminded the senators—in case they missed his first approach—that adoption of the Nineteenth Amendment, "is, in my judgment, clearly necessary to the successful prosecution of the war and the successful realization of the objects for which the war is being fought."

Brilliantly, then, he brought the war argument full circle to the matter at hand and placed suffrage among universal truths for which the country was fighting.

Through many, many channels I have been made aware what the plain, struggling, workaday folk are thinking upon whom the chief terror and suffering of this tragic war falls. They are looking to the great, powerful, famous Democracy of the West to lead them to the new day for which they have so long waited; and they think, in their logical simplicity, that democracy means that women shall play their part in affairs alongside men and upon an equal footing with them. If we reject measures like this, in ignorance or defiance of what a new age has brought forth, of what they have seen but we have not, they will cease to believe in us; they will cease to follow or to trust us.

Noting that America's allies had already given women full voting rights, Wilson sought to shame the Senate into action.

> Are we alone to refuse to learn the lesson? Are we alone to ask and take the utmost that our women can give—service and sacrifice of every kind—and still say we do not see what title that gives them to stand by our sides in the guidance of the affairs of their nation and ours? We have made partners of the women in this war; shall we admit them only to a partnership of suffering and sacrifice and toil and not to a partnership of privilege and right? This war could not have been fought, either by the other nations engaged or by America, if it had not been for the services of the women—services rendered in every sphere—not merely in the fields of effort in which we have been accustomed to see them work, but wherever men have worked and upon the very skirts and edges of the battle itself. We shall not only be distrusted but shall deserve to be distrusted if we do not enfranchise them with the fullest possible enfranchisement, as it is now certain that the other great free nations will enfranchise them. We cannot isolate our thought and action in such a matter from the thought of the rest of the world. We must either conform or deliberately reject what they propose and resign the leadership of liberal minds to others.

Then he turned away from the war and toward the time of peace that would surely follow, and he made a final, moral, and even practical case for elevating women in American society. "We shall need then in our vision of affairs, as we have never needed them before, the sympathy and insight and clear moral instinct of the women of the world....We shall need their moral sense to preserve what is right and fine and worthy in our system of life as well as to discover just what it is that ought to be purified and reformed. Without their counsellings we shall be only half wise."[26]

It was a bold, full-throated, and eloquent endorsement of the amendment—everything Maud Wood Park, Carrie Catt, and their fellow suffragists could have hoped for, and more.

"For a while our fears were at rest and Monday afternoon when the words of that noble speech fell upon our ears it seemed impossible that a third of the senate could refuse the never-to-be-forgotten plea," Park said.[27] "To me, those words were the most impassioned that I had ever heard the President utter, and it seemed impossible that they could be spoken in vain."[28]

But they were.

Before a vote, some senators decided a packed gallery was an irresistible temptation that demanded additional speechifying. "Perhaps if the vote had been taken immediately, the result might have been different," Park mused, but "the afternoon dragged on. I felt as if I were at a funeral service, waiting for the arrival of the officiating clergyman."[29] In addition to the speeches, opponents of the amendment were working hard to hold their votes. "Our chief enemies moved about the floor to see whether their forces were still unbroken. The two floor leaders, Lodge of Massachusetts and Martin of Virginia, were arm in arm comparing votes—'the unholy alliance' we called them."[30]

The speeches stretched into the evening, and the Senate ended its session for the day without a vote. "After adjournment, I went down to see as many of our friends as possible and ask whether they knew of any votes that had been changed by the president's speech.

"They feared none had been."[31]

CHAPTER 17

TURNING THE CORNER

SEPTEMBER 25–30

The stark message relayed by Dr. William Welch from Camp Devens to higher military command had spurred acting Army Surgeon General Charles Richard, in charge while General William Gorgas was at the front in France, finally into action. He isolated Camp Devens in an order that left no doubt as to the seriousness of the viral threat. "No disease which the army surgeon is likely to see in this war will tax more severely his judgment and initiative," he wrote. "It is important that the influenza be kept out of the camps, as far as practicable. In transferring men from Camp Devens a virulent form of the disease will almost surely be conveyed to other stations. During the epidemic new men should not be sent to Camp Devens, nor should men be sent away from that camp."[1]

It was the right idea, but it came too late. At Camp Upton on Long Island, for instance, there had been just a few isolated cases of influenza. Now, a single barracks primarily filled with troops from Massachusetts had erupted with 2,000 cases.

Drs. Welch, Vaughan, and Cole, along with Dr. Simeon Wolbach of the Harvard Medical School, met with Lieutenant Colonel McCornack, the Camp Devens division surgeon, to impress upon him the gravity of the situation in his own cantonment. The team of prominent epidemiologists also convinced the Devens commanding officer, Major General McCain, to act. He took a series of steps characterized as "drastic" in the press but seemingly mild, if practical, given the circumstances. He closed the camp's theater and the recreation centers, and he canceled all movies, dances, or other activities at the Knights of Columbus and YMCA facilities in the camp. Meanwhile, sixty-six more people died at Devens on September 24 and seventy-seven more the next day, including Dorothy Crosby of Chestnut Hill, the second nurse to lose her life caring for sick soldiers in the camp.

The Massachusetts state health commissioner, Eugene Kelly, appealed to the federal government for 500 doctors, in a telegram to his Massachusetts predecessor, Colonel Allan McLaughlin of the Public Health Service in Washington. He was far more dire than in any statement he had previously made to the public. "Deaths increasing at alarming rate," he wired. "Coordinated force of doctors and nurses from Public Health Service, Army, Navy and Red Cross for short period emergency service appears only chance for necessary assistance."[2]

As another 105 people died in Boston, acting Governor Coolidge appointed an Emergency Health Committee and put Henry Endicott, a millionaire shoe manufacturer and chairman of the statewide Committee on Public Safety, in charge. Almost immediately, the committee doubled down on the previous day's ban on large gatherings. "It is requested that no gatherings of any name or nature that can be possibly avoided during the period of the epidemic shall be held in any section of the Commonwealth," Endicott announced.[3] Citizens' freedom of assembly was not being revoked, but they were under a very strong suggestion to refrain from exercising that freedom. If the bans were observed, one reporter noted, the coming Sunday would be the first since the time of the pilgrims on which there would be no church services of any denomination in Massachusetts.

The crisis did not lessen in any way the importance of the war effort, at least to Endicott's mind. His effort to shut down public gatherings was now in direct conflict with fundraising plans for the upcoming Fourth Liberty Loan drive, due for the weekend. In keeping with the demands of the time, Endicott cast the two imperatives as just one more challenge in the cause of freedom. "The cancellation of all Liberty Loan meetings places upon the people of Massachusetts a responsibility for individual effort far greater than that which the citizens of any other state are called upon to bear," he said.

> It is comparatively easy to subscribe generously when the emotions are stirred by the appeal of a soldier fresh from overseas, or by the thrill of patriotic music, or by the sight of a neighbor's response. Massachusetts will have the benefit of none of these rallying forces to arouse the generosity of her subscribers. The very absence of parades and oratory, however, makes the duty of each man and woman clearer than ever before. Subscriptions which have heretofore been made in the excitement of public gatherings must be offset by the appeal to each man's conscience. It will never be said of Massachusetts that she was so immersed in her own private troubles that for one moment she failed to heed the nation's call to practical service. Massachusetts must and will do her part.[4]

Epidemic or not, there was an existential cause to be funded, and Bay Staters would just have to do their part regardless. In Boston, Mayor Peters appointed a five-member committee of his own to coordinate with state officials. Finally, the gears of government were turning in response to the crisis. A centralized response was being planned and instituted. Suddenly, every possible precaution was being considered. Boston Superintendent of Police Michael Crowley even ordered the arrest of any person seen spitting on a sidewalk.

Even as the government at last became far more serious about battling the epidemic and the press became more comfortable in reporting the reality of the tragedy, there remained an undercurrent of naiveté among the public that some authorities were content to foster. At the end of a long story detailing the area deaths, the severity of the cases, and the steps being taken to combat the disease, the *Boston Globe* felt compelled to add advice it apparently felt would be helpful. "Mrs. Minnie Pendelsohn offers this recipe, used in her family for three generations, as a cure for the grippe," the paper read. "Three pounds of onions, to one pound of garlic, mix and make into a poultice, to be applied to feet, under the knees and around the neck every three to four hours." In addition, the story added a detail critical, one would imagine, given the nature of the influenza symptoms and the subsequent pneumonia killing so many: "If the lungs are affected, mix lard into the poultice."[5]

Pharmacies did not seem to have much more to offer than home remedies of this sort, as a pair of contrasting advertisements in the *Lowell Sun* demonstrated. Stacked atop each other in the same column, both ads ran under bold headlines that read simply "Spanish Influenza." "The only persons who are likely to be affected by the germs of the disease are those with poor blood, a run down system or whose vitality is lowered temporarily," read the Dow's Drug Store ad on the top, which promoted a "blood builder" called Vitalitas.

Directly below it, Dow's ran another ad which cautioned readers "Don't dose your stomach with patent medicines" and instead recommended the store's own menthol cream. "Place a little in the nostril. It dissolves rapidly."

At least the newspapers were now fully engaged. Morning headlines on September 25 announced the highest daily death toll so far. A boxed statement on the front page of the *Globe* begged for more nurses. Grace O'Bryan, associate director of the District Nursing Association, appealed for people to volunteer the use of their automobiles to transport sick people to hospitals or carry nurses to the homes of those too ill to travel. "Each auto helps to double the efficiency of our work," she explained. "It is like supplying an extra nurse."[6]

Through it all, the city's health commissioner remained steadfast. "I will not issue any direct order which will close theaters and churches at this time," Dr. Woodward insisted. "I have not got enough evidence to show that these institutions are in any way responsible for the spread of influenza."[7]

That Wednesday was the first day classes were canceled, and Boston's school children stayed home. The school-closing order must have come as a relief to many. Even as a child, Francis Russell could see the toll the stress of living and working in a disease-ravaged city had taken on adults like his teacher, whose classroom overlooked the route to a nearby cemetery. "In those weeks the plague had stretched out its fingertips toward Miss Sykes and she could feel that substance-less touch each day," Russell remembered later, blaming the near-constant parade of funerals outside the school's windows. "Trying as best she could to conceal it from us, she became sharp and tense-voiced. The rattle of the hacks and the hiss of vacuum-cup tires had broken her nerve."[8]

As President Wilson had planned, the effects of the war and the all-out effort to support America's engagement in it extended into nearly every aspect of life in Massachusetts, even in those homes that had not been touched directly by death and disease, like Russell's. "Instead of sugar we used Karo Corn Syrup," he said. "The red Karo cans had yellow syrup and the blue ones white. Neither tasted very good, and there was no frosting any more even for birthday cakes, because the sugar had to go to saving the Belgians."[9]

Whether those sacrifices played much practical purpose to American soldiers was very much in question, however. "We got some mail, and the letters mentioned heatless days, meatless days, sugarless days, etc. so that the boys overseas could have those things," noted Private Connell Albertine of Somerville and the 104th Infantry. "Some of us wondered particularly where the sugar was going. Sure, our cooks did receive some sugar, but to put that little bit in a batch of coffee would really be wasting it, because it did not make the coffee any sweeter. The cooks told us that they were saving it until they had enough to make the coffee taste sweet, but travelling through this kind of country it got lost or got so wet from the rain that it was no use to anyone."[10]

Acting Army Surgeon General Richard continued to sound the alarm in Washington. On September 25 he sent a stark and urgent message to General March which could not be misconstrued. "Epidemic influenza has become a very serious menace and threatens not only to retard the military program, but to exact a heavy toll on human life before the disease has run its course throughout the country."[11] War planners did not know that peace was on the horizon, of course, but the mushrooming influenza epidemic was spreading through stateside training camps. Major General Enoch Crowder canceled plans that would have inducted 142,000 more draftees and shipped them off to Army bases and into the teeth of the deadly viral storm. Those soon-to-be soldiers got a reprieve until the epidemic could be assessed further in October.

On September 26, the medical staff at Camp Devens finally surrendered in the face of overwhelming biological forces. Unable to keep up with the tide of incoming cases, the Camp Devens medical team simply halted all new admissions to the base's hospitals.[12] At the start of the month, there had been twenty-five doctors at Camp Devens. Now there were 250, and still they could not keep up. Each nurse was responsible for forty to fifty patients; doctors cared for more than 150 men at a time. There was no way to provide real care. Infected men either lived or died, and there was little the medical professionals could do to affect the outcome either way. Men could die in their barracks as easily as on a hospital floor.

More than seventy-five men had succumbed the day before, and sixty more would die of influenza on this day.[13] The Red Cross sent a dozen more nurses. Eight would fall ill, and two of them would die.

"It is horrible," a Devens-based doctor wrote to a colleague.

One can stand it to see one, two or twenty men die, but to see these poor devils dropping like flies sort of gets on your nerves. We have been averaging about 100 deaths per day, and still keeping it up. There is no doubt in my mind that there is a new mixed infection here, but what I don't know. We have lost an outrageous number of nurses and doctors, and the little town of Ayer is a sight. It takes special trains to carry away the dead. For several days there were no coffins and the bodies piled up something fierce, we used to go down to the morgue (which is just back of my ward) and look at the boys laid out in long rows. It beats any sight they ever had in France after a battle. An extra long barracks has been vacated for the use of the morgue, and it would make any man sit up and take notice to walk down the long lines of dead soldiers all dressed up and laid out in double rows. We have no relief here; you get up in the morning at 5:30 and work steady till about 9:30 p. m., sleep, then go at it again. Some of the men of course have been here all the time, and they are tired.[14]

In the face of it all, some still failed to grasp the severity of the crisis. In Ayer, outside the gates of Camp Devens, a group of local merchants was furious at town officials for instituting a quarantine. Without the free flow of men in and out of the camp, who would they sell their goods to? They circulated a petition asking that military authorities at the War Department in Washington be given control of town government, saying the decision to keep soldiers out of the town "borders on the spreading of panic and giving aid and comfort to the enemy."[15] The chairman of the town's Board of Health was at a loss. "It simply shows the lure of the dollar is a very potent factor," he said.[16]

William Welch and Victor Vaughan traveled from Devens to Boston for a meeting with Mayor Andrew Peters. The civilian fight was not going any better than the military battle. The Massachusetts State Health Office appealed to the surgeon general for immediate aid, but few medical officers were available. Boston's health commissioner, Dr. William Woodward, continued to provide evidence that he was woefully unequipped to deal with the crisis. He blamed the day's rainy weather for a worsening of health conditions. In a joint order issued with the mayor, Woodward then reversed his earlier decisions and banned public gatherings through October 7. Either isolation brought on by rainy weather put people at greater risk, or socialization and exposure to others put them at risk. Woodward couldn't seem to decide. In another curious move, after meeting with the health commissioners of Quincy, Braintree, Hingham, and Weymouth, Woodward announced that he was suddenly suspicious the epidemic might be the result of "milk which is not up to standard." So he ordered that guards from the Fore River Shipbuilding Company's security department be stationed to watch over two milk stations. Were they somehow going to keep milk from spoiling? Or was Woodward fantasizing about a nefarious plot to poison the milk supply?

Acting Governor Calvin Coolidge sent a telegram to President Wilson and the governors of neighboring states seeking assistance. "Massachusetts urgently in need of additional doctors and nurses to check growing epidemic of influenza," Coolidge's wire read. "Our doctors and nurses are being thoroughly mobilized and worked to the limit. Many cases can receive no attention whatever. Hospitals are full, but arrangements can be made for outside facilities. Earnestly solicit your influence in obtaining for us this needed assurance in any way you can."[17] He reached out as far as the mayor of Toronto in requesting more nurses. The notoriously thrifty politician hinted at the desperation of the times when he even made sure to note that, "Massachusetts will, of course, bear all expenses."[18]

As Coolidge's pleas spread across the continent, 156 more people died of influenza and pneumonia on September 26 in Boston alone, the highest one-day death toll yet and a jump of 50 percent. Nearly 900 people had perished in Boston in less than two weeks. Two doctors and a nurse at City Hospital died on the same day. But it was the storm before the calm.

"It seemed as if all the city was dying," a nurse later recalled. "In the homes, serious illness. On the streets, funeral processions."[19]

Already, the string of funerals trudging toward New Calvary cemetery in the Boston suburb of Dorchester was nearly constant. Seven-year-old Francis Russell lived nearby and saw them pass his school on Walk Hill Street on their way down to the burial ground in Canterbury Hollow.

"There were not enough grave diggers, and coffins were beginning to pile up in the yard behind the disintegrating mansard-roofed house that served as a chapel," Russell recalled.

Finally, Pig Eye John Mulvey, who owned the land, set up a second hand circus tent next to the chapel, and the coffins were stacked inside. After the gravediggers had put up the tent most of them got drunk for several days, and still more coffins accumulated. The tent lay there, white and billowing, like some grotesque autumn carnival among the withered leaves, with the somber line of vehicles trailing through New Calvary gate. Even the undertakers fell behind. Sometimes we would see a touring car with the top down headed for New Calvary, an unboxed coffin stacked in the rear seat.[20]

Five miles down the road, in Quincy, unclaimed bodies were also piling up at the hospital on Chubbuck Street. The War Department managed to find twenty-nine nurses in Buffalo, New York, and they arrived in Quincy just as yet another local nurse died of influenza. At the massive Fore River shipyard, assistant general manager Joseph P. Kennedy—son-in-law of former Mayor John "Honey Fitz" Fitzgerald and father of young John F. Kennedy—sent a telegram to Congressman Richard Olney pleading for more doctors to care for his employees.

The shortage of doctors was severe. At the Boston Dispensary, where physicians were sent out on house calls, Dr. M. M. Davis was doing the best he could. "Yesterday we had 150 new calls, and today it has been the same," he said in frustration. "Out of a staff of eight doctors, we have but three available for work. The others are sick."[21] This in a city where visiting doctors were now the only hope, as every Boston hospital was refusing new influenza cases. There were no beds, no doctors, no nurses available to care for the cresting wave of the sick.

The epidemic was reaching into every aspect of life in Massachusetts. New England Telephone and Telegraph reported that 400 of its 8,000 operators, responsible for manually connecting every phone call in the state, were sick. Company officials asked the public to refrain from making all but the most urgent calls. With temperatures dipping into the fifties, and health officials stressing the importance of keeping the sick warm, the federal Fuel Administration urged people to burn wood for heat so coal could be preserved for the war effort.

Across the state, tragedy continued to devastate families. Joint funeral services were held for Julia and James Toomey at St. Benedict's in Somerville following her death on a Tuesday and her husband's on Wednesday. In Brockton, the Taulcelli family was hit even harder. The father and mother died two hours apart on Saturday, their fourteen-year-old son on Monday, and their four-year-old son on Thursday, while two more brothers remained gravely ill. In the north shore town of Gloucester, five members of an extended family perished: Charles Nolan, his two sisters, and two of their sons. In Boston, public funerals were banned.

In the midst of this plague, every effort was being made to keep the war's demand for shared sacrifice uppermost in the minds of the public. Plastered across the front page of the morning's *Boston Globe* on September 27, even as influenza claimed a new victim every ten minutes in the city, was a headline about the massive Liberty Bond drive set to kick off over the upcoming weekend. "Grippe Unable to Block Loan," it read, over a story that outlined how fundraising tactics would change in light of the city's new ban on public meetings.

Slowly, and far too late, the widespread factions of a bureaucratic government began to react to the health crisis. An 11:00 a.m. meeting was called at Boston City Hall on that Friday, where representatives of the Army, Navy, and twenty-five area hospitals met to coordinate responses.

In Ayer, the District Health officer estimated there were 1,500 influenza cases, in a town with a permanent population of 2,500, but also inexplicably reported "conditions very good for the control of the disease."[22] Still, unclaimed bodies of dead soldiers were being laid to rest in the town's cemetery.

Just outside the town, the influenza epidemic actually had reached its peak at Camp Devens with the deaths of eighty-one soldiers in a day, though no one yet knew it.[23] On September 28, only 240 new cases were admitted to camp hospitals, a decrease of 50 percent, coinciding with a doubling in the number of discharges. The number of infected men was starting to subside, if for no other reason than that the virus had used up all its available fuel. In less than four weeks, more than 10,000 influenza cases had been identified in the cantonment. Every soldier had already been exposed, troop movement was virtually non-existent, and there were simply no more available victims to be found. At this location, at least, the epidemic quickly began to burn itself out.

William Blake had been sick with influenza for less than 48 hours, but he was dying, and he knew it. Doctors at Brockton Hospital had told him as much on Friday. The thirty-three-year-old was engaged to Sophia Chillingworth who was, literally, the girl next door. He lived at 14 Waverly Street. She lived at 16 Waverly Street. When he got the news of his imminent demise, Blake asked hospital officials to help him with one thing. They managed to arrange with City Hall to waive the five-day waiting period following the issuance of a marriage license and, on Saturday afternoon, Reverend David Matthews, rector of St. Paul's Episcopal Church, presided over the wedding of Sophia and William in his hospital room.

Two hours later, he was dead.[24]

Health officials in Brockton estimated there were 8,000 cases in their city and another 4,000 in the towns just around it. The situation was even worse in Lynn, with an estimated 12,000 cases. In Boston, overwhelmed public health officials began grasping at straws in a desperate attempt to control the epidemic.[25] Woodward sent a letter to local undertakers banning wakes. He suggested that they enforce the order by refusing to supply chairs to grieving families, though he allowed that friends and relatives might still be permitted to privately call at the homes of families that had lost a loved one.

The Boston Health Department ordered that local restaurants and soda shops begin washing utensils and scalding them with boiling water after they were used by each customer. Many soda fountains were reportedly so flummoxed by such an elementary step toward good hygiene that they stopped serving drinks altogether rather than thoroughly wash every glass.

The Red Cross was producing 3,000 gauze masks per day and handing them out at locations around downtown Boston. A train with forty beds, plus a contingent of doctors and nurses, was sent to Quincy by the Public Health Service to supplement the thinly stretched local medical facilities. Lieutenant Stowe, the naval officer given command of the city's health services, noted that there were over 2,000 cases in a city with just five ambulances.

Dr. John Keegan published a report in the *Journal of the American Medical Association* on his efforts, under the direction of Dr. Milton Rosenau at the Chelsea Naval Hospital, to isolate, identify, and combat the influenza virus. It was a stark assessment. "The disease is similar to the familiar endemic influenza, except that it is often more severe, the complications are more frequent and serious, and it shows an extraordinary degree of contagiousness," Keegan wrote, abandoning the usually reserved language used in medical journals. "We, therefore, have every indication that this outbreak will soon spread all over the United States."[26] He predicted, based on what he had already seen in Boston, that 30 to 40 percent of the American population would ultimately become infected. On the day the report was published, another of Keegan's fellow Chelsea doctors died.

Fear was rampant and the government continued to fail the people. In Somerville, within view of Boston, four police officers refused—one after another—to drive the force's ambulance to transport flu victims to the hospital. Each said they were afraid they would bring the infection home to their own families. Finally, the dispatcher called the police chief, who came from home and did it himself. Governor Samuel McCall wired his private secretary from his vacation in Quebec, offering assurance that he would come back to the state, but only if it were believed that he was really needed. Then he headed for Halifax, Nova Scotia.

Often, information seemed to be in as short supply as hospital beds or gauze masks. One nurse recalled the case of a sick twenty-five-year-old woman with an eight-week-old infant. "Then came news that her husband was very ill at Camp Devens," she reported. "His relatives told me that a telegram had come telling of his death. Next day she died. I went in half an hour later and not one of his people wanted to take the baby. They wanted me to take it. I told them it was their duty to take it, and they must, which they finally did. About two weeks later, the husband returned in time to see them dividing his furniture among his relatives. Poor fellow came to find no wife, baby or home."[27]

Military officials were quick to deny other misinformation, however. Admiral Spencer Wood, commander of the First Naval District, saw the need to put down one story that was apparently making the rounds about Camp Devens. "There isn't a particle of truth," he announced, "in the rumors in circulation in all parts of the state concerning a French doctor inoculating soldiers at this cantonment and of his being caught after killing a number of men and being driven out of camp to a nearby field and filled full of bullets."[28]

The statistics published in the Sunday newspapers on September 29 told a chilling story. In the city of Boston, weekly deaths from influenza had risen over the last three weeks of September from 46 to 270 to 775.

Was it ignorance, misguided patriotism, or wishful thinking, then, that prompted the nonsensical announcement from state Health Commissioner Dr. Eugene Kelly? "No large communities report an alarming extension of the disease yesterday," he said, "and I believe that in Boston, which is by far the worst effected district, the epidemic has reached its peak." With the country's most eminent scientists working non-stop to isolate and identify the virus in a frantic search for treatment and cure, Kelly blamed deaths over the previous few days on the rain and predicted that fatality rates would come down over the next few days based on a better weather forecast.[29]

The stunning contrast between real scientists and those entrusted with public health was also evident in another pair of head-scratching statements from Woodward. He advised those seeking to avoid contracting influenza to "eat your meals regularly and slowly."[30] Displaying his total detachment from the reality around him, he grumbled, "I believe that because of the number of deaths some timid folks are becoming panicky."[31] What cause did people have to fear, Woodward apparently wondered, even as 144 people died in his city on Friday and 152 more perished on Saturday? "Unreasoning fear is overcoming judgment and the ordinary instincts of humanity. Panic or fear, either in the individual or in the mass, is unjustified by the situation."[32] His milk guards remained on duty, however.

A more realistic appraisal of the crisis appeared two pages further into the newspaper. Under a picture of an ornate coffin, an advertisement for undertaker W. H. Graham promoted a $75 funeral package and promised that "the collective strength of five large establishments in the big cities of New England is working night and day to give you this opportunity to save money when it is needed most."[33]

So ingrained was war fervor that many government officials could not see their way to separate even a crisis this grave from the omnipresent struggle to defeat the Germans. When Henry Endicott was chosen by Coolidge to chair the state's Emergency Public Health Committee, he could not help but elevate the war efforts above the rampant death. "I am certain that the people of Massachusetts will show the same courage in meeting this calamity at home as those splendid boys of ours are showing on the plains of France, where they are fighting with such wonderful results for the liberty of the world," he said. "This courage shown by each one of us in doing the work of the day to the best of our ability will be a real help toward that on which our hearts are set—the winning of the war. It is today equally our duty and our privilege, on the one hand, to do everything essential, and on the other, to avoid everything that is not essential."[34]

Whatever we do or don't do, he claimed, both must be in the service of war—epidemic or no epidemic.

Sunday was an eerily quiet day in Boston, which Oliver Wendell Holmes had once famously called "the hub of the solar system." Once again, driving for all but the most urgent needs was virtually banned on another Gasless Sunday designated to conserve fuel, so cars were nearly non-existent. At the government's strong urging, church services were curtailed, though every Catholic church held at least a short Mass and more Protestant churches than expected held services despite the admonitions. No other public gatherings were held, however, and even healthy people remained largely locked in their homes in fear of infection.

Sad stories seemed endless. A man died in a hotel in Boston's North End, but his signature on the guest register was unclear, so no one knew his name, where he was from, or how to contact whatever family he might have. On Beach Street, Wang Lee, a thirty-five-year-old laundryman, stepped into a doorway to make a delivery and dropped to the ground dead. Overall, 149 more people died in Boston in a day.

"Not a day has passed that the dead wagon hasn't gone by our house," said a woman living on Beacon Street near the foot of Corey Hill, site of the outdoor naval hospital. "Ambulances loaded with the sick are going up, the dead being brought down. It has been a sad sight for all of us living here."[35]

Boston's parochial schools were finally closed, with no classes scheduled for that Monday morning, September 30. Just under 1,000 deaths were reported in the city in the final week of the month, though the inconsistency of record keeping under the circumstances likely means that the toll was much higher. The Massachusetts state health commissioner wired the surgeon general that there were 85,000 people in the state currently suffering the effects of influenza.

More than 500 men had fallen fatally ill at Camp Devens during the month, but the camp's chief of staff, Colonel A. G. Lot, proudly claimed that "training of the division has not been retarded in any way." Except for the deaths. And the thousands of bedridden men. And the soldiers pulled out of combat training to act as apprentice embalmers.

For Health Commissioner William Woodward, the fifteenth time was apparently the charm. "The climax of the crisis has been reached," he announced yet again, "and if the mortality or the number of new cases appear greater tomorrow, it should be little or no cause for worry on the part of the public, who may attribute the increase—if it comes—to the aftermath of the wave which is to be expected in every epidemic."[36]

This time, he was right. As quickly as the epidemic wave had swelled, it now crested. Nearly every person in the Commonwealth of Massachusetts had been exposed to influenza. Many had fought off the infection with little consequence. Others had taken gravely ill but ultimately survived. Thousands had perished. Now, there was almost no one left for the Spanish flu to kill.

As if on cue, Governor Samuel McCall returned from his Canadian vacation and went almost immediately to inspect the facilities on Corey Hill.

The intertwined fates of the military and civilian epidemics at Camp Devens and in Boston struck home with the Olson family of East Cambridge. As the death toll began to subside at the cantonment and reached its peak in the state as a whole, Robert Olson, who worked for the Independent Ice Co., died of influenza at his home on Fourth Street. Later that same night, his brother, Private Olaf Olson, died of influenza as well, in the hospital at Camp Devens. The two were mourned at a double funeral service with the Reverend C. O. Swanson of the local Swedish Congregational Church presiding.

The last day of September was sunny and warm, a classic New England Indian Summer day, and the clear signs that the epidemic was running its course were finally evident. Hospitals in Boston, Brockton, and Lynn all reported a decrease in the number of cases. At Camp Devens, as 118 soldiers checked in to the hospital, 248 men were released.

As September 1918 came to a close, for the first time in weeks, there were reasons to be hopeful.

EPILOGUE

On October 1, the Woman Suffrage amendment passed in the Senate by a 62–34 vote. Maud Wood Park and her allies had won, but not by enough. They were two votes short of the two-thirds majority needed. Two days later, Park attended a meeting at the White House between the movement's leadership and the president. "I do not deserve your gratitude," Wilson told them. "When my conversion to this idea came, it came with an overwhelming command that made it necessary I should omit nothing and use the position I occupied to enforce it, if I could possibly do so. History will deal very candidly with the circumstances in which the head of a government asked the kind of support that I asked the other day and did not get it."[1]

As it turned out, the suffrage vote was a forerunner of things to come. After the war, Wilson would once again appeal directly for a cause in which he deeply believed—a League of Nations to rebind Europe and the world in the aftermath of the conflict—only to suffer a bitter defeat at the hands of Henry Cabot Lodge.

Deeply disappointed but undaunted, the suffragists chose their next battle the day after the vote. Convinced they would not change any current senator's mind, they decided they would just find themselves new senators. They chose one Democrat, from Delaware, and one Republican, John Weeks of Massachusetts, and began planning a massive campaign against each for the election just over a month away. In the Bay State, they formed the Non-Partisan Suffrage Committee with the aim of electing Weeks's opponent and a suffrage supporter, David Walsh. The committee was chaired by Blanche Ames, the granddaughter of one Republican governor and the daughter-in-law of another, so as to emphasize that this was a moral, not a party, issue.

The whirlwind campaign was impressive, even by today's standards. They prepared flyers outlining Weeks's stand on thirteen issues, not just suffrage, and mailed them to every Republican and Progressive voter in the state. They also sent it to 35,000 suffrage-supporting women, urging them "as a woman denied political self-expression at the ballot box, to get at least one vote through a voter in your family or among your friends, against Weeks."[2] They conducted specific campaigns targeting Catholic and Jewish women and traveled across the state speaking to trade union women from the sideboard of automobiles.

It worked. Both targeted senators were defeated. In the next session of Congress, the Nineteenth Amendment to the United States Constitution was passed and American women were finally guaranteed the right to vote.

Also on October 1, Dr. William Welch was unable to attend ceremonies in which he was installed as the first dean of the Johns Hopkins School of Hygiene and Public Health. As it turned out, Welch had actually contracted influenza during his brief but disturbing visit to Camp Devens the week before. He ended up bedridden for three weeks, and away from work in seclusion for six weeks, before finally recovering.

On October 2, *Boston Globe* sportswriter Ed Martin, who had reported on all the details of the Red Sox World Series victory, lost his wife Delia to influenza. The two had gone on vacation following the baseball season, and she fell ill. He cared for her until he became infected as well. He died, at age thirty-four, the day after she did.

A week later, the folks at home in Massachusetts read in their news-papers the first details of the critical role the Yankee Division had played in the victory at St. Mihiel. The men of the Twenty-Sixth would see sporadic action before the war ended, but they would not return to the United States and sail into Boston Harbor until the early part of 1919. On October 27, Calvin Coolidge and John Weeks were among the speak-ers at a memorial service for Lieutenant David Putnam, America's young "Ace of Aces," at Newton Highlands Congregational Church.

The influenza epidemic spread to Philadelphia, where the death toll was even higher than in Boston, and then across the entire country. Some cities, like New York, learned from early mistakes in Boston. Others did not. In Baltimore, the city health commissioner told the local newspaper that "drastic measures only excite people, throw them into a nervous state and lower their resistance to disease."[3] In Chicago, the health com-missioner echoed those sentiments. "It is our duty to keep the people from fear," he said. "Worry kills more people than the epidemic. For my part, let them wear a rabbit's foot on a watch-chain if they want it and it will help them get rid of the physiological action of fear."[4]

It was all eerily reminiscent of the nonsensical pronouncements that had so often been issued by Dr. William Woodward in Boston.

American scientists and medical researchers continued to pursue prevention measures, to little avail. "It encircled the world, visited the remotest corners, taking toll of the most robust, sparing neither soldier nor civilian, and flaunting its red flag in the face of science," Dr. Vincent Vaughan wrote of the pandemic.[5] In the end, somewhere between 50 and 100 million people worldwide died—likely a low estimate given the patchy record keeping across the globe. Almost one in four Americans were infected, and nearly 700,000 people died in the United States. By comparison, that is the proportional equivalent of more than two million American deaths today.

Despite careful planning and remarkable foresight, men who under-stood disease were unable to prevent it and helpless to stop it once it began to devour the population. The devastation humbled the country's foremost medical authorities. "We entered the outbreak with a notion that we knew the cause of the disease, and were quite sure we knew how it was transmitted from person to person," Dr. Milton Rosenau of Chelsea Naval Hospital said later. "Perhaps, if we learned anything, it is that we are not quite sure what we know about this disease."[6]

"We are inclined to boast that the age of pestilence has passed," noted Vaughan. "I dare say the world has never before known a pestilence more widespread, more intensive and appalling in its progress or more destructive to life, than the epidemic of influenza."[7] Later in life, he often spoke of his visit to Camp Devens as a turning point in his view of medicine. "The saddest part of my life was when I witnessed the hundreds of deaths of the soldiers in the army camp and did not know what to do. At that moment I decided never again to prate about the great achievements of medical science and to humbly admit our dense ignorance."[8]

As one doctor put it, "the epidemic seemed to care little for authorities. [It] showed no respect for its human opponents, spread in spite of all methods used to prevent it, increased in spite of all the precautions undertaken and the means employed to combat it, and declined seemingly without any regard to measures used against it."[9]

Before Massachusetts could fully come to grips with what had happened, an armistice was reached, and the war ended on November 11. The euphoria that followed somehow masked the deep tragedy that had peaked just weeks earlier.

"By November the influenza had passed, and in the turbulence of the war's ending it tended to be forgotten quickly," wrote Francis Russell, whose school-aged memories remained vivid when he recounted them more than four decades later. "So many had died since 1914; but it was over now, all the killing and the dying, and better to start again and put death out of mind. For all its deaths the influenza did not last long enough to stamp itself permanently on the popular imagination. And in any case, like the war, it was part of the past. The present was what mattered."[10]

ACKNOWLEDGMENTS

Writing a book, I always imagined, was a solitary endeavor.

I was wrong.

Sure, I wrote most of this book on commuter trains and airplanes and in hotel rooms, away from everyone I know. If you sat next to someone in an aisle seat who spent the entire flight nose-down in a laptop, that might have been me. I'd apologize for not engaging with you, but the reality is that even if I wasn't writing, I likely would have given you a short response signaling to "leave me alone." I'm not what you'd call a social traveler.

While writing this book I came to realize that the process is so much more than typing. You'd think I'd have figured that out before I began. Nevertheless, thanks are in order.

I first had the germ of an idea for this book after reading Dennis Lehane's novel, *The Given Day*. Lehane is a Boston guy and someone whose writing I greatly admire and respect from afar. His story is set in Boston in 1919 and features Babe Ruth of the Red Sox. I was taken by the mental image he painted of Ruth, not as a stove-bellied, pigeon-toed character in sped-up, grainy newsreels, but as a vibrant, athletic hero coming into his prime. I connected the story to that of my own family in that time, when the great aunts and uncles I grew up with were New England teenagers whose father, family lore has it, died of the Spanish flu. The more I looked into the period, the more I discovered the amazing string of events that took place in Boston over the course of a single month, and *September 1918* began to take form.

It would have remained just an idea if my agent, John Rudolph of Dystel, Goderich and Bourret, hadn't first agreed that the idea could be turned into a compelling book, and then completely torn my initial effort apart and forced me to rebuild it. Happily, he was completely right. More happily, Alex Novak of Regnery History thought so too and agreed to publish the book.

At the risk of sounding self-serving, I could not have done the research required for a book like this without the miraculous technology developed by my employer, Google. It astounds me—even from inside the machine, as it were—that all of us have ready access to all of mankind's knowledge and can reach it with a few taps on a keyboard or swipes on a phone screen. I used the Google search engine continuously during this process, and Google Books gave me the ability to see inside books and publications long out of print without having to criss-cross the country visiting libraries. That eliminated a barrier I could not otherwise have overcome. Humans helped in the research too, and I'm grateful to lots of librarians, particularly the helpful professionals at the Boston Public Library and the Trinity College Library in Hartford.

I've been blessed to have amazing writers around me in my life. My brother, the historian Tom Desjardin, is the foremost expert on Maine's Civil War hero, Joshua Chamberlain, and the real author in the family. My dear friend from Notre Dame, Frank LaGrotta, was an early influence on my writing style, and he is still the person I'd most like to write like. My son, Michael, is the most innately talented writer I know, with a unique voice and a gift for dialogue. I'm certain he'll surpass the rest of us if that's what he decides he wants. He understands me in ways no one else does and, for some reason, still seems to like me a bit—for which I am continually thankful.

My family made me what I am today, in countless ways. My daughter, Aimee, is a revelation to me: an artist and a dreamer in the best sense of the word, full of empathy and big plans. She makes me proud in many ways but never more than in the joy she takes at touching the lives of others. My parents, Ron and Fern Desjardin, sacrificed and struggled but always encouraged me, enabled me, and loved me. I miss them both and wish they were here to share this. My sister Beth showed me where life's priorities really should lie—in the quiet dignity of doing good regardless of cost.

Then there is Karen Smith, who came later to my life but changed it in ways wondrous and fundamental. This book would not exist without her. I never would have started it, never would have dared believe I could make it happen. Except for her, I would have given it up at several points along the way—I've thought about it, and she was right. She amazes me, understands me, makes me laugh, and inspires me to be a better person tomorrow than I am today. For that, I owe a debt I will try to repay for a lifetime. Hold my hand and see the world with me.

NOTES

Prologue

1. Stephen Vaughn, *Holding Fast the Inner Lines: Democracy, Nationalism and the Committee on Public Information* (Chapel Hill: University of North Carolina Press, 1980), 4.
2. Eugene L. Fisk, "Military Medicine & Surgery," *Journal of the American Medical Association* 70, no. 1 (February 2, 1918): 302.
3. David M. Kennedy, *Over Here: The First World War and American Society* (New York: Oxford University Press, 1980), 46.
4. Thomas Gregory, *Annual Report of the Attorney General of the United States* (Washington, DC: Government Printing Office, 1918), 21.
5. *Official U.S. Bulletin* 1, no. 30 (June 14, 1917), 1.
6. Vaughn, *Holding Fast the Inner Lines*, 4.
7. George Creel, *How We Advertised America* (New York: Harper & Brothers, 1920), 5.
8. Ibid., 7.
9. Ibid., 3.
10. "America's War Craze," *New York Times*, August 19, 1918.

Chapter 1

1. Michael T. Lynch, *Harry Frazee, Ban Johnson and the Feud That Nearly Killed the American League* (Jefferson, NC: McFarland & Co., 2008), 42.

2.   Sean Deveney, *The Original Curse:* Did the Cubs Throw the 1918 World
        Series to Babe Ruth's Red Sox and Incite the Black Sox Scandal? (New
        York: McGraw Hill, 2010), 29.
3.   "Cubs And Red Sox Scattering Money," *New York Times*, January 6,
        1918.
4.   Lynch, *Harry Frazee, Ban Johnson and the Feud That Nearly Killed the
        American League*, 49.
5.   "May Yet Be Engineers," *Washington Post*, July 3, 1918, p. 5.
6.   Leigh Montville, *Big Bam: The Life and Times of Babe Ruth* (New York:
        Broadway Books, 2006), 74.
7.   Ibid., 69.
8.   Paul J. Zingg, *Harry Hooper: An American Baseball Life* (Urbana, IL:
        University of Illinois Press, 2004), 161.
9.   Montville, *Big Bam*, 73.
10.   Daniel R. Levitt, *Ed Barrow: The Bulldog Who Built the Yankees' First
        Dynasty* (Lincoln, NE: University of Nebraska Press, 2008), 137.
11.   Ibid., 133.
12.   Ibid., 134.
13.   Ibid., 134.
14.   "Boston To Clash With Chicago For The First Time Ever," *Boston Sunday
        Advertiser*, September 1, 1918, p. 6B.
15.   Arthur Duffey, "Sport Comment," *Boston Post*, August 8, 1918.
16.   Edward F. Martin, "Red Sox Finish by Dividing with Yanks," *Boston
        Globe*, September 3, 1918.
17.   Burt Whitman, "Red Sox Will Begin By Leading Their Ace," *Boston
        Herald*, September 2, 1918, p. 6.
18.   "Sox and Cubs Fit for World Series," *New York Times*, September 4,
        1918.
19.   Eddie Hurley, "Red Sox Banking On Ability Of Babe Ruth To Come
        Through," *Boston Evening Record*, September 4, 1918, p. 8.
20.   Ty Waterman and Mel Springer, *The Year the Red Sox Won the Series: A
        Chronicle of the 1918 Championship Season* (Boston: Northeastern
        University Press, 1999), 214.
21.   Burt Whitman, "World Series Starts Today," *Boston Herald*, September 4,
        1918, p. 1.
22.   Hugh Fullerton, "Fullerton Had Dope On Bush," *Boston American*,
        September 7, 1918, p. 10.

Chapter 2

1.   "Few N. E. Names in the List," *Boston Post*, September 2, 1918.
2.   Michael E. Shay, *The Yankee Division in the First World War: The Highest
        Tradition* (College Station, TX: Texas A&M University Press, 2008), 143.
3.   Frank P. Sibley, *With the Yankee Division in France* (Boston: Little, Brown,
        and Co., 1919), 251.
4.   Connell Albertine, *The Yankee Doughboy* (Boston: Branden Press, 1968),
        178.

5. Russell G. Carter, The 101st Field Artillery, A. E. F., 1917–1919 (Boston: Houghton Mifflin, 1940), 190.
6. Albertine, *The Yankee Doughboy*, 178.
7. Harvey Cushing, *From a Surgeon's Journal, 1915–1918* (Boston: Little, Brown, and Co., 1936), 435.
8. Shay, *The Yankee Division in the First World War*, 146.
9. Ibid., 147.
10. "Doughnuts at the Front," *Boston Post*, September 4, 1918.
11. Albertine, *The Yankee Doughboy*, 179.
12. Eddie V. Rickenbacker, *Fighting the Flying Circus: The Greatest True Air Adventure to Come Out of World War I* (Garden City, NY: Doubleday & Co., 1965), 245.
13. "American 'Ace of Aces' Dies in Battle," *El Paso Herald*, September 19, 1918, p. 1.
14. James Norman Hall and Charles B. Nordhoff, eds., *The Lafayette Flying Corps*, vol. 2 (Boston: Houghton Mifflin, 1920), 11.
15. Ibid., 52.
16. Ibid., 397.
17. Ibid., 253–54.
18. Caroline Ticknor, *New England Aviators 1914–1918: Their Portraits and Their Records* (Boston: Houghton Mifflin, 1920), 5.
19. Ibid., 4.

Chapter 3

1. "All America in War to Win," *Boston Post*, September 2, 1918.
2. "Patriotism in Labor Parade," *Boston Post*, September 3, 1918.
3. "'Win War is Labor's Message,'" *Boston Post*, September 2, 1918.
4. John M. Barry, *The Great Influenza: The Epic Story of the Deadliest Plague in History* (New York: Penguin Books, 2005), 186.
5. William J. Robinson, *Forging the Sword: The Story of Camp Devens, New England's Army Cantonment* (Concord, NH: The Rumford Press, 1920), 9.
6. Karl G. Baker, "Dr. Rosenau of Harvard Tells of His Battle with the Grip Germ," *Boston Sunday Post*, February 9, 1919.
7. "Col. Gorgas Called to Africa to Fight Grippe Plague," *New York Times*, October 26, 1913.
8. Nancy K. Bristow, *American Pandemic: The Lost Worlds of the 1918 Influenza Epidemic* (New York: Oxford University Press, 2012), 33.
9. Baker, "Dr. Rosenau of Harvard Tells of His Battle with the Grip Germ."
10. Edwin O. Jordan, *Epidemic Influenza: A Survey*, American Medical Association, 1927, 101.
11. Alfred W. Crosby, *America's Forgotten Pandemic* (Cambridge: Cambridge University Press, 1989), 40.
12. "Draftees from Bay State Reach Camp," *Boston Daily Globe*, September 4, 1918.

Chapter 4

1.   John A. Garraty, *Henry Cabot Lodge: A Biography* (New York: Alfred A. Knopf, 1968), 295.
2.   Henry Cabot Lodge, *War Addresses, 1915–1917* (Boston: Houghton Mifflin, 1917), 39.
3.   Garraty, *Henry Cabot Lodge*, 326.
4.   "Gillett Raps Administration," *Boston Herald*, September 22, 1918, p. 6.
5.   Karl Schriftgiesser, *The Gentleman from Massachusetts: Henry Cabot Lodge* (Boston: Little, Brown & Co., 1944), 275.
6.   "Speeches Naming Eleven Candidates," *New York Times*, June 10, 1916.
7.   Garraty, *Henry Cabot Lodge*, 325.
8.   Ibid.
9.   Ibid., 333.
10. David Kennedy, *Over Here: The First World War and American Society* (New York: Oxford University Press, 1980), 233.
11. Schriftgiesser, *The Gentleman from Massachusetts*, 270.
12. George Creel, *How We Advertised America* (New York: Harper & Brothers, 1920), 59.
13. Schriftgiesser, *The Gentleman from Massachusetts*, 295.
14. "Lodge Demands A Dictated Peace Won By Victory," *New York Times*, August 24, 1918, p. 5.
15. HCL to John T. Morse, Jr., September 11, 1918, Papers of Henry Cabot Lodge, Massachusetts Historical Society Archives.
16. Charles G. Washburn, *The Life of John W. Weeks* (Boston: Houghton Mifflin, 1928), 213–15.
17. HCL to George Bacon, September 9, 1918, MSHA
18. George Bacon to HCL, September 16, 1918, MSHA
19. HCL to George Bacon, September 18, 1918, MSHA
20. Oliver M. Gale, *Americanism: Woodrow Wilson's Speeches on the War—Why He Made Them and What They Have Done* (Chicago: Baldwin Syndicate, 1918), 129.
21. "Lodge Backs Wilson," *Washington Post*, September 18, 1918.

Chapter 5

1.   William A. Cook, *August "Garry" Herrmann, A Baseball Biography* (Jefferson, NC: McFarland & Co., 2008), 65.
2.   Ibid.
3.   "Boston To Clash With Chicago For The First Time Ever," *Boston Sunday Advertiser & American*, September 1, 1918, p. 6B.
4.   Ty Waterman and Mel Springer, *The Year the Red Sox Won the Series: A Chronicle of the 1918 Championship Season* (Boston: Northeastern University Press, 1999), 219.
5.   "Statement of Manager Barrow of Red Sox," *Boston Post*, September 4, 1918.
6.   *Boston Herald*, September 4, 1918, p. 4.

7. "4 Killed, 75 Hurt in Chicago Bomb Outrage," *Boston Globe*, September 5, 1918.

8. "Cool Wave Grips Ball Park Today," *New Castle News*, September 5, 1918, p. 16.

9. Gene Fowler, *Skyline: A Reporter's Reminiscence of the 1920s* (New York: Macfadden Publications, 1962), 108.

10. Fowler, *Skyline*, 109.

11. "Statement of Manager Mitchell of Cubs," *Boston Post*, September 4, 1918.

12. "Mail Aviator Flying to Chicago in Accident," *Boston Post*, September 6, 1918.

13. Fred Lieb, *The Boston Red Sox* (New York: G.P. Putnam's Sons, 1947), 167.

14. "First Blood for Red Sox," *Boston Post*, September 6, 1918.

15. "Mitch's Statement Boosts Babe Ruth," *Boston Post*, September 6, 1918.

16. Edward F. Martin, "Vacant Seats and Lack of Cheers Show War's Effects," *Boston Globe*, September 6, 1918.

17. "One Run Gives Red Sox First Game of Series," *New York Times*, September 6, 1918.

18. Edward F. Martin, "Hooper, the Reliable, and Ruth, the Fence Breaker, Big Assets," *Boston Globe*, September 3, 1918.

19. Burt Whitman, "Red Sox Will Begin By Leading Their Ace," *Boston Herald*, September 2, 1918, p. 6.

20. Charley Dryden, "Wagner and Knabe Enliven Game By Coming To Blows," *Boston American*, September 7, 1918, p. 10.

21. Waterman and Springer, *The Year the Red Sox Won the Series*, 235–56.

22. Charley Dryden, "Wagner and Knabe Enliven Game By Coming To Blows," *Boston American*, September 7, 1918, p. 10.

23. Waterman and Springer, *The Year the Red Sox Won the Series*, 228.

24. "Red Sox And Cubs Play Final Game At Chicago Today," *Boston Evening Record*, September 7, 1918, p. 6.

25. "'Cubs Had Bulk of Breaks,' Says Barrow," *Boston Post*, September 7, 1918.

26. Edward F. Martin, "Tyler Stops Sox Despite Late Rally," *Boston Globe*, September 7, 1918.

27. Edward F. Martin, "Red Sox' Big Fourth Undoing of Vaughn," *Boston Sunday Globe*, September 8, 1918.

28. "Barrow Prediction Runs True to Form," *Boston Sunday Post*, September 8, 1918.

29. Edward F. Martin, "Ruth-Tyler Likely in Game Here Today," *Boston Globe*, September 9, 1918.

30. Daniel R. Levitt, *Ed Barrow: The Bulldog Who Built the Yankees' First Dynasty* (Lincoln, NE: University of Nebraska Press, 2008), 141.

31. "Boston To Clash With Chicago For The First Time Ever," *Boston Sunday Advertiser & American*, September 1, 1918, p. 6B.

32. Martin, "Ruth-Tyler Likely in Game Here Today."

Chapter 6

1.   Francis Russell, "A Journal of the Plague: The 1918 Influenza," *The Yale Review* 47 (December 1957): 222.
2.   *Pacific Coast Gazette* XIII, no. 8 (August 1918): p. 12.
3.   "Drive For Peach Stones Wins Support," *Boston American*, September 7, 1918, p. 5.
4.   "Peach Stones Pour In," *Boston Post*, September 5, 1918.
5.   Russell, "A Journal of the Plague," 222.
6.   "Thousands at Radio School Dedication," *Cambridge Tribune*, September 14, 1918, p. 5.
7.   *American Journal of Public Health*, November 1917, p. 931.
8.   Rexmond C. Cochrane, *The National Academy of Sciences: The First Hundred Years, 1863–1963* (Washington, DC: National Academies Press, 1978).
9.   Dorothy Ann Petit and Janice Bailie, *A Cruel Wind: Pandemic Flu in America, 1918–1920* (Murfreesboro, TN: Timberlane Books, 2008), 85.
10. J. J. Keegan, "The Prevailing Pandemic of Influenza," *Journal of the American Medical Association* vol. 71 (September 28, 1918): p. 1051.
11. "Fear Influenza Outbreak Among Sailors May Spread," *Boston Daily Globe*, September 6, 1918.
12. John M. Barry, *The Great Influenza: The Epic Story of the Deadliest Plague in History* (New York: Penguin Books, 2005), 186.
13. "Warns Public of Grip Epidemic," *Boston Herald*, September 6, 1918, p. 7.
14. Barry, *The Great Influenza*, 192.

Chapter 7

1.   Nick Flatley, "Pick Mays To Stop Cubs," *Boston American*, September 7, 1918, p. 1.
2.   Edward F. Martin, "Ruth-Tyler Likely in Game Here Today," *Boston Globe*, September 9, 1918.
3.   Babe Ruth and Bob Considine, *The Babe Ruth Story* (New York: Penguin, 1976), 57.
4.   Allan Wood, *Babe Ruth and the 1918 Red Sox* (Lincoln, NE: iUniverse, 2000), 302.
5.   "Heroes from France Enjoy Sox' Victory," *Boston Globe*, September 10, 1918.
6.   Edward F. Martin, "Wonderful Support When Babe Wobbles," *Boston Globe*, September 10, 1918.
7.   Ruth and Considine, *The Babe Ruth Story*, 58.
8.   Burt Whitman, "Red Sox Win Fourth Game in World Series," *Boston Herald*, September 10, 1918, p. 1.
9.   Wood, *Babe Ruth and the 1918 Red Sox*, 313.
10. Daniel E. Ginsburg, *The Fix Is In: A History of Baseball Gambling and Game Fixing Scandals* (Jefferson, NC: McFarland & Co., 1995), 85.

11. Michael T. Lynch, *Harry Frazee, Ban Johnson and the Feud That Nearly Killed the American League* (Jefferson, NC: McFarland & Co., 2008), 47.

12. Francis Eaton, "Under the Sport Tree," *Boston Sunday Advertiser & American*, September 1, 1918, p. 7.

13. Martin, "Wonderful Support When Babe Wobbles."

14. Wood, *Babe Ruth and the 1918 Red Sox*, 313.

15. Ruth and Considine, *The Babe Ruth Story*, 58.

16. "Barrow Will Top Off With Jones," *Boston Post*, September 10, 1918.

17. "Cubs Threaten to Call Off Series," *Boston Post*, September 10, 1918.

18. "Bullseyes Punctured at Devens," *Boston Post*, September 10, 1918.

19. Ty Waterman and Mel Springer, *The Year the Red Sox Won the Series: A Chronicle of the 1918 Championship Season* (Boston: Northeastern University Press, 1999), 246.

20. Nick Flatley, "Pick Mays To Stop Cubs," *Boston American*, September 7, 1918, p. 1.

21. Wood, *Babe Ruth and the 1918 Red Sox*, 318.

22. Ibid., 319.

23. Daniel R. Levitt, *Ed Barrow: The Bulldog Who Built the Yankees' First Dynasty* (Lincoln, NE: University of Nebraska Press, 2008), 142.

24. "Ball Stars Clash Over Coin," *Boston American*, September 9, 1918, p. 10.

25. Wood, *Babe Ruth and the 1918 Red Sox*, 320.

26. Ibid.

27. Fred Lieb, *The Boston Red Sox* (New York: G. P. Putnam's Sons, 1947), 173.

28. Wood, *Babe Ruth and the 1918 Red Sox*, 323.

29. Ibid., 324.

30. Ibid., 325.

31. Ibid., 326.

32. Levitt, *Ed Barrow*, 142.

33. *Boston American*, September 11, 1918, p. 10

34. Wood, *Babe Ruth and the 1918 Red Sox*, 331.

35. Ibid., 321.

36. Levitt, *Ed Barrow*, 143.

37. Wood, *Babe Ruth and the 1918 Red Sox*, 340.

38. "Red Sox Beat Cubs 2 to 1 and Put World's Series of 1918 to Their Credit," *New York Times*, September 12, 1918.

39. Edward F. Martin, "Red Sox Win Sixth Game and the Title," *Boston Globe*, September 12, 1918.

40. Ibid.

41. "Red Sox Beat Cubs 2 to 1 and Put World's Series of 1918 to Their Credit."

42. Nick Flatley, "Strike! Strike! Strike!" *Boston American*, September 11, 1918, p. 10.

43. Martin, "Red Sox Win Sixth Game and the Title."

44. Burt Whitman, "Red Sox Sound Baseball Taps By Beating Cubs," *Boston Herald*, September 12, 1918, p. 1.

45. Martin, "Red Sox Win Sixth Game and the Title."

46.   Ibid.

Chapter 8

1.   Connell Albertine, *The Yankee Doughboy* (Boston: Branden Press, 1968), 179.
2.   Edward S. Sirois and William McGinnis, *Smashing through "The World War"* (Salem, MA: The Meek Press, 1919), 100.
3.   Frank P. Sibley, *With the Yankee Division in France* (Boston: Little, Brown, and Co., 1919), 261.
4.   Ibid.
5.   "To Aid 101ˢᵗ Auxiliary," *Boston Globe*, September 6, 1918.
6.   "Bushels of Money for 101ˢᵗ Regiment," *Boston Globe*, September 8, 1918.
7.   Bert Ford, *The Fighting Yankees Overseas* (Boston: Atlantic Printing Co., 1919), 91–92.
8.   Michael E. Shay, *The Yankee Division in the First World War: The Highest Tradition* (College Station, TX: Texas A&M University Press, 2008), 147.
9.   Ford, *The Fighting Yankees Overseas*, 91.
10.   Sibley, *With the Yankee Division in France*, 262.
11.   Sirois and McGinnis, *Smashing through "The World War,"* 100.
12.   Charles Merrill Mount, *John Singer Sargent: A Biography* (New York: W. W. Norton & Co., 1955), 360.
13.   Ibid.
14.   Stanley Olson, *John Singer Sargent: His Portrait* (New York: St. Martin's Press, 1986), 260.
15.   Sibley, *With the Yankee Division in France*, 264.
16.   Albertine, *The Yankee Doughboy*, 180.
17.   John J. Pershing, *My Experiences in the World War*, vol. 2 (New York: Frederick A. Stokes Co., 1931), 267.
18.   Sibley, *With the Yankee Division in France*, 265.
19.   Don Martin, "Yankees Reached All Objectives," *New York Herald*, September 13, 1918.
20.   Sirois and McGinnis, *Smashing through "The World War,"* 101–2.
21.   Albertine, *The Yankee Doughboy*, 180.
22.   David Bonk, *St. Mihiel 1918: The American Expeditionary Forces' Trial by Fire* (Long Island City, NY: Osprey, 2011), 41.
23.   Sibley, *With the Yankee Division in France*, 265.
24.   Sirois and McGinnis, *Smashing through "The World War,"* 103.
25.   Shay, *The Yankee Division in the First World War*, 149.
26.   Sirois, and McGinnis, *Smashing through "The World War,"* 102.
27.   Charles Coulter, "Was in Big Drive: Captain Charles Coulter Tells of Capture of St. Mihiel Salient," *Concord Enterprise*, October 30, 1918.
28.   Sibley, *With the Yankee Division in France*, 267.
29.   Albertine, *The Yankee Doughboy*, 181.
30.   "Found Women Machine Gunners," *Boston Sunday Globe*, October 27, 1918.
31.   Ford, *The Fighting Yankees Overseas*, 91.

32. Sibley, *With the Yankee Division in France*, 268.
33. Albertine, *The Yankee Doughboy*, 210–11.
34. Sibley, *With the Yankee Division in France*, 269–70.
35. Albertine, *The Yankee Doughboy*, 183.
36. Eddie V. Rickenbacker, *Fighting the Flying Circus: The Greatest True Air Adventure to Come Out of World War I* (Garden City, NY: Doubleday & Co., 1965), 238.
37. Lowell, A. Lawrence. *New England Aviators 1914–1918: Their Portraits and Their Records* (Boston: Houghton Mifflin Company, 1920), 6.
38. Pershing, *My Experiences in the World War*, vol. 2, 269.
39. David Woodward, *The American Army and the First World War* (Cambridge: Cambridge University Press, 2014), 316.
40. Shay, *The Yankee Division in the First World War*, 151.
41. Pershing, *My Experiences in the World War*, vol. 2, 266.
42. Sirois, and McGinnis, *Smashing through "The World War,"* 104.
43. Sibley, *With the Yankee Division in France*, 274–75.
44. Sirois, and McGinnis, *Smashing through "The World War,"* 105.
45. Pershing, *My Experiences in the World War*, vol. 2, 272–73

Chapter 9

1. William C. Gorgas, "Battle On Ills Stars At Camp," *Boston Sunday Advertiser & American*, September 8, 1918, p. B1.
2. *Providence Journal*, September 9, 1918, quoted in John M. Barry, *The Great Influenza: The Story of the Deadliest Pandemic in History*, p. 310.
3. "Dr. Woodward on Problems of Health Board," *Boston Sunday Post*, August 4, 1918.
4. Lavinia L. Dock, et al., *History of American Red Cross Nursing* (New York: The Macmillan Co., 1922), 969.
5. "Roads Expected to be Autoless Today," *Boston Globe*, September 8, 1918.
6. "Senate Accepts Sedition Bill," *New York Times*, May 5, 1918.
7. *Providence Journal*, September 9, 1918, quoted in John M. Barry, *The Great Influenza: The Story of the Deadliest Pandemic in History*, p. 310.
8. "Brookline Gets 200 Sick Sailors," *Boston Globe*, September 10, 1918.
9. "Influenza On Increase Here," *Boston Herald*, September 11, 1918, p. 14.
10. "Trying to Prevent Spread of Grippe," *Boston Globe*, September 11, 1918.
11. "Influenza On Increase Here," *Boston Herald*, September 11, 1918, p. 14.
12. "2 Spanish Grip Deaths Here; Many Cases," *Boston American*, September 10, 1918, p. 1.
13. "Influenza On Increase Here," *Boston Herald*, September 11, 1918, p. 14.
14. "Must Keep from Boston," *Boston Post*, September 10, 1918.
15. Lynette Iezzoni, *Influenza 1918* (New York: TV Books, 1999), 47.
16. "Edgar Reports Grip Causes 6 Deaths," *Boston American*, September 11, 1918, p. 3.
17. "Navy Surgeon Victim of Grippe Epidemic," *Boston Globe*, September 13, 1918.

18. "Grippe Abating at Naval Stations," *Boston Globe*, September 14, 1918.
19. "Deaths," *Boston Globe*, September 13, 1918.
20. "Edward H. Winslow Dead," *Boston Globe*, September 14, 1918.
21. "Surg Gen Blue Tells How to Treat Disease," *Boston Globe*, September 14, 1918.
22. "20 Die In Day From Influenza," *Boston Herald*, September 17, 1918, p. 10.
23. William J. Robinson, "McCain Proud of His 12ᵗʰ Division," *Boston Globe*, September 15, 1918.
24. Victor C. Vaughan, *A Doctor's Memories* (Indianapolis: Bobbs Merrill, 1926), 424.
25. N. R. Grist, letter to "Burt," September 29, 1918, archives of the Department of Epidemiology, University of Michigan.
26. "2000 Men at Devens Have Grip," *Boston Sunday Post*, September 15, 1918.
27. "Sees No Cause for Alarm," *Boston Globe*, September 14, 1918.
28. "Simply Grippe, Rear Admiral Wood Says," *Boston Sunday Globe*, September 15, 1918.
29. Francis Russell, "A Journal of the Plague: The 1918 Influenza," *The Yale Review* 47 (December 1957), 223.
30. Kelley Colihan, "Witness to 1918 Flu: 'Death Was There All the Time,'" CNN.com (November 2, 2005), http://www.cnn.com/2005/HEALTH/ conditions/10/07/1918.flu.witness/.
31. Edward R. Ellis, *Echoes of Distant Thunder: Life in the United States, 1914–1918* (New York: Kodansha International, 1996), 463.
32. "Avoid Spanish Grippe," *Boston Sunday Post*, September 15, 1918.
33. Ellis, *Echoes of Distant Thunder*, 464
34. *Four Minute Men Bulletin*, no. 21, as quoted in Vaughn, *A Doctor's Memories*, 126.
35. "No Influenza Scare," *Lowell Sun*, September 16, 1918.
36. "2000 Men at Devens Have Grip."
37. Edwin O. Jordan, *Epidemic Influenza: A Survey* (Chicago: American Medical Association, 1927), 101.
38. Carol R. Byerly, *Fever of War: The Influenza Epidemic in the U.S. Army During World War I* (New York: New York University Press, 2005), 86.
39. Ibid., 74.
40. "Two Thousand Men Ill With grip At Camp Devens," *Boston Sunday Advertiser & American*, September 15, 1918, p. 3.
41. Richard S. Kennedy, *Dreams in the Mirror: A Biography of E. E. Cummings* (New York: Liveright Publishing, 1980), 137.
42. Ibid., 146.
43. Ibid., 170.
44. Ibid., 171.
45. Ibid., 176.
46. Thomas F. Phelan, "Camp Hospital Quarantined For Grip," *Boston American*, September 17, 1918, p. 5.

47. *Boston American*, September 14, 1918, p. 3.
48. *Hotline* newsletter, Massachusetts General Hospital, January 18, 2013.
49. *Boston Evening Record*, September 16, 1918, p. 5.

Chapter 10
1.   "American Drive a Great Victory; German Front in Lorraine Crushed,"
     Boston Globe, September 13, 1918.
2.   Fred J. Wilson, "Yankees Take 'First Step On The Road To Berlin,'"
     Boston American, September 12, 1918, p. 8.
3.   Russell, "A Journal of the Plague: The 1918 Influenza," *The Yale Review*
     47 (December 1957): 225.
4.   George Creel, *How We Advertised America* (New York: Harper &
     Brothers, 1920), 5.
5.   "Public Is Asked to Get Facts," *Boston Sunday Post*, August 25, 1918.
6.   Creel, *How We Advertised America*, 94.
7.   Roger Babson, *Action and Reactions: An Autobiography* (New York:
     Harper, 1950), 178.
8.   James R. Mock and Cedric Larson, *Words that Won the War: The Story of
     the Committee on Public Information 1917–1919* (New York: Russell &
     Russell, 1939), 192.
9.   Babson, *Action and Reactions*, 78–79.
10. "Smith & Wesson Plant Taken Over," *Boston Globe*, September 14, 1918.
11. David Kennedy, *Over Here: The First World War and American Society*
     (New York: Oxford University Press, 1980), 72.
12. Ibid., 72.
13. Creel, *How We Advertised America*, 133–34.
14. Edward L. Bernays, *Public Relations* (Norman, OK: University of
     Oklahoma Press, 1980), 78.
15. Alfred B. Cornebise, *War as Advertised: The Four Minute Men and
     America's Crusade, 1917–1918* (Philadelphia: American Philosophical
     Society, 1984), 115.
16. "Board to Control Building in State," *Boston Globe*, September 14, 1918.
17. John A. Garraty, *Henry Cabot Lodge: A Biography* (New York: Alfred A.
     Knopf, 1968), 341.
18. William C. Widenor, *Henry Cabot Lodge and the Search for an American
     Foreign Policy* (Berkeley, CA: University of California Press, 1980), 208.
19. Garraty, *Henry Cabot Lodge*, 312.
20. "Eighteen to Forty-Five," *New York Times*, September 15, 1918.
21. Edward F. Martin, "Each Sox Regular Receives $1108.35," *Boston Globe*,
     September 13, 1918.
22. Allan Wood, *Babe Ruth and the 1918 Red Sox* (Lincoln, NE: iUniverse,
     2000), 343.
23. "Attacks Congressional Record of J. F. Fitzgerald," *Boston Globe*,
     September 5, 1918.
24. "Curley Spy Suspect, Gallivan Charges," *Boston Globe*, September 5,
     1918.

25. "Curley Declares Gallivan a Liar," *Boston Globe*, September 6, 1918.
26. "Opens G.O.P. Campaign," *Washington Post*, September 22, 1918.
27. "Orgy of U.S. Printing," *Washington Post*, September 15, 1918.
28. "Lieut. Putnam Has Downed 26 Planes," *Boston American*, September 18, 1918, p. 6.
29. "Football Knockout by War Department," *Boston Globe*, September 13, 1918.
30. *Students' Army Training Corps Regulations* (Washington, D.C.: Government Printing Office, 1918).
31. "Football Season Opens This Week," *New York Times*, September 22, 1918.
32. "Draw Line on College Athletics," *Boston Post*, September 15, 1918.
33. "Notre Dame Football—1918," *Notre Dame Scholastic* 52, no. 4 (January 11, 1919): 154.
34. "Football Season Opens This Week," *New York Times*, September 22, 1918.
35. Jack Cavanaugh, *The Gipper: George Gipp, Knute Rockne and the Dramatic Rise of Notre Dame Football* (New York: Skyhorse Publishing, 2010), 74.
36. Ibid., 75.
37. "Notre Dame Football—1918," *Notre Dame Scholastic*, 153.
38. "Baseball Up to Baker," *Boston Globe*, September 27, 1918.
39. "Lock Up Red Sox Ball Yard," *Boston Sunday Post*, September 15, 1918.
40. "Send Dr. Muck Back, Roosevelt Advises," *New York Times*, November 3, 1917.
41. "Dr. Muck Resigns, Then Plays Anthem," *New York Times*, November 3, 1917.
42. "Dr. Muck Bitter at Sailing," *New York Times*, August 22, 1919.

Chapter 11

1. "Many More Women Must Enter Industries," *Boston Globe*, September 5, 1918.
2. Jacqueline Van Voris, *Carrie Chapman Catt: A Public Life* (New York: The Feminist Press, 1987), 135.
3. "Republican Party Platform of 1916," June 7, 1916, Political Party Platforms, The American Presidency Project, http://www.presidency.ucsb.edu/ws/?pid=29634 (accessed April 24, 2017).
4. Maud Wood Park, *Front Door Lobby* (Boston: Beacon Press, 1960), 13.
5. "Plank on Woman Suffrage Adopted," *Boston Globe*, June 9, 1916.
6. Park, *Front Door Lobby*, 39.
7. Elizabeth Cady Stanton, *History of Woman Suffrage: 1900–1920*, vol. 5 (New York: J. J. Little & Ives Co., 1922), 639.
8. Woman's Rights Collection, Mary Garrett Hay Series, Schlesinger Library, Radcliffe College (Women's Studies Manuscript Collection microfilm, part B: New York, reel 1, frame 454).
9. Stanton, *History of Woman Suffrage*, vol. 5, 564

10. "Women Will Never Read Boston Meters 'The Lord Forbid!'" *Boston Evening Record*, September 5, 1918, p. 1.
11. Ray Stannard Baker, *Woodrow Wilson: Life and Letters*, vol. 8 (New York: Doubleday, Doran & Co., 1939), 404.
12. "Suffragists Burn President's Words," *New York Times*, September 17, 1918.

Chapter 12

1. *Boston Medical & Surgical Journal* 179 (Boston: Cupples, Upham & Co.), 463.
2. John Van R. Hoff and Louis A. LaGarde, "Editorial," *The Military Surgeon: Journal of the Association of Military Surgeons of the United States* 43 (August 1918): 208.
3. William J. Robinson, "Devens Excited by Spanish Influenza," *Boston Globe*, September 18, 1918.
4. "Influenza Causes 70 New England Deaths," *Lewiston Daily Sun*, September 18, 1918, p. 1.
5. Thomas F. Phelan, "3,500 Influenza Cases At Camp; Two Deaths," *Boston American*, September 17, 1918, p. 1.
6. *Cambridge Chronicle*, September 14, 1918, p. 2.
7. Marian Moser Jones, "The American Red Cross and Local Response to the 1918 Influenza Pandemic: A Four-City Case Study," *Public Health Reports* 125, no. 3 (2010): p. 95.
8. "14 New Deaths Are Laid To Influenza," *Boston American*, September 16, 1918, p. 1.
9. "Vigorous Action to Stamp Out Grippe," *Boston Globe*, September 18, 1918.
10. "Much Better Situation Reported In 1st Naval District," *Boston American*, September 19, 1918, p. 3.
11. "Alien Teacher's Pay Is Ordered Stopped," *Boston Globe*, September 18, 1918.
12. "Schools May Cut German," *Boston Sunday Post*, June 9, 1918.
13. Charles E. Folsom, "McCain rebukes Boston Lawyer," *Boston Herald*, September 16, 1918, p. 8.
14. "Grippe Making Great Headway," *Boston Globe*, September 17, 1918.
15. John M. Barry, *The Great Influenza: The Epic Story of the Deadliest Plague in History* (New York: Penguin Books, 2005), 203.
16. Nancy K. Bristow, *American Pandemic: The Lost Worlds of the 1918 Influenza Epidemic* (New York: Oxford University Press, 2012), 67.
17. Gertrude Farmer and Janet Schoenfeld, "Epidemic Work at the Boston City Hospital," *The Boston Medical and Surgical Journal* 180 (May 29, 1919): p. 608.
18. *Boston American*, September 20, 1918, p. 1.
19. "Worry Will Not Help," *Boston Globe*, September 19, 1918.
20. "Woodward Resigns as Health Officer," *Washington Post*, July 2, 1918.

21. "Wants Boston Schools Closed," *Boston Evening Globe*, September 20, 1918.
22. Barry, *The Great Influenza*, 303.
23. Ibid., 336.
24. Ibid., 343.
25. Patricia J. Fanning, *Influenza and Inequality: One Town's Tragic Response to the Great Epidemic of 1918* (Amherst, MA: University of Massachusetts Press, 2010), 73.
26. Edward R. Ellis, *Echoes of Distant Thunder: Life in the United States, 1914–1918* (New York: Kodansha International, 1996), 468.
27. Bristow, *American Pandemic*, 67.
28. Fanning, *Influenza and Inequality*, 74.
29. Ibid., 82.
30. Miss Coolidge, "Personal Experiences During the Epidemic," Simmons College.
31. Barry, *The Great Influenza*, 240.
32. Lynette Iezzoni, *Influenza 1918* (New York: TV Books, 1999), 51.
33. Fanning, *Influenza and Inequality*, 79.
34. Ibid., 78.
35. "Influenza Found in Several Cities," *Boston Globe*, September 14, 1918.
36. William J. Robinson, "Ayers Quarantined Against Influenza," *Boston Globe*, September 20, 1918.
37. "Doctors Declare Grippe Is On Wane," *Boston Globe*, September 20, 1918.
38. "Believe Influenza Has Passed The High Point," *Boston Herald*, September 21, 1918, p. 4.
39. "Three Deaths in One Newton Family," *Boston Globe*, September 20, 1918.
40. "Epidemic Of Grip Is Spreading Rapidly," *Boston Herald*, September 20, 1918, p. 4.
41. "Naturalized at Camp Devens," *Boston Globe*, September 21, 1918.
42. "Believe Influenza Has Passed The High Point," *Boston Herald*, September 21, 1918, p. 4.
43. "New England Honor Roll in France Now Exceeds 6000," *Boston Globe*, September 20, 1918.
44. "20 Deaths at Camp Devens—No Quarantine," *Boston Globe*, September 22, 1918.
45. "City's Death Toll Reduced To 63 Sunday," *Boston Herald*, September 23, 1918, p. 1.
46. Miss Donahue, "Personal Experiences During the Epidemic," Simmons College.
47. Barry, *Influenza and Inequality*, 311.
48. "Death Rate for Boston Takes Rise," *Boston Post*, September 22, 1918.
49. "Influenza Is On the Wane," *Boston Post*, September 21, 1918.
50. "Ban at Quincy on Public Funerals," *Boston Globe*, September 24, 1918.
51. "Influenza Toll in Boston for Day 87," *Boston Globe*, September 24, 1918.

52. Ibid.

Chapter 13

1. "Governor Acts on Grippe Situation," *Boston Globe*, September 25, 1918.
2. Calvin Coolidge, *The Autobiography of Calvin Coolidge* (New York: Cosmopolitan Book Corporation, 1929), 121.
3. Ibid., 121.
4. Calvin Coolidge, *Your Son, Calvin Coolidge* (Montpelier: Vermont Historical Society, 1968), 139.
5. Claude M. Fuess, *Calvin Coolidge: The Man from Vermont* (Boston: Little, Brown and Co., 1940), 166.
6. HCL to George Bacon, September 6, 1918, MSHA
7. Robert Sobel, *Coolidge: An American Enigma* (Washington, DC: Regnery Publishing, 1998), 114.
8. Coolidge, *Your Son, Calvin Coolidge*, 141.
9. Fuess, *Calvin Coolidge*, 170
10. "Essex Republicans Gather at Suntaug," *Boston Sunday Globe*, September 15, 1918.
11. "Boston Victims of Grippe," *Boston Globe*, September 24, 1918.
12. "17 More Dead Of Grip Yesterday," *Boston Herald*, September 19, 1918, p. 3.

Chapter 14

1. Victor C. Vaughan, *A Doctor's Memories: An Autobiography by Victor Clarence Vaughan* (Indianapolis: Bobbs Merrill, 1926), 402.
2. Ibid.
3. Jim Duffy, "The Blue Death," *John Hopkins Public Health* (Fall 2004).
4. John M. Barry, *The Great Influenza: The Epic Story of the Deadliest Plague in History* (New York: Penguin Books, 2005), 189.
5. Mary T. Sarnecky, *A History of the U.S. Army Nurse Corps* (Philadelphia: University of Pennsylvania Press, 1999), 120–21.
6. William J. Robinson, *Forging the Sword: The Story of Camp Devens, New England's Army Cantonment* (Concord, NH: The Rumford Press, 1920), 171.
7. Ibid., 133.
8. Rufus I. Cole, *The Etiology and Presentation of Influenza*, The Practitioners' Society of New York lecture, February 1, 1946, Rufus Cole Papers [B/C671]. American Philosophical Society
9. Lynette Iezzoni, *Influenza 1918* (New York: TV Books, 1999), 48.
10. Barry, *The Great Influenza*, 189.
11. Edward R. Ellis, *Echoes of Distant Thunder: Life in the United States, 1914–1918* (New York: Kodansha International, 1996), 472.
12. Robinson, *Forging the Sword*, 131.
13. Barry, *The Great Influenza*, 190.

14.   Rufus I. Cole, "The Etiology and Presentation of Influenza," The
      Practitioners' Society of New York lecture, February 1, 1946, *Rufus Cole
      Papers* B/C671 (American Philosophical Society).
15.   Barry, *The Great Influenza*, 190.
16.   Ibid.
17.   Cole, "The Etiology and Presentation of Influenza."
18.   Richard Collier, *The Plague of the Spanish Lady: The Influenza Pandemic
      of 1918–1919* (London: Allison & Busby, 1974), 266.
19.   Dorothy Ann Pettit and Janice Bailie, *A Cruel Wind: Pandemic Flu in
      America, 1918–1920* (Murfreesboro, TN: Timberlane Books, 2008), 88.
20.   Carol R. Byerly, *Fever of War: The Influenza Epidemic in the U.S. Army
      During World War I* (New York: New York University Press, 2005), 75.
21.   Carol R. Byerly, "The U.S. Military and the Influenza Pandemic of 1918–
      1919," Public Health Report 125, Supplement 3 (2010).
22.   Peyton C. March, *The Nation at War* (Garden City, NJ: Doubleday, Doran
      & Co., 1932), 360.
23.   "Camps Have 20,211 Cases of Influenza," *Boston Globe*, September 24,
      1918.
24.   "Famed Doctors Work At Devens," *Boston Herald*, September 24, 1918, p.
      7.
25.   William J. Robinson, "Grippe Falls Off at Camp Devens," *Boston Globe*,
      September 24, 1918.

Chapter 15

1.   "David Putnam Killed In Air," *Boston Herald*, September 20, 1918, p. 9.
2.   "David Putnam Killed In Air," *Boston Herald*, September 20, 1918, p. 9.
3.   Burt Whitman, "Dave' Putnam A Synonym For All That Is Epic and
      Brave," *Boston Herald*, September 20, 1918, p. 4.
4.   Edward S. Sirois and William McGinnis, *Smashing through "the World
      War"* (Salem, MA: The Meek Press, 1919), 106.
5.   Frank P. Sibley, *With the Yankee Division in France* (Boston: Little, Brown,
      and Co., 1919), 269.
6.   Bert Ford, *The Fighting Yankees Overseas* (Boston: Atlantic Printing Co.,
      1919), 90.
7.   Sirois and McGinnis, *Smashing through "the World War,"* 109.
8.   Ibid.
9.   Sibley, *With the Yankee Division in France*, 285.
10.   Ibid., 286.
11.   Sirois and McGinnis, *Smashing through "the World War,"* 110.
12.   M. C. Liekind, "Stanhope Bayne-Jones," *Bulletin of New York Academy
      of Medicine* (April 1972): p. 588.
13.   Michael E. Shay, *The Yankee Division in the First World War: The Highest
      Tradition* (College Station, TX: Texas A&M University Press, 2008), 171.
14.   Ibid., 245–47.
15.   Frank P. Sibley, "Bitterest Fight Yankee Division Has Had Yet," *Boston
      Sunday Globe*, October 20, 1918.

16. United States Army, *Being A Narrative of Battery A of the 101ˢᵗ Field Artillery* (Boston: Loomis & Co., 1919), 170.

17. Emerson G. Taylor, *New England in France 1917–1919: A History of the Twenty-Sixth Division U.S.A.* (Boston: Houghton Mifflin, 1920), 237.

18. Sibley, *With the Yankee Division in France*, 297.

19. United States Army, *Being A Narrative of Battery A of the 101ˢᵗ Field Artillery*, 170–71.

20. Major L. Vernon Briggs, *The New England Medical Gazette* 53, no. 1 (January 1918): p. 5–6.

21. Rexmond C. Cochrane, *The 26ᵗʰ Division East of the Meuse* (Army Chemical Center, MD: Army Chemical Corps Historical Office, 1960), 1.

22. Ibid., 42.

23. Connell Albertine, *The Yankee Doughboy* (Boston: Branden Press, 1968), 58–59.

24. Briggs, *The New England Medical Gazette*, 6.

25. Cochrane, *The 26ᵗʰ Division East of the Meuse*, 5.

26. Ibid., 20.

27. Charles Merrill Mount, *John Singer Sargent: A Biography* (New York: W. W. Norton & Co., 1955), 360.

28. Ibid., 361.

Chapter 16

1. John A. Garraty, *Henry Cabot Lodge: A Biography* (New York: Alfred A. Knopf, 1968), 341.

2. Oliver M. Gale, *Americanism: Woodrow Wilson's Speeches on the War— Why He Made Them and What They Have Done* (Chicago: Baldwin Syndicate, 1918), 130–33.

3. Garraty, *Henry Cabot Lodge: A Biography*, 341–42.

4. "Asks for $1,000,000," *Boston Post*, September 28, 1918.

5. Carol R. Byerly, "The U.S. Military and the Influenza Pandemic of 1918– 1919," *Public Health Report* 125, supplement 3 (2010): p. 80.

6. Lynette Iezzoni, *Influenza 1918* (New York: TV Books, 1999), 101.

7. "Suffragist Defeat in Senate Averted," *New York Times*, September 28, 1918.

8. Iezzoni, *Influenza 1918*, 101.

9. Ray Stannard Baker, *Woodrow Wilson: Life and Letters*, vol. 6 (New York: Doubleday, Doran & Co., 1939), 412.

10. Ibid., 413.

11. "Women Deluge Senate For Vote," *Boston Sunday Advertiser*, September 22, 1918, p.III-W-1.

12. Mrs. Charles Sumner Bird, "A Protest," *Boston Post*, September 25, 1918.

13. "Is Woman Suffrage Pro-German?" pamphlet issued by the Massachusetts Public Interests League of Anti-Suffragists (September 16, 1918).

14. "Women Deluge Senate For Vote," *Boston Sunday Advertiser*, September 22, 1918, p. III-W-1.

15.   Anne Biller Clark, "My dear Mrs. Ames: a study of the life of suffragist
      cartoonist and birth control reformer Blanche Ames Ames, 1878-1969"
      (1996), Doctoral Dissertations 1896–February 2014, Paper 1228, p. 167.
16.   Maud Wood Park, *Front Door Lobby* (Boston: Beacon Press, 1960), 193.
17.   Ibid., 202.
18.   Ibid., 195–96
19.   "Suffragist Defeat in Senate Averted," *New York Times*, September 28,
      1918.
20.   Park, *Front Door Lobby*, 206.
21.   Van Voris, Jacqueline. "Carrie Chapman Cott: A Public Life." New York:
      The Feminist Press, 1987, p. 151.
22.   Baker, *Woodrow Wilson: Life and Letters*, 434.
23.   Park, *Front Door Lobby*, 207.
24.   Ibid., 209.
25.   Baker, *Woodrow Wilson: Life and Letters*, 436.
26.   Woodrow Wilson, "Address of the President of the United States; Delivered
      in the Senate of the United States, September 30, 1918," U.S. Government
      Printing Office, 1918.
27.   Ida Husted Harper, ed., *History of Woman Suffrage*, vol. 5 (New York: J.
      J. Little & Ives Co., 1922), 640.
28.   Park, *Front Door Lobby*, 210.
29.   Ibid., 210.
30.   National American Woman Suffrage Association, *Victory: How Women
      Won It: A Centennial Symposium, 1840–1940* (New York: H. W. Wilson,
      1940), 136.
31.   Park, *Front Door Lobby*, 210–11.

Chapter 17

1.   John M. Barry, *The Great Influenza: The Epic Story of the Deadliest Plague
      in History* (New York: Penguin Books, 2005), 191.
2.   "New Serum May Give Influenza A Knockout," *Boston American*,
      September 26, 1918, p. 4.
3.   "State-Wide Call to Stop All Gatherings," *Boston Globe*, September 26,
      1918.
4.   Wendell Endicott, *Henry B. Endicott: A Brief Memoir of his Life and his
      Services to the State and Nation* (Boston: Privately printed, 1921), 33–34.
5.   "Three Deaths in Malden," *Boston Globe*, September 25, 1918.
6.   "Appeal for Autos for Use of Nurses," *Boston Globe*, September 25, 1918.
7.   "Woodward Urges Open Cars To Halt Grip," *Boston American*,
      September 25, 1918, p. 4.
8.   Francis Russell, "A Journal of the Plague: The 1918 Influenza," *The Yale
      Review* 47 (December 1957): p. 224.
9.   Ibid., 222.
10.   Connell Albertine, *The Yankee Doughboy* (Boston: Branden Press, 1968),
      193.

11. Carol R. Byerly, *Fever of War: The Influenza Epidemic in the U.S. Army During World War I* (New York: New York University Press, 2005), 104.
12. Barry, *The Great Influenza*, 187.
13. William J., Robinson, *Forging the Sword: The Story of Camp Devens, New England's Army Cantonment* (Concord, NH: The Rumford Press, 1920), 131.
14. N. R. Grist, "Pandemic Influenza 1918," *British Medical Journal* 2, no. 6205 (December 22, 1979): pp. 1632–33.
15. "Ask Army To Take Over Ayer," *Boston Herald*, September 26, 1918, p. 3.
16. Thomas F. Phelan, "Open Hospital For Visitors At Ayer," *Boston American*, September 28, 1918, p. 6.
17. "Public Gatherings Barred Until Oct 7," *Boston Globe*, September 27, 1918.
18. Ibid.
19. Miss Franklin, *Personal Experiences During the Epidemic*, Simmons College.
20. Russell, "A Journal of the Plague," 225.
21. "Need Big Force Of Nurses," *Boston American*, September 27, 1918, p. 10.
22. "Improvement in Grip Epidemic Looked For," *Boston Sunday Post*, September 29, 1918.
23. Robinson, *Forging the Sword*, 131.
24. "Is Married on His Deathbed," *Boston Sunday Post*, September 29, 1918.
25. "No Wakes to Be Held During Grip Epidemic," *Boston Sunday Post*, September 29, 1918.
26. J. J. Keegan, "The Prevailing Pandemic of Influenza," *Journal of the American Medical Association* 71 (September 28, 1918): p. 1051.
27. Miss Murray, *Personal Experiences During the Epidemic*, Simmons College.
28. Thomas F. Phelan, "'Nail 'Doctor' Yarn About Ayer Canp," *Boston Sunday Advertiser*, September 29, 1918, p. B-5.
29. "Improvement in Grip Epidemic Looked for," *Boston Sunday Post*.
30. William C. Woodward, "What to Do When Grip Case Is Discovered," *Boston Sunday Post*, September 29, 1918.
31. "Influenza Deaths in Boston Fewer," *Boston Globe*, September 28, 1918.
32. "Grip Epidemic Appears To Be On The Wane Here," *Boston Herald*, September 29, 1918, p. 5.
33. W. H. Graham Undertaker, "Advertisement," *Boston Post*, September 29, 1918.
34. Henry B. Endicott, "Patience and Courage Urged by Endicott," *Boston Globe*, September 28, 1918.
35. Ethel Armes, "Heroic Girls of Vincent Club Rener Valuable Aid In Epidemic," *Boston Herald*, September 30, 1918, p. 7.
36. "Worst Stage of Epidemic Over," *Boston Herald*, October 1, 1918, p. 5.

EPILOGUE

1.   Ray Stannard Baker, *Woodrow Wilson: Life and Letters*, vol. 8 (New York: Doubleday, Doran & Co., 1939), 446.

2.   Maud Wood Park, *Front Door Lobby* (Boston: Beacon Press, 1960), 215.

3.   Jim Duffy, "The Blue Death," *Johns Hopkins Public Health* (Fall 2004).

4.   George M. Price, "Influenza—Destroyer and Teacher," *The Survey* XLI, no. 12 (December 21, 1918): p. 368.

5.   Victor C. Vaughan, *A Doctor's Memories: An Autobiography by Victor Clarence Vaughan* (Indianapolis: Bobbs Merrill, 1926), 432.

6.   Milton J. Rosenau, "Experiments to Determine Mode of Spread of Influenza," *Journal of the American Medical Association* 73, no. 5 (1919), 311.

7.   Carol R. Byerly, "The U.S. Military and the Influenza Pandemic of 1918–1919," *Public Health Report* 125, Supplement 3 (2010): p. 69.

8.   Price, "Influenza—Destroyer and Teacher," 367.

9.   Ibid., 368.

10.   Francis Russell, "A Journal of the Plague: The 1918 Influenza," *The Yale Review* 47 (December 1957): p. 229.

INDEX

A

Abbott, George, 182
Albany, NY, 162
Amherst College, 189, 224
Anthony, Susan B., 162
Appalachian Mountains, 150
Associated Press, 178
Avery, Oswald, 205

B

Babson, Roger, 141–44, 146
Baker, Newton, 5, 9, 142, 146
Baltimore, MD, 6–8, 13, 47,
    157–58, 255

Barrow, Ed, 1, 4, 6–9, 11–12,
    46–47, 51–53, 55, 57–58, 60,
    75, 77, 80, 87, 89, 92
Baruch, Bernard, 162
Battle of Bunker Hill, 21
Battle of Chateau-Thierry, 16
Battle of St. Mihiel, 95–114, 211
Bearss, Hiram, 112
Benet, Christie, 227
Berlin, Germany, 140, 158
Bethlehem Steel, 157–58
Black Death, 125
Blake, William, 247
Boston American, 56, 73, 81, 91

Boston Globe, 11, 17, 53, 58, 76, 91, 96, 121, 123, 148, 175, 208–9, 214, 240, 246, 254

Boston Herald, 12, 196, 208

Boston Herald & Journal, 121

Boston Post, 11, 15, 80–81, 88, 98, 123, 157, 187, 228

Boston Record, 13, 46, 58

Boston Sunday Advertiser, 10

Bower, Jean Stewart, 179

Braisted, William C., 67

Bulgaria, 231

Bunker Hill, 194

Bush, Joe, 3, 51, 55–56, 58, 89

C

Cambridge Chronicle, 172

Canada, 192

Cape Cod, 149

Capitol Hill, 229, 231

Capone, Al, 12

Catolina, Francisco, 197

Catt, Carrie Chapman, 169, 231–32, 235

Charles River, 67, 172, 191

Charleston, SC, 121

Chicago, IL, 2–3, 8, 10–13, 38, 45–57, 59–61, 71, 73, 77–78, 80–81, 83, 87–89, 93, 147, 163, 255

Chicago Herald & Examiner, 89

Chicago Journal, 50

Chicago Tribune, 56

Chillingworth, Sophia, 247

Clexton, Mary, 98

Columbia University, 212

Comiskey Park, 12, 45–46, 49, 51, 53–54, 59

Commonwealth Pier, 28, 30, 32, 69–70, 121–22, 136, 196

Concord, MA, 183

Cone, Sarah, 182

Coolidge, Calvin, 164, 189–97, 224, 238, 244, 250, 255

Cornell University, 150

Creel, George, xiii, 19, 40, 46, 73, 81, 140–43, 146, 158–59, 195, 224

Croix de Guerre, 111

Crowder, Enoch, 5, 9, 29, 134, 146, 242

Cummings, E. E., 131–36

D

Damrosch, Walter, 159–60

Devine, William, 123, 173

Distinguished Service Cross, 111, 216

Doane, Philip, 178

Dourhauer, Caroline, 174

E

Edgar, John, 120, 147, 174, 184, 186

Edwards, Clarence, 95, 99, 112, 208–9, 213–15

Endicott, Henry, 145, 238–39, 250

Espionage Act, 47, 118

Experience, 81

F

Flagg, James Montgomery, 144

Florence, Italy, 100–1

Foch, Ferdinand, 16–17, 210

Ford Motor Company, 117

Fore River, 5, 28, 183, 186, 245

Four Minute Men, xiii, 129, 140–42

Frazee, Harry, 2–4, 6–7, 9, 60–61, 78, 81, 85, 88, 92, 147, 151, 156

Frothingham, Channing, 130

G

Galleani, Luigi, 48

Gardner, Augustus Peabody, 41, 100

Gardner, Isabella Stewart, 100

General Motors, 143

Georgetown University, 116

Georgia, 41, 160

Gillett, Frederick, 37, 149, 224–25

Gipp, George, 154–56

Girl Scouts, 179

Gloucester, MA, 4, 100, 173, 246

Gompers, Samuel, 28, 143

Gorgas, William, 31, 69, 115, 212–13, 237

Green Bay, WI, 154, 156

Greenfield, MA, 129

Greenwood, Levi, 164

Gregory, Thomas, xii

H

Hale, Edward Everett, 134

Harper, Jess, 153

Hartford, CT, 157, 258

Harvard Medical School, 18, 171, 238

Harvard University, 22, 30, 35, 67, 120, 131–33, 150–51, 162

Heydler, John, 49, 54, 75, 81, 85

Hicks, Frederick, 166

Higginson, George, xiv, 105

Higginson, Henry, 158–59

Hines, Paul, 210–11, 216

Hitchcock, John, 70–71, 120–21

Holmes, Oliver Wendell, 250

Hooper, Harry, 6–7, 11, 59, 61, 63, 74–75, 81–88, 148

Hughes, Charles Evans, 39

I

Illinois, 166

Indian Packing Company, 156

J

Johnson, Ban, 2, 74, 78, 84
Journal of the American Medical Association, 248

K

Kansas, 119
Keegan, John, 31–33, 69–70, 205, 248
Kelley, Eugene, 188–89
Kennedy, David, xii
Kennedy, John F., 245
Key, Francis Scott, 53
Knabe, Otto, 56
Knights of Columbus, 238
Knute Rockne, All American, 156

L

Lambeau, Curly, 154–56
Landis, Kenesaw Mountain, 48
Laurium, MI, 154
Lawrence, MA, 48, 95, 99, 103, 128, 209, 211
Lebanon, PA, 157
Legion d'Honneur, 111
Lieb, Fred, 52, 84
Linton, Frederick, 112, 215–16
Lodge, Henry Cabot, 35–44, 100, 145, 149, 164–65, 168, 192, 224–28, 230, 235
London, England, 28, 101, 221

Long Island, NY, 237
Lowell Sun, 130, 240

M

Mann, James, 166
March, Peyton, 177
Mass, 127, 183, 196, 250
Maynard, MA, 105
McAdoo, William, 231
McAuliffe, John, 174
McCain, Henry P., 29, 65, 123–25, 130, 174–75, 184–85, 205, 238
McCall, Samuel, 75, 77, 91, 175, 177, 189–92, 194, 196, 248, 252
McConnell, Joseph, 98, 106–8, 209
McCornack, Condon C., 125, 129–30, 136, 172, 184, 201, 238
McLaughlin, Allan, 238
McQueen, John, 131
Meagher, Patrick, 183
Metz, France, 212
Meuse River, 16, 21
Mexico, 98
Michigan, 150, 154, 168
Milford, MA, 136, 182–83
Military Surgeon, 172
Mississippi, 167, 230
Missouri, 230, 232

Mitchell, Fred, 13, 51, 53, 57–60

Moran, Pat, 50

Moselle River, 21

Muck, Karl, 158–60

Murphy, John, 129

Murray, Stephen, 196

Murray, William F., 186

N

National Football League, 156

Naval Radio School, 67, 126, 172

New Orleans, LA, 212

New York Herald, 103

New York Times, xiv, 3, 12, 31,
    54, 90–91, 142, 146, 152, 155

Newton, MA, 21–22, 110, 183,
    208, 255

Nord, France, 23

Northampton, MA, 190

Norwood, MA, 178–79

Notre Dame Scholastic, 154

O

O'Bryan, Grace, 240

O'Connell, William, 116

O'Connor, Michael, 107–8, 209

O'Rourke, Simon, 183

Ohio, 163

Oklahoma, 228

Olney, Richard, 245

Oman, Joseph, 121

Owen, Robert, 228

P

Paris, France, 100, 132–33, 135

Park, Maud Wood, 162, 226,
    230, 235, 253

Patton, George, 102

Peters, Andrew, 28, 116, 196–97,
    239, 243

Plymouth Notch, VT, 189

Price, Norman, 23

Providence Journal, 159

Providence, RI, 157, 159

Putnam, David, 21–25, 110–11,
    150, 207–8, 255

Putnam, Israel, 21

Putnam, Janet, 207

Q

Quincy, MA, 28, 122, 157, 183,
    186, 188, 244–45, 248

R

Rabaud, Henri, 158

Radcliffe College, 162

Reagan, Ronald, 156

Red Cross, 19, 66, 76, 116–17,
    173, 179, 189, 210, 238, 242,
    247

Reed, James, 230

Revolutionary War, 21, 97, 194

Rhode Island, 121, 157, 159

Rockefeller Institute of Medical
    Research, 67

Rockne, Knute, 153–56

Roosevelt, Theodore, 36–40, 145, 159, 164, 166, 190, 224–25

Rosenau, Milton, 30–33, 69–70, 121, 128, 205, 248, 256

Royal Rooters, 2, 76

Runyon, Damon, 46

Rupert, Jacob, 6

Russell, Francis, 65–66, 126, 140, 199–200, 241, 244, 256

Russia, 143, 175

S

Salem, MA, 173, 194

Sargent, John Singer, 99–101, 220–21

Saturday Evening Post, 142

Seattle, WA, 71

Shubert-Majestic Theater, 81

Sirois, Edward, 95, 103, 105, 113–14, 209–10, 212, 214

Somerville, MA, 95, 177, 182, 241, 246, 248

Spain, 118–1

Spanish-American War, 29, 38, 41, 200, 204

Springfield, MA, 74, 143, 149

St. Agnes School, 162

Stanton, Elizabeth Cady, 168

"Star-Spangled Banner, The," 53–54, 159–60

Sullivan, Lewis R., 177, 183

Sullivan, Sport, 78

T

Tate Gallery, 101

Thayer, Elaine, 135

Thayer, Scofield, 135

Toul, France, 21, 110

U

Uffizi Gallery, 101

University of Leipzig, 158

University of Michigan School of Medicine, 68

University of Notre Dame, 150–56

U.S. Constitution, 35, 164, 166, 191, 254

USS *Aztec*, 69

V

Vaughan, Victor, 68, 124, 199–200, 202, 204, 238, 243, 255–256

W

Wagner, Heinie, 8, 56

Walsh, David, 147, 254

Weeghman, Charlie, 3, 61, 85, 88, 93

Weeghman Park, 8, 12, 59

Welch, William, 67–69, 117,
    199–205, 212–13, 237–38,
    243, 254
Wellesley, MA, 141–42
Whitman, Burt, 12–13, 77, 90,
    92, 208
Williams College, 98
Wilson, Woodrow, xi–xiii, 3, 27,
    36–44, 53, 68, 117–18, 132,
    140, 142–43, 145, 158, 160,
    166, 169, 186, 195, 223–25,
    227, 231–32, 234, 241, 244,
    253
Wisconsin, 154
Wolbach, Simeon, 238
Woodward, William C., 116–17,
    120, 136–37, 173–74, 177,
    181–83, 185, 187–89, 196,
    241, 243–44, 247, 249, 251,
    255

Y

Yale University, 150, 212
Yankee Stadium, 156
YMCA, 238